S0-AZP-300

A Primer on Animal Rights

# A Primer on Animal Rights

## Leading Experts Write about
## Animal Cruelty and Exploitation

KIM W. STALLWOOD, EDITOR

Lantern Books • New York
A Division of Booklight Inc.

2002
Lantern Books
One Union Square West, Suite 201
New York, NY 10003

Copyright © Kim W. Stallwood 2002

All rights reserved. No part of this book may be reproduced, stored in a retrieval system, or transmitted in any form or by any means, electronic, mechanical, photocopying, recording, or otherwise, without the written permission of Lantern Books.

Printed in the United States of America

Library of Congress Cataloging-in-Publication Data

Stallwood, Kim W.
  A primer on animal rights : leading experts write about animal cruelty and exploitation / Kim W. Stallwood.
      p. cm.
Includes bibliographical references.
  ISBN 1-59056-003-5 (alk. paper)
  1. Animal rights—United States. 2. Animal welfare—United States.
I. Title.
  HV4764 .S73 2002
  179.3'0973—dc21

                                    2002006010

To the animals who have no voice,
and to the people who
selflessly speak out for them

# ✻ Table of Contents

# ❧ Foreword

HISTORIANS HAVE USED many benchmarks to assess progress over the millennia. In recent times, scientific accomplishments, technological proficiency, and material gain have topped the list of most-favored measurements. While these three categories are deserving of attention, it should be noted that none of them is without its drawbacks. Certainly the twentieth century bears witness to the fact that science, technology, and commerce can be applied in ways that are cruel and divisive as well as ameliorative and harmonious.

There is, however, another benchmark for measuring human progress, one overlooked by historians, I suspect, for the reason that it is less quantifiable. I'm thinking of empathy, that most precious of all expressions that is at once both a feeling and a value. To empathize is to cross over and experience, in the most profound way, the very being of another—especially the other's struggle to endure and prevail in his or her own life journey. While empathy has deep biological roots, like language, it too has to be practiced and continually renewed to be of use. Empathy is the ultimate expression of communication between beings.

In the long sweep of human history, what becomes clear is that the human journey is, at its core, about the extension of empathy to broader and more inclusive domains. Parents' empathy for their child is the first classroom. At this stage, the process is both biologically driven and socially constructed. Each step beyond this most biologically rooted connection requires patient learning—the kind that comes not from control and mastery but rather surrender and revelation. Empathy is something that reveals itself to us if we are open to the experience. And we are most often open when we have experienced personal hardships and travails in our own individual journeys to endure and prevail.

While the human sojourn is often littered with defeats, failures, and suffering of immense magnitude, the saving grace is that the hardships we endure, both individually and collectively, can prepare us to be open to the plight of others, to console them and champion their cause.

To "Do unto others as we would have others do unto us" is the operational expression of the empathetic process. At first, the golden rule extended only to kin and tribe. Eventually it was extended to people of like-minded values—those who shared a common religion, nationality or ideology. In the 19th century, the first humane societies were established, extending the empathetic journey to include our fellow creatures. Today, millions of people all around the world, under the banner of the animal rights movement, are continuing to deepen and to expand human concern for, and empathy toward, our fellow creatures.

My wife, Carol Grunewald, once said to me something I will never forget: Every other creature alive today, she observed, is a fellow traveler who shares some connection to us by dint of our being here on earth together at the same time. We have, therefore, a bond of history. But all creatures also have their own journey to attend to, their own destiny to live, and their own inheritance to pass along.

To the extent that we can empathize with their journey and appreciate our common time on earth together we will be made more whole and our lives enriched.

*A Primer on Animal Rights* is a learning tool for helping all of us find our connections to our fellow creatures and to champion their journey. To live fully and to live well is to be an empathetic soul. By sharing their own experience as animal rights activists, the contributors to this book both inspire and encourage the rest of us in our quest to extend the golden rule to our fellow travelers, the many animals who share this moment on earth with us.

Jeremy Rifkin

# ❦ Acknowledgments

THIS ANTHOLOGY WOULD not have been possible if it were not for the contributors who generously donated their time and expertise, first when their articles were published in *The Animals' Agenda* magazine, and now, when they have given their permission to publish those articles in this anthology. Further, the animal advocacy organizations that many of these authors are affiliated with deserve special appreciation for the challenging work that they do on behalf of animals.

The small but dedicated staff at *The Animals' Agenda*—Jill Howard Church, Rachelle Detweiler, Suzanne McMillan, and Kirsten Rosenberg—demonstrate every day a complete commitment to animal liberation and to the ethics of professional journalism. Quite simply, this anthology and *The Animals' Agenda* would not be possible without them. Nor would *The Animals' Agenda* and its not-for-profit publisher, the Animal Rights Network Inc. (ARN), be possible if it were not for additional staff stalwarts Shannon Bowman, Peter Hoyt, Laura Moretti, and Jacque West.

I also want to thank the ARN board of directors and advisory board for their heartfelt dedication, commitment, and endurance in steering a minuscule but muscular organization. The hardy group of generous individuals known as the Friends of *The Animals' Agenda*, who, along with like-minded organizations and foundations, provide much-needed financial sustenance, deserve a standing ovation.

Finally, I wish to acknowledge the animals whom you will read about in this volume. Please know that one day you will be free.

Kim W. Stallwood

# ❦ Introduction

KIM W. STALLWOOD

> Once you have discovered what is happening, you can't
> pretend not to know, you can't abdicate responsibility.
> —**P. D. James**, British novelist

FIRST OF ALL, you need to know what this book is *not*. It is
not a philosophical guide to the theories of animal rights.
For nearly thirty years, many thinkers have written extensively
on the subject of animal rights, and some of the considerable
work done in this important area is listed in the bibliography at
the back of this book. Nor is this book is a comprehensive catalog of animal exploitation. Unfortunately, so pervasive is our
cruelty toward animals that it would be impossible to encompass the entirety of it in a hundred volumes, let alone one.

What this book does instead is to present a snapshot of a
number of areas where animal advocates are active. Some articles are broad outlines, some cover individual cases; some
pieces offer clear solutions, others reveal the complexity of the
issue at hand. I hope these investigations will provide readers
who may be concerned about our relationship with other animals and who remain uncertain of where to begin, an entry
point to work to limit, or better yet halt, the misery we, the
human species, inflict on our fellow creatures.

No one is born an animal rights activist. Granted, there are
many people who have a natural affinity for animals, and some

would say that all of us start life with an innate affection for other animals; it is simply custom and prejudice that drum it out of us. But those of us who care enough to dedicate our lives to improving the lives of others—many of whom we may never see or personally know—are the products of an epiphany, a moment in time that we often vividly recall as an emotional turning point. The day before that moment, we were clueless; the day after, we were unstoppable.

For more than two decades, *The Animals' Agenda* magazine, from which these articles are drawn, has been devoted to publishing the kind of information that can change lives, both human and nonhuman. Animals of all kinds are used and abused in so many different ways by human society that most people have become inured to commonplace cruelties. But once the animals' story is told with unflinching, uncensored honesty, it becomes nearly impossible to ignore reality.

Most steak lovers have never seen the inside of a slaughterhouse; most circusgoers have never seen an elephant being "trained"; most fur-wearers don't know what "anal electrocution" involves; most cosmetics users couldn't define an "LD-50" test; and even the legions of self-proclaimed cat and dog lovers have rarely stopped to consider what life is like for animals unlucky enough to fall outside the "pet" category.

But once you learn about things you were neither meant nor inclined to see, you can never use ignorance as an excuse for letting evil continue. *The Animals' Agenda* routinely receives letters from individuals who picked up their first copy of the magazine on a newsstand, or received a gift subscription, and were astounded and horrified by what they read. And instead of turning away, they got involved. Regardless of whether or how they define themselves as "activists," just changing their eating habits or shunning certain forms of so-called entertainment results in a paradigm shift toward liberation. The magazine's stated role in this movement is "helping people help animals," and the first step is knowledge.

*A Primer on Animal Rights* is a compilation of some of the magazine's best investigative pieces. Each of the six parts covers a different aspect of animal cruelty, from education and entertainment to agriculture and wildlife. Many of these institutionalized systems of abuse represent major business and economic interests, a clue as to why the cruelty continues. Those who are vested in vivisection or prejudiced against predators often thrive in the shadow that public ignorance affords them. The light of scrutiny can be an eye-opener indeed.

We deeply regret that this edition cannot, for reasons of sheer scope and size, include all of the important investigations we have covered. We greatly value such stories as Mike Markarian's "Tally-ho, Dude" exposé of U.S. fox hunting, as well as his coverage of the "Migratory Massacre" of bird hunting. Teri Barnato's "Canine Consumer Report" can be found on the web site of the Association of Veterinarians for Animal Rights (www.avar.org). The issue of "Pork, Politics, and Pollution" by Ellen Bring and Sheila Schwartz's "Humane Hypothesis" are other notable stories we will endeavor to include in a future compilation.

For now, however, there is much to learn and much to be done with that knowledge. Every one of these stories has a real-life component that each reader can put into practice in his or her own life and community. We realize that the harsh realities depicted in these articles are difficult for caring people to read about, but we cannot help the animals until we fully understand their predicament. We must, at least, bear witness to their suffering. And we can, at most, do whatever is necessary to stop it.

Welcome, then, to the second anthology of articles from *The Animals' Agenda*. The first, *Speaking Out for Animals* (also published by Lantern Books), gathered together moving and inspiring stories from many who are involved with animal advocacy at the most fundamental level—rescuing animals from torture, deprivation, or despair. Read *A Primer on Animal Rights* and *Speaking Out for Animals* together and you will surely become an animal rights activist—and perhaps even believe that you were born one.

# PART 1

# COMPANION ANIMALS

# 1: Caring for Companions

KIM STURLA

FROM INSIDE KENNEL number three he peers out, ears back, hunched, eyes searching. His paperwork identifies him as Cody, an unneutered, two-year-old terrier/basset mix whose people are moving to Texas. Odds are not in Cody's favor, since 60 percent of all dogs entering California shelters are destroyed. If he makes it out of the shelter, chances are he will suffer from some of the 35 genetic defects (such as osteodystrophy, diseases involving the development of the bones) that are prevalent in bassets. Humans began domesticating dogs about 8,000 to 10,000 years ago. The American Kennel Club registers 135 dog breeds, most of which suffer from at least one of more than 300 genetically transmitted abnormalities. Cats began life with humans just 3,000 to 4,000 years ago, and 39 cat breeds are now recognized.

More than 110 million dogs and cats live in this country. About half of all U.S. households include a dog, a cat, or both. A survey conducted by the American Animal Hospital Association reveals that 65 percent of animal guardians claim they give their nonhuman companions as much attention as they would their children. Yet, despite such popularity, animal shelters kill five to 10 million unwanted dogs and cats a year. (There are no exact figures because no national animal data reporting system exists for shelters.)

It seems ironic to some that euthanasia is the number one "disease" killing dogs and cats. To understand the reason, one must understand the root of the problem: why people do not sterilize their animals. A study conducted by Penn & Shoen Associates discovered that 27 percent of those surveyed believed that sterilizing their dogs and cats was unnecessary. This conclusion likely involves people not realizing the reproductive potential of an animal, being unaware of the severity of dog and cat overpopulation, or believing they can control their animal's reproductive behavior. Twenty percent of the people who do not sterilize their dogs or cats wish to breed them, and 7.5 percent feel the surgery is too expensive.

The Penn & Shoen data provides helpful insight about how to address this problem. It appears there are three strategies to solve dog and cat overpopulation:

- *Education*: Educate people about why sterilizing their animals is important. Besides the ethical consequence of breeding animals and thus contributing to the surplus problem, scientific data that show that sterilized animals live longer and are less likely to develop certain cancers.
- *Legislation*: Enact spay/neuter incentive laws to discourage people from breeding their animals.
- *Sterilization*: Provide affordable and accessible spay/neuter services.

Changing the attitudes, values, and behaviors of animal guardians through education is the most difficult challenge. Several different approaches—humane education curriculums in schools, teacher workshops, adult education, animal training and behavior classes, and other community outreach education programs—are all needed. For example, the Kentucky Humane Society conducts summer camps for children at its shelter. The campers' week-long session includes hands-on animal care, speakers, and activities. The Peninsula Humane Society (PHS) in California holds regular education and training classes for prospective volunteers. During the multi-session course, participants learn about animal behavior, shelter operations, euthanasia, and animal control laws. As a result, PHS has an educated and trained team of more than 400 volunteers working in several capacities at the shelter.

The Association of Veterinarians for Animal Rights (AVAR) is educating veterinary medical students about how they can help. AVAR is building bridges between veterinary medical schools and animal shelters. Teri Barnato, AVAR's national director, explains, "Our externship program gives veterinary medical students firsthand exposure to dog and cat overpopulation when working in animal shelters. This educational opportunity creates a greater interest in young veterinarians to work with shelters to solve the problem."

Legislation is the second component to the solution. Spay/neuter laws take many forms: some are directed at specific parties (i.e., animal shelters, guardians, breeders, or puppy mills), and others simply provide funds to support affordable or free sterilization. A comprehensive dog and cat overpopulation ordinance includes several components: it prohibits the free roaming of animals (if exceptions are allowed for cats to roam outdoors, they must be sterilized); it includes a differential licensing program that sets a high fee for unneutered dogs and cats and a low one for those sterilized (many communities charge as little as $5 to license sterilized animals and $50 for intact ones); it mandates sterilization of animals adopted from shelters; and it strictly enforces all aspects of adoption contracts. Shelters need to be a part of the solution and not allow animals in their care to contribute to the surplus. In other words, animal rescue groups should release only neutered animals for adoption.

Creating a permanent source of funding for a spay/neuter subsidy is also achievable through legislation. Spokane, Washington, allocates a portion of the general fund for free spaying and neutering, which raises about $100,000 a year. New Jersey and New York have a $3 surcharge on licenses for unaltered dogs that is used for spay/neuter subsidies. New Jersey also raises money for a spay/neuter fund through "Animal Friendly" license plates, a program that generated more than $500,000 in its first year. Bob Monyer of the New Jersey Department of Health is proud to announce, "In the first 11 months of our license plate program, we subsidized more than 8,000 sterilizations." King County, Washington, sends a $25 spay/neuter voucher to every person who licenses an intact dog or cat (such licenses cost $55). In Fort Myers, Florida, when someone buys a dog license from a veterinarian, 100 percent of the license fee goes into that individual veterinarian's spay/neuter account.

Feral cats, whose population may be almost as high as the housecat population (about 57 million), are a group often ignored. Several communities, however, have passed precedent-setting legislation to help feral cats. Santa Cruz, California, and Cape May, New Jersey, have ordinances allowing people to care for feral cats if they agree to trap the cats and have them sterilized, tested for feline leukemia, vaccinated against rabies, and registered with animal control at no fee.

Funding spay/neuter subsidies can be achieved through legislation, but this is not the only option. Compromises and agreements with private veterinarians to provide affordable sterilization offer another route. The accessibility of a spay/neuter service is being addressed in some communities through mobile spay/neuter vans.

A crucial ingredient of a progressive spay/neuter program is the age at which the animal is sterilized. Although six months used to be considered the minimum age for these surgeries, the veterinary community now recognizes that they can be done as early as eight weeks of age. Moreover, the American Veterinary Medical Association encourages this prepubescent surgery. The reason for sterilizing animals at a younger age is that it reduces the chance that they will contribute to the endless cycle of more births and deaths. Some private practitioners, however, are reluctant to change their standard operating procedures.

Whether it is humane education curricula for the schools, veterinary students working in shelters, mobile spay/neuter vans, or working cooperatively with feral cat caretakers, forming new partnerships is the key to solving the animal overpopulation problem. New alliances must be developed and differences must be put aside for the benefit of the animals, like Cody, who need help.

Cody's first family will never know his fate. He was adopted and lives with two other canines, two humans, and an array of other rescued animals on 60 acres. Also, he willingly shares our communal king-size bed. And yes—he is now neutered.

# 2: Scapegoats and Underdogs

Ariana Huemer

scapegoat n. [Scape (for escape) + goat.]
1. (Jewish Antiq.) A goat upon whose head were symbolically placed the sins of the people, after which he was suffered to escape into the wilderness.
2. Hence, a person or thing that is made to bear blame for others.

WHEN PRE-LAW STUDENT Rebecca Sandler left for her morning classes in the fall of 1999, she little anticipated the ordeal that was about to consume her life for the next several months. Upon returning to her Greenbelt, Maryland, home, Rebecca found a chilling notice from animal control authorities, who had stopped by only minutes earlier in search of her dog, Diesel. The official notice demanded that Rebecca surrender

Diesel to the authorities immediately in accordance with a new, countywide provision. Panicked, Rebecca hurried Diesel away to the safety of a friend's house in another county.

History is rife with examples of minority groups targeted by members of a disgruntled society, based on sins real or imagined. In this case, Rebecca and Diesel were the targets of new legislation banning the ownership of pit bull dogs in Prince George's County, Maryland. Their sin? Diesel fit the description of a "pit bull," a catchall term referring to several distinct dog breeds: the American bulldog, the American Staffordshire Terrier, and the American pit bull terrier.

Prince George's County is just one of an increasing number of localities nationwide that have enacted legislation to ban or severely restrict pit bull ownership. The emergence of this type of legislation is not entirely arbitrary or surprising; the last two decades have seen an alarming rise in the number of reported human fatalities related to pit bull encounters. The public outcry against this apparent social menace has prompted towns in at least 37 states to enact this kind of breed-specific legislation (BSL), ostensibly to protect the public.

The Humane Society of the United States (HSUS) estimates that every year 4.7 million Americans suffer dog bites, 6,000 of which require hospitalization and 12 of which end fatally. However, according to Julie Gilchrist, M.D., an epidemiologist at the Centers for Disease Control and Prevention (CDC), little information regarding dog bite statistics by breed is available, because there is no national reporting system for dog bites or national registry system for dogs by breed. Hence, there is no way to arrive at comparisons of bite rates by breed. When it comes to bite risk, Gilchrist suggests that far more relevant than breed are other factors such as animal guardianship, early training, and socialization. She advises that "one must keep in mind that while many dog qualities such as temperament and trainability differ, in general, by breed and owner, environmental factors are likely much more important in determining risk for biting." Further CDC data shows that male dogs are six times more likely to bite than female dogs, and that dogs who have not been spayed or neutered are three times more likely to bite.

Nonetheless, the nation's largest animal rights organization, People for the Ethical Treatment of Animals (PETA), has publicly declared a solution to the pit bull problem: ban the breed, for the sake of both the public and the dogs. In a January 2000 letter printed in the *Knight Ridder Tribune*, PETA director and former Washington Humane Society (WHS) executive director Ingrid Newkirk explains, "These dogs were designed specifically to fight other animals and kill them, for human sport. Hence the barrel chest, the thick hammer-like head, the strong jaws, the perseverance, and the stamina. Pits can take down a bull weighing in at over a thousand pounds, so a human being a tenth of that weight is small potatoes to them. Pit bulls are perhaps the most abused dogs on the planet. These days, they are kept for protection by almost every drug dealer and pimp in every major city and beyond....People who genuinely care about dogs won't be affected by a ban on pits. They can go to the shelter and save one of the countless other breeds and lovable mutts sitting on death row through no fault of their own. We can only stop killing pits if we stop creating new ones."

**Crisis in the Capital**
One of the more high-profile cities considering a pit bull ban is Washington, D.C. The Pit Bull Public Protection Amendment Act, supported by D.C. city council members Jim Graham and Kevin Chavous, would amend the city's laws to declare pit bulls de facto dangerous dogs—a move that will, in effect, expurgate them from the city. Although the Act would prohibit new pit bulls from entering the city, it would allow those with proof of residency prior to the ban to remain, provided they adhere to a strict set of regulations: registration with local animal control authorities, sterilization, at least $50,000 liability insurance coverage, posting of "Dangerous Dog" signs at the dog's resi-

dence, and mandatory muzzling in public—a modern version of the Scarlet Letter.

As in many big cities, violence underscores the poverty that blankets much of the District. Councilman Chavous speaks in terms of a city under siege, "inundated with pit bulls that terrorize our citizens." In the November 2, 1999, *Washington Post* he gripes, "I'm tired of having senior citizens call my office saying they do not feel comfortable sitting on their porches or walking down the streets of their own neighborhoods because they are afraid of pit bulls."

In a grim parallel to the city's police department, WHS has its hands full with cases of animal fighting, vicious dogs, and a kennel that often seems nothing more than a pit bull holding facility. No surprise, then, that its director, Mary Healy, has penned several public pleas for a pit bull ban. Also not surprising is the WHS' strict prohibition on pit bull adoptions, a preventive measure that translates into obligatory euthanasia for all pit bulls without proper identification who find their way to the shelter doors. Many shelters nationwide similarly refuse to adopt out pit bulls, partly because of the ponderous legal liability they present and partly as a preemptive strike against potential abusers with a taste for dog fighting. In a February 2000 letter to *The Washington Post*, Healy bemoans her city's predicament: "The District's dangerous-dog law, which worked well until pit bulls came on the scene in the mid-'80s, is now inadequate. It looks at each dog's case individually, after the animal has demonstrated aggression, but it does not prevent attacks. With a ban in place, problem pit bulls could be removed from the community before they maul someone."

Her point is well taken. It is difficult to ignore the lethal potential of the prototypical pit bull terrier—the wide mandible, exaggerated musculature, and tenacious character are traits that have been reinforced through generations of selective breeding for dog fighting. These traits can also make them the perfect instrument of violence against humans when exploited by criminals and other violent individuals. At the same time, this criminal element also spurs many fearful citizens to acquire pit bulls as a defensive measure. Jeffrey Sacks, M.D., an injury prevention specialist with the CDC, says that while "it used to be that people got dogs for pets, now more get them out of fear of crime. That's spawning a movement toward bigger dogs," who may be improperly socialized and cared for by uneducated guardians.

**Crawling Out of the Pits**
Originally bred in England in the early 1800s to fight bulls for the amusement of human spectators, the pit bull is generally considered to be the most powerful dog, pound for pound, ever developed. When England outlawed bull baiting for humane reasons in 1835, organized dog fighting became popular, especially in the Staffordshire coal-mining areas, and later in the United States around the time of the Civil War. It would be more than a century before U.S. laws began to seriously address the scourge of dog fighting, with a spate of states passing felony dog fighting laws starting in 1970.

Ironically, another trait bred into pit bulls to maximize their fighting success is a strong inhibition against biting humans, who typically hover over the fighting pit and have to be able to step in at any time, even in the midst of the most vicious dog fight, without fear of being bitten. In organized fighting rings, any dog who exhibits aggression toward a handler or referee is immediately disqualified. Hence, the same aggressive drive crucial to a fighting dog's success in the ring would prove disastrous to his fighting career if misdirected toward humans.

"In my work as a canine behaviorist, I deal primarily with difficult dogs," says Tamara Zaluzney, owner of the Natural Way dog training school in Virginia. "The type of dog I see least often is one of the breeds commonly referred to by the generic term 'pit bull.' The reason for this is simple: they are not, by definition, difficult dogs...whatever the background, the one common

denominator, the single underlying fact, is a stability of temperament. Even in cases of severe abuse."

What, then, can account for the disproportionate number of
human fatalities attributed to pit bull attacks in recent years?
Much, it appears, can be traced to a confluence of irresponsible
guardianship and classic media hype. In a self-fulfilling prophe-
cy, as the media builds the pit bull into a fiend of mythical pro-
portions, throngs of unscrupulous individuals, from gang members to drug dealers, are encouraged to acquire them simply to
bolster their own "bad" image. The relentless media focus on pit
bulls as "dangerous" and "vicious" dogs has sealed their fate as
pawns of humankind's penchant for violence.

As Zaluzney explains, "It is possible to make a 'pit bull'-type
dog vicious toward people, but it is against their nature and
therefore not a simple feat. They have been bred for generations
to show no human aggression, even in the heat of battle....[A]ny
dog can be made to be vicious when subjected to the torture
that these dogs often are at the hands of less-than-scrupulous
individuals....The dogs only do what is asked of them...."

The effects of abuse are further cited by Dr. Leslie Sinclair, a
veterinarian formerly employed by HSUS, who observes, "A lot
of pit bulls involved in attacks have never had a chance to be
around people."

The WHS' Healy blames the combination of "dog fighting,
inhumane confinement, starvation, and beatings administered
as 'training' " that fill the lives of so many pit bulls in her city.
Taken in concert with a pit bull's redoubtable physical profile,
the potentially tragic ends are impossible to overlook: "Most
dogs bite and release; pit bulls bite, hold, grind, and shake,
often doing horrendous damage to their victims."

An HSUS training manual for law enforcement officials further explains the dangerous potential unique to pit bulls. The
manual describes how "animals selected for fighting gain an
advantage by not revealing their intentions and by not being
inhibited by displays of submission in their opponents. These

animals offer little or no indication that an attack is imminent. In fights, they often appear to be insensitive to normal 'cut off' behaviors that signal an end to aggression...they will fight to the point of complete exhaustion or death with minimal provocation."

In contrast with this grim image, recent generations of selective breeding for temperament and docility have successfully produced family companions renowned by breed devotees for their loyalty and stability. Petey, the memorable canine character in the *Little Rascals* television series, is perhaps the best-known pit bull who exemplified these traits. Not only an endearing television character, Petey was also the very first Staffordshire Terrier to be registered by the American Kennel Club in 1936.

What has been the pit bull's asset in the fighting ring— indomitable strength, courage, and willingness to please—has been its biggest liability in modern times. And as long as dog fighting continues as a forum for violent individuals, the pit bull problem will only continue to grow. In the end, it will be a curb on human misdeeds, rather than on the behavior of the dogs, that will stunt the cycle. Even the CDC, in its analysis of dog bite fatalities, warns that "breed-specific approaches to the control of dog bites do not address the issue that many breeds are involved in the problem and that most of the factors contributing to dog bites are related to the level of responsibility exercised by dog owners."

Stronger dog-fighting laws are one step, as are laws addressing animal cruelty as a whole. Says Paul Shapiro, campaigns manager of Compassion Over Killing and guardian of a mixed-breed pit bull, "While I oppose making pit bulls de facto dangerous in the way the D.C. legislation is trying, I'm not certain that we should oppose a breeding ban....Any ban on dog breeding is a fresh breath of air and a beginning to the solution of overpopulation which claims the lives of literally millions each year....Instead of treating all pit bulls as if they were inherently aggressive, the solution lies in taking our obligation to prevent animal cruelty more seriously. At a bare minimum, felonizing animal cruelty would seem to be a good start."

Indeed, the growing mainstream acceptance of animal rights and animal welfare issues in recent years has spawned an unprecedented wave of animal protection legislation at every level of government. Animal cruelty in general and dog fighting in particular are illegal in every state and are now considered felony offenses in 35 and 46 states, respectively. Despite these legislative advances, however, dog fighting and its attendant problems still appear to be on the rise, much to the dismay of humane organizations and animal welfare advocates.

"The reasons for illegal animal fighting to be on the rise despite better laws are complex and manifold," says Eric Sakach, West Coast regional director of HSUS and a veteran dogfight investigator. "Passing legislation for felony laws is only part of the solution...no law is any better than its enforcement and prosecution. Education is a key. We've been hammering away at that with our courses and materials. Statistically, the chances that a dog fighter will get busted are still low, low, low."

## Physical Wounds, Psychological Salve

Proponents of pit bull bans claim that those who wish to tackle the problem through stricter animal control laws are naive to the extent of the problem, which they believe can only be affected by drastic measures. However, it may be equally naive to assume that exterminating pit bulls from an area will remove the problem of dangerous dogs. In fact, some experts believe that breed-specific legislation may unwittingly create more dangerous dog problems by fostering a false sense of security in a community, making it more vulnerable to hazards posed by all dogs. Furthermore, such laws would likely compel many owners of targeted breeds to resort to chaining or confining their dogs out of sight for long periods, virtually guaranteeing a neurotic, unpredictable animal.

In March 2000, the city of Wilmington, Delaware, passed restrictions against pit bulls, allocating an extra $50,000 to pay an animal-control officer to accompany police officers on sweeps for the dogs that summer. The result so far has been a double-edged sword: as of June 2000, while 17 pit bulls had been duly registered in compliance with the new law, the Delaware SPCA and the Delaware Humane Association reported that at least 44 other dogs had been turned in to shelters for euthanasia, with people citing the stringent registration requirements as the reason for giving up their dogs. Councilman Gerard Kelly, who sponsored the new law, thinks that the fact that more pit bulls are being left at animal shelters is a positive thing. "People are making better decisions," Kelly says. "They realize if they are not going to invest a great deal of attention in this animal, it's better not to have it."

As with any disease, treating only the symptoms does not guarantee that the malady will not manifest itself in an alternate form. Many speculate that a pit bull ban could very well precipitate a rise in Rottweiler, Doberman, or German shepherd abuses and related human fatalities. According to Marianne Radziewicz, associate director of the American Society for the Prevention of Cruelty to Animals, "If potentially aggressive breeds such as the pit bull or the Rottweiler are banned by a community, those renegade members of the community who wish to own inappropriately aggressive dogs can readily train another breed and inflict damage as bad or worse. There are 157 breeds now registered by the American Kennel Club, and there are probably more than 800 breeds worldwide, offering an endless supply from which aggressive dogs may be bred."

As for the pit bull ban in Prince George's County—adjacent to Washington, D.C., and similar in size and demographics—animal control statistics show that since the ban began in 1997, pit bull bites have not decreased. The statistics also show that both German shepherds (including mixes) and mixed-breed dogs were each responsible for more bites than pit bulls

(American pit bull terriers, American Staffordshire Terriers, and pit bull mixes).

The effectiveness of breed bans becomes even hazier when considering the long-term results of such laws. For example, ten years after it initiated a sweeping ban against all pit bulls, the Cincinnati city council's law committee recommended that the ban be repealed, based on inherent difficulties ranging from prohibitive enforcement costs to the logistics of accurate identification. According to Carol Walker, assistant to the safety director for the city, the police department spent more than $160,000 a year attempting to enforce the law. A dog warden had to perform identity checks on suspected "pit bulls," finding among the seized dogs such breeds as boxers and golden retrievers.

Finally, the National Animal Control Association opposes labeling animals "dangerous" based solely on breed. Echoing the CDC's analysis of the dog bite problem, Executive Director John Mays cautions, "Any animal may exhibit aggressive behavior regardless of breed. Accurately identifying a specific animal's lineage for prosecution purposes may be extremely difficult. Additionally, breed-specific legislation may create an undue burden to owners who otherwise have demonstrated proper pet management and responsibility."

**The Slippery Slope**
With respect to human populations, most progressive leaders have systematically rejected the tenets of biological reductionism as socially destructive and inherently unjust. Indeed, law enforcement agencies in many large cities from California to New Jersey have come under fire recently for employing the related tactic of "racial profiling" to identify potentially threatening individuals, most often young minority men. In racial profiling, the assumption of innocence seems conveniently discarded under the auspices of public welfare; law enforcement officials earmark suspects based primarily upon a set of physi-

cal agenda, substituting skin color for evidence as grounds for
suspicion. Much like the "preemptive strike" against threatening canines championed by D.C. officials, it is in one sense an
easy way to provide reassurance of community safety. In another sense, racial profiling, like breed bans, targets a convenient
scapegoat in order to assuage public paranoia.

This point is not lost on pit bull owners in Berlin, Germany,
where lawmakers passed a ban against pit bulls and other fighting dog breeds. To protest this mandate, pit bull owners
planned a march upon the capitol with their dogs emblazoned
with yellow Stars of David—a symbol that the protesters say is
an appropriate representation of what they call racist attempts
to wipe out their dogs.

Like racial profiling, breed bans can stir up conflicts even
more troubling than those they seek to resolve. Before embrac-
ing draconian measures, citizens ought to look beyond the
immediate effects of a measure to how it will affect communities in the long run. Whatever potential panacea breed-specific
legislation may hold for communities, it most certainly does so
at the expense of the individuals, who for the most part are
unwilling reflections of a culture of violence. In short, it is a
slippery slope from recognizing individual problems within a
group to adopting policies that reflect a genocidal attitude.

Hilary Twining, a former agent with the Animal Rescue
League of Boston, is personally familiar with the ambivalence
many animal shelter workers feel regarding pit bulls. "The shelter where I worked chose not to place pit bulls for adoption, and
it broke my heart to see young, friendly pit bull puppies and
adolescents euthanized based solely on their breed," she recalls.
"Ironically, the American Canine Temperament Testing
Association reports that 95 percent of the pit bulls that have
taken its temperament test passed, as compared to a 77 percent
passing rate for all breeds on average. Although I can appreciate
that placing pit bulls for adoption may present significant liabil-

ity issues for shelters, I feel that breed-specific bans are unnecessarily restrictive and are ultimately short-sighted."

The point we have reached with pit bulls is only a symptom of the greater, deeply rooted malady couched within contemporary culture. The same culture of violence that has shaped certain groups of humans into societal threats has spawned a group of threatening dogs.

In 2000, when law enforcement authorities raided the Nebraska home of New York Giants linebacker LeShon Johnson for allegedly running a dog-fighting operation, they found almost 70 pit bulls staked in the woods near the house, many bloodied from battle. Just weeks earlier, humane organizations lambasted rap star DMX for his music video depicting snarling pit bulls. Both media stories seem compelled by common demons: a society that disproportionately emphasizes domination as a passageway to power, supposed "heroes" who thrive on the exploitation of the weak, and masses quick to pinion a victim for the resultant undercurrent of anxiety. We are witnessing in modern times the allegorical scapegoat recast in the mold of the pit bull terrier—an animal forced to bear the sins of humans and cast out by his keepers.

# 3: You Can Teach a Dog Cruel Tricks

MICHAEL MARKARIAN

A GROUP OF friends interested in training their golden retrievers attended a "hunt test" in Houston, and were appalled by what they witnessed. Hundreds of live birds (mainly pigeons and ducks) were shackled, their wings broken to prevent them from flying. "Bird boys" used slingshots to propel the birds 30 to 50 feet in the air; upon landing, each bird was located and retrieved by a canine contestant. Dead birds were replaced with live ones, but surviving birds were used repeatedly—sometimes for hours—until they died.

Typical hunt tests, such as those sanctioned by the American Kennel Club (AKC), may use live birds in some shooting and hunting simulations, but they do not use live birds in retrieval exercises like those described above. At hunt tests sanctioned by the younger and smaller United Kennel Club (UKC), however, such scenes are not uncommon. This little-known practice has received virtually no attention from the humane community.

Live birds are also used to train hunting dogs. Private companies around the country breed, train, and sell such dogs, and will train a hunter's own dogs for a fee. A kennel worker (who wishes to remain anonymous) at one Midwestern training business described it this way: "My boss would buy live birds on a regular basis. In a slow month, he would buy at least 80 ducks and 40 pigeons. I have personally watched over 250 ducks and about 150 pigeons get tortured to death in the three months that I worked there during hunting season. People think that the birds' necks are broken before the training begins, but it is simply not true. We would shackle the birds' wings together and their legs together. If it was a duck that really wanted to live and would bite at the dogs, its beak would be taped shut. So you see there was no hope for their survival."

Such abuse is not illegal; most states specifically exempt hunting activities and related training from their animal cruelty or wildlife statutes. (Canada, however, specifically prohibits the use of live birds to train hunting dogs.) Winged wildlife are not the only ones who suffer during dog training; the four-legged variety—mainly raccoons, rabbits, coyotes, and foxes—are also thrown to the hounds, so to speak. In Virginia, it is legal to capture foxes in the wild and transport them to pens where foxhounds are trained to chase them and maul them to shreds. North Dakota officials capture thousands of foxes and coyotes with neck snares and leghold traps and export them to Southern states that use the animals as live bait to train hounds. Only a handful of states still accept the shipments, because studies indicate that 70 to 90 percent of North Dakota's foxes carry *Echinococcus multilocularis*, a deadly parasite that kills more than half the people it infects.

The March 1988 issue of *Outdoor Life* magazine recommended an "easy way" to train coonhounds: Keep a live raccoon in a cylindrical cage, allowing the dogs to follow the scent while the raccoon runs and rolls the cage away. Ironically, the article states that "the coon lives in the cage," making a "delightful pet." The cage prevents the dogs from killing the raccoon, but it is a Pyrrhic victory at best—living terrified inside a cramped cage, constantly running from yelping dogs, cannot be a suitable life for a wild animal.

State wildlife agencies generally frown on the private possession of wildlife, but they gladly give special permits to hunters and clubs that use these animals in dog training. Each state has different regulations on the types and numbers of animals that hunters and trainers can possess. The Michigan Natural Resources Commission, for example, considered a proposal that would allow beagle clubs to trap rabbits and hares and relocate them to training enclosures.

Aside from the obvious harm to the prey animals, there have also been rampant reports of dogs being injured during training. Repeated beatings with "heeling sticks" have resulted in dogs with blood pouring out of their mouths, and welts that don't go down for hours. A process called "force breaking" includes the use of a shock collar placed around a female dog's leg to shock her vagina, or around a male dog's stomach to shock his penis. The dogs' owners are generally unaware of these methods.

The AKC and the UKC are breed registry clubs, not enforcement entities, and they have no control over what goes on in the woods, at hunting clubs, or behind the closed doors of private training companies. It is surprising, however, that neither group has publicly addressed this issue, especially considering that they have issued position statements and guidelines regarding other humane concerns such as puppy mills. These groups should recognize that allowing dogs to torture wild animals is the humane equivalent of dog fighting and cock fighting, and they should encourage their members not to participate in these activities.

# 4: Nowhere to Run

JOAN EIDINGER, SUSAN NETBOY,
LAUREL WILLIAMS, AND MELANI NARDONE

THE EMOTIONALLY CHARGED battle to ban greyhound racing in a state where it has existed for 65 years ended November 8, 2000, with the defeat of Grey2K's ballot initiative by a narrow margin of less than two percent. According to final election results, 2,733,831 votes were cast. Of those, 1,276,708 voted yes on Question 3 to ban dog racing and 1,328,374 voted against the ban, a difference of 51,666 votes. Nearly 130,000 voters left Question 3 blank. Nevertheless, the work that went into bringing the ballot to the public and the amount of information disseminated more than suggests that greyhound racing will shortly be banned.

For the first time in the 75-year history of greyhound racing in America, the future of the pastime was to be decided by the number of citizens who went to the polls rather than the betting booth. If voters had approved the initiative, Massachusetts—which has two greyhound tracks—would have become the first to ban greyhound racing by such a referendum. Ballot initiatives like the one in Massachusetts allow the voters to pass a statute or constitutional amendment directly, without involving the legislature. With the ban, Massachusetts would have followed seven other states (Maine, Virginia, Vermont, Idaho, Washington, Nevada, and North Carolina) to ban live dog racing and/or simulcasting. This was the mission of GREY2K (Greyhound Racing Ends Year 2000), a grassroots group consisting of more than 1,000 animal welfare advocates throughout Massachusetts that began organizing in 1999 after it appeared that a third legislative attempt to ban dog racing would fail. GREY2K collected 150,000 signatures to place the proposition on the November 2000 ballot.

The first commercial greyhound racetrack opened in St. Petersburg, Florida, in 1925. It was quickly followed by the Biscayne Kennel Club in Miami in 1926, and in the next decade eight more tracks opened in Florida. By 1960, 28 greyhound tracks were operating in seven states. By 1990, 19 states had legalized pari-mutuel wagering, and the number of racetracks had doubled to 56. This rapid expansion fueled a breeding frenzy to supply them. In the 1980s alone, an estimated 450,000 racing greyhounds were born.

In less than a century, the greyhound—revered for millennia by pharaohs and kings—had been reduced to an easily replaceable object upon which to place a bet. The greyhound's speed and agility had doomed the breed to servitude under a people whose only interest was gambling profits.

Maine banned dog racing in 1993, followed by Virginia and Vermont in 1995, Idaho and Washington in 1996, and Nevada in 1997. Greyhound racing never existed in Maine, Virginia, or Washington; the legislation was a proactive move to prevent any attempt by the industry to expand into new territory. Nevada had a brief courtship with dog racing when the Las Vegas Downs track opened in Henderson in January 1981, but it closed 11 months later. North Carolina, which outlawed dog racing in the 1950s, updated its gambling laws in 1998 and banned the televised transmission (simulcasting) of dog races into the state.

Vermont and Idaho, however, each had a long and infamous history of dog racing marked by allegations of abuse and atrocities. Media exposure by the *Bennington Free Press* in 1992 and

*The Spokesman-Review* in 1992 and 1995 eventually led to the closure of the Green Mountain track in Pownal, Vermont, and the Coeur d'Alene track in Post Falls, Idaho.

## Dog Race About-Face

Greyhound racing was an accepted, state-sanctioned spectacle in this country for 60 years before the general public had any idea of the horrors taking place behind the scenes. In the mid-1980s information began to surface in the mainstream media about the grim fate of racing greyhounds and the slaughter of tens of thousands of other small animals in the training process.

A racing greyhound's welfare at each stage of life is largely dependent on the dog's ability to generate money. Greyhounds typically begin racing at the age of 18 months. To qualify at an official track, the dogs must finish in the top four in two schooling races. If successful, the dogs enter maiden races. As they win, the dogs advance up through grades D, C, B, and finally grade A, as they finish in first, second, or third place in three consecutive races. Alternately, as they begin losing, they decline in grades using the same criteria in reverse. By failing in D, the lowest grade, a dog is considered "graded off" and may be sent to a less competitive track. Once a dog has graded off at an end-of-the-line track, he or she is either killed, kept for breeding, or turned over for adoption.

Each track requires approximately 15 kennels to keep an adequate supply of dogs. Each of these privately owned kennels maintains an average of 50 to 60 dogs. Kennel operators typically lease the dogs from their owners in return for 35 percent of the dogs' winnings. Dog owners are often people who invest in greyhounds as a sideline business or hobby, and may never actually see the dogs. In other cases—usually large farms of 600 dogs or more—the dogs are bred, trained, and raced by the owner.

In 13 of the 15 racing states, the dogs are housed at a kennel compound on the racetrack grounds. They are often kept muzzled in stacked metal cages or wooden crates for 20 or more hours a day. Bedding is shredded newspaper or small carpet remnants; flea and tick infestation is common. The typical diet is raw "4-D" meat (taken from diseased, dying, downed, or dead livestock).

At about six months of age, greyhound puppies are sent to training farms where they race around a track in pursuit of a lure. To encourage this behavior, trainers traditionally used "live lures"—rabbits, cats, and other small animals—tied to the lure mechanism. The dogs are encouraged to shred the animals to build a taste for blood and instill the instinct of running after the fake lure at the track.

This training method was well chronicled by The Humane Society of the United States (HSUS) in several undercover investigations in the 1980s. HSUS estimated that more than 100,000 small animals were killed every year to train racing dogs. Today, the industry insists that most greyhounds are trained with mechanical lures and that only about 10 percent of trainers still use live lures.

Greyhounds are at risk throughout their racing lives. Many die because of hazardous kennel or track conditions, negligent handling during transport, preventable diseases due to a lack of basic veterinary care, and epidemic outbreaks of highly contagious illnesses.

Despite industry claims that allegations of abuse are outdated and therefore no longer valid, horrific stories continue to surface at an alarming rate. At Alabama's Birmingham Race Course on June 21, 2000, the lure operator failed to stop the lure when the race ended and Randad, a two-year-old male, became trapped inside the rail. Investigators concluded the greyhound was dead before the returning mechanical lure struck him. In Massachusetts, 87 greyhounds burned to death on Valentine's Day 1992 at the Lynn Kennel Compound, a 50-year-old facility that houses 1,600 dogs in 28 wooden buildings for the Wonderland track in Revere. Eight more greyhounds perished there in another fire in June 1999. Nearly 100 grey-hounds nationwide died of complications from kennel cough in two large outbreaks in the last decade; a 1999 epidemic affecting 5,000 dogs placed every track in the country under quarantine for weeks. A condition later identified as canine streptococcal toxic syndrome killed 24 dogs in Florida, Kansas, New Hampshire, and Wisconsin. The afflicted dogs developed fevers of 107 degrees, hemorrhaged nasally, rectally, and from their urinary tracts, and died within 24 hours.

**Disposable Dogs**

Racing greyhounds are the disposable commodities of a gambling industry. Despite nationwide rescue efforts and a decline in the number of greyhounds bred, it is estimated that 20,000 to 25,000 greyhounds are still being killed annually. Animal advocates conservatively estimate that this "sport" has claimed the lives of more than one million greyhounds in its 75-year U.S. history.

Any greyhound bred to race on an official racetrack must be registered with the National Greyhound Association (NGA) at the age of three months and again at 18 months. According to industry breeding reports published in *The Greyhound Review*, 65,601 litters were registered by the NGA between 1989 and 1998. Multiplying these litters by an average of 6.5 pups per litter results in a minimum total of 426,407 greyhounds born during this period. By comparing the number of dogs registered by litter at age three months against the number of dogs registered individually at 18 months, the attrition rate for puppies and young dogs averaged nearly 20 percent, or 84,385 greyhounds culled from the system in one decade. According to industry insiders, unwanted puppies are disposed of by being drowned in a bucket of water or by being deliberately separated from nursing mothers.

An analysis by the Greyhound Protection League and *Greyhound Network News* (GNN) of the published numbers and the estimated number of dogs who are still racing, on breeding or training farms, and those who have been adopted, indicates that more than 200,000 greyhounds have disappeared from the record in this 10-year period.

Puppies and young dogs deemed unsuitable for racing, and older dogs graded off from the racetrack when they can no longer "run in the money," are disposed of by various means, including lethal injection, gunshot, starvation, bludgeoning, electrocution, and abandonment. They also are sold or donated to medical research laboratories, sold to coyote and rabbit hunters and amateur "match" racers, and sold to racing interests in other countries.

In 1999, approximately 27,000 greyhounds entered the racing system, but greyhound advocates estimate that an equal, if not greater, number also exited the system. While approximately 12,000 graded-off dogs found safety in adoption programs, at least 7,170 puppies and young dogs did not survive to the age of 18 months. Adding the 13,000 grade-offs who were not rescued to the number of young dogs who died, advocates estimate that a minimum of 20,170 racing greyhounds were killed in 1999. This number does not include an untold number of old dogs (brood bitches and stud dogs) killed after they were no longer productive as breeding stock.

According to a November 1996 *Pensacola News Journal* article, 600 to 800 greyhounds at the Pensacola Greyhound Track are euthanized every year and dumped in the Perdido Landfill. "It's not wonderful what I do, but as long as greyhound racing is legal, we need to be sure that when these animals are disposed of, it's done in the most compassionate way possible," said Andy Hillman, veterinarian at the 54-year-old Florida track. In Pittsfield, Massachusetts, from 1987 to 1992, more than 1,200 racing dogs were killed at a local shelter. Also in 1992 in Chandler Heights, Arizona, the decomposing bodies of 143 racing greyhounds were discovered in an abandoned citrus orchard 30 miles southeast of Phoenix. Each dog had been shot in the right temple with a .22-caliber pistol, and their tattooed left ears had been cut off to prevent identification.

Other killing methods are more crude and protracted. Two hundred racing greyhounds were found starving to death on an Ocala, Florida farm in November 1991. According to an eyewitness, the five-acre property was littered with shallow graves and burial pits. Of the 101 greyhounds found in 1990 starving at a private kennel that served the Tucson Greyhound Park in Arizona, only 40 survived.

In 1991 a trainer at the Coeur d'Alene track in Idaho described the electrocution of greyhounds using a device called the "Tijuana hot plate," so called because "in Mexico they used to electrocute their dogs." It consisted of a metal rod that was placed in the dog's rectum plus a metal clip that was attached to the dog's lip; electrocution resulted when the device was plugged into a wall outlet. According to the trainer, the killings took place in a "party-like" atmosphere.

Some dogs who manage to survive the racing industry face additional exploitation at the hands of the vivisection industry. For decades both public and private medical research facilities have been the end of the line for an incalculable number of racing greyhounds. Twenty years ago the New England Anti-Vivisection Society reported that more than 2,000 "retired" racing dogs flowed into Massachusetts research institutions each year. More recently, activists using the federal Freedom of Information Act (FOIA) and state open records laws have discovered that the flow of racing dogs into research labs has continued unabated.

The first publicly exposed case of greyhounds used in research came to light in 1989 and involved more than 600 greyhounds collected over a one-year period from Arizona dog farms and racetracks. The greyhounds, obtained by two Class B animal dealers with close ties to the racing industry, were sold to public and private research facilities in California and Arizona.

Susan Netboy, who later founded the Greyhound Protection League (GPL), a national greyhound advocacy organization, received information from In Defense of Animals (IDA) that 20 greyhounds had been sold to the Letterman Army Institute of Research (LAIR) in San Francisco. The dogs were to be used for bone-breaking experiments in a pilot study that would have ultimately involved hundreds of greyhounds had it continued. After tracing the dogs' tattoo numbers and working with IDA's president, Elliot Katz, D.V.M., Netboy filed a lawsuit against the Army, proving that the dogs were sold without the permission of their legal owners. Eventually all 19 of the surviving dogs were rescued. After obtaining the release of the LAIR greyhounds, Netboy made a FOIA request; she later received dealer records on more than 600 greyhounds sold by the two Arizona dog dealers. Four hundred of the dogs had been sold to W. L. Gore Industries, a private research facility in Flagstaff, Arizona. Despite a lengthy battle, none of the Gore dogs was saved. Shortly thereafter, the NGA extended registration privileges to Gore as an officially recognized kennel, thus providing the legal loophole for continued use of greyhounds by the facility.

Other southwestern facilities that bought dogs from the Arizona dealers included the University of California at Los Angeles, Cedars Sinai Hospital, the University of California at Davis, the University of California at San Diego, the University of the Pacific, Humana Hospital, St. Joseph's Hospital (Phoenix), and Harrington Arthritis Research Center. By the time Netboy's FOIA request was honored, most of the dogs were already dead; only 24 were rescued. Pursuit of such cases was predicated on owner consent issues. Because racing greyhounds are tattooed, and thereby traceable, they present a unique opportunity for animal advocates to establish that the dogs are frequently obtained from unscrupulous trainers and sold by Class B dealers without the knowledge or consent of their legal owners. Owners who check on the status of a dog may be told that the dog either was adopted or was injured and euthanized.

One of the most shocking research cases came to light two years ago. Documents obtained under a public records request sent to Colorado State University (CSU) by GNN in March 1998 revealed that 2,652 racing greyhounds had been euthanized at CSU's School of Veterinary Medicine between January 1995 and March 1998. The 320 pages of acquisition sheets listed dogs who ranged in age from puppies to 10-year-olds; nearly half were two-year-olds. Approximately one-third of the dogs were anesthetized and used to teach surgical procedures before being destroyed. Two-thirds of the greyhounds donated to the school were considered "excess" and were killed immediately after arrival.

A Denver *Rocky Mountain News* investigation revealed that CSU had a decade-long relationship with the state's greyhound breeders. CSU collected many of the dogs from track kennels and state dog farms, processed them, and disposed of the carcasses. Many of the greyhounds were delivered to CSU personally by their owners, often as many as 17 at a time.

In all, 70 individuals, including greyhound breeders, kennel operators, and trainers, appeared on the pages of CSU's acquisition records. Among them were some of the racing industry's most celebrated kennel owners, one of whom was honored by the NGA and had personally donated 320 greyhounds to CSU.

When the story broke in June 1998, James Voss, dean of the CSU vet school, defended the university's alliance with the racing industry, telling the *News* that the dogs being used would "likely die anyway, but by clubbing, shooting, or other inhumane methods." But public outcry forced CSU to sever its racing ties. Basic anatomy is now taught using interactive CD-ROM software, and students get hands-on surgical experience by spaying and neutering shelter animals under the supervision of a staff veterinarian.

But in a new low even for the racing industry, a greyhounds-in-research case involves a racing kennel owner who operates an adoption service and also holds a Class B dealer license. Until a few years ago, NGA member Daniel Shonka operated a racing kennel at the St. Croix Meadows track in Hudson, Wisconsin, and operated Greyhound Adoption of Iowa from his residence in Cedar Rapids. Shonka is under investigation by the U.S. Department of Agriculture, the Wisconsin Division of Gaming, and the Wisconsin Division of Criminal Investigation for allegedly obtaining greyhounds from unsuspecting owners who believed their dogs were being adopted and then selling them for $400 to $500 each to a private research lab. State gaming officials estimate Shonka's dealings netted him at least $500,000 in three years.

Most of the dogs were sold to Guidant Corp.'s Rhythm Management Group, a cardiac research lab in St. Paul, Minnesota. As of June 20, 2000, the USDA and the gaming division had traced 1,086 greyhounds on Guidant's records directly to Shonka. All but 108 greyhounds died at the lab, and Guidant agreed to reverse the surgical procedures on the remaining dogs and release them for adoption.

The resolution of this case is atypical, however. Throughout the past decade activists have repeatedly brought the greyhound acquisition issue to the attention of the USDA, but the agency has refused to take any significant action that would redress this ongoing tragedy.

Other state universities have received a total of more than 1,000 greyhounds donated by their legal owners in recent years. The dogs have ended up at Arizona State University, the University of Arizona, Mississippi State University, Auburn University, Iowa State University, and Kansas State University.

## The Adoption Angle

Once the systematic abuse of greyhounds became known in the mid-1980s, the racing industry was forced into a defensive position that encouraged adoption and discouraged the use of live lures. Part of the public relations makeover included the formation of the American Greyhound Council in 1987 to "provide for the welfare of the racing greyhound and the betterment of the greyhound industry." It provides funding for a toll-free adoption inquiry number for the industry-controlled Greyhound Pets of America (GPA), a national adoption group, and provides yearly stipends to GPA chapters and track adoption programs. However, only those groups that promote a positive image of greyhound racing are eligible for financial assistance. The industry continues to spend more money on public relations and lobbyists than it does on the rescue and adoption of greyhounds.

It was during this time that the fledgling greyhound adoption movement began with a handful of individuals in Florida and Massachusetts. Since then, more than 150 privately funded independent rescue and adoption groups have been formed. These groups are responsible for placing the majority of an estimated 12,000 to 13,000 discarded greyhounds into adoptive homes annually. Greyhounds lucky enough to reach the safety net of an adoption program typically arrive underweight, covered with ticks and fleas, and riddled with both external and internal parasites. Many have open pressure sores on their hips and shoulders caused by long confinement in small crates, and broken legs that have been left untreated for weeks.

Ironically, it will be the adoption movement that will ultimately bring about dog racing's demise. The adoption of tens of thousands of greyhounds in the last 15 years has turned thousands of animal lovers into greyhound welfare advocates, many of whom have become politically active in the battle to end dog racing. Docile and loving dogs, greyhounds have been their own best ambassadors. Just ten years ago, an adopter walking a greyhound often heard such comments as, "I bet I lost money on that dog." Today, greyhound guardians are more likely to be asked, "Is that one of those abused greyhounds?"

### An Industry on Its Last Legs

It is not just the image of greyhound racing but also the very nature of the business itself that has changed dramatically in the last decade. The industry peaked in 1991 with a wagering handle (total amount of money bet on races) of $3.4 billion, making it the sixth most popular spectator sport. By 1995, attendance had dropped 25 percent and the total handle had dropped 26 percent to $2.5 billion. Attendance and handle continue to drop steadily with each passing year.

The dog racing industry currently holds less than a one percent share of the entire $54.3 billion annual U.S. gambling market. After payouts (more than 80 percent of the handle is returned to the public as winnings), the industry netted approximately $493.7 million in 1998. Its dramatic decline is due largely to competition from the rapidly expanding casino gaming industry. In a February 27 *Washington Post* article, reporter Andrew Beyer noted that dog racing has lost much of its customer base to other forms of gambling, adding, "Never again will this industry be able to stand on its own."

State revenue from dog racing has also dropped significantly. Florida, widely considered to be the last bastion of dog racing with 17 racetracks, has seen its pari-mutuel tax revenue drop 71 percent, from $100 million in 1990 to $28.7 million in 1998. In May 2000, Florida lawmakers approved a $20 million tax break for the state's pari-mutuel industry, which includes horse and dog tracks and jai alai frontons; $14 million will be used to bail out the dog tracks.

In 1994 the Arizona legislature approved a $6 million tax break for the state's three ailing racetracks. As a result, Tucson Greyhound Park has paid no pari-mutuel taxes to the state since mid-1995, despite annual gross simulcast earnings of about $5 million. Taxpayer dollars are now subsidizing the existence of this end-of-the-line track.

Other states also have experienced drastic revenue declines between 1990 and 1998. In Kansas, tax income from dog racing fell 59 percent; in Arizona, 68 percent; in Massachusetts, 69 percent; in Oregon, 70 percent; in Connecticut, 79 percent; and New Hampshire, 84 percent.

Twelve U.S. tracks have closed since 1990, and 49 privately owned racetracks continue to operate in 15 states, although many of them are awash in red ink. The exceptions are the five tracks in Iowa, West Virginia, and Rhode Island, where state lawmakers, pressured by racetrack lobbyists, amended their gambling statutes and allowed the tracks to operate either slot machines or video lottery terminals.

Casinos have become the racing dogs' best allies. A casino operating within 100 miles of a dog track will eventually pull the plug on that track; conversely, allowing dog tracks to morph into casinos will keep those tracks on life support for the foreseeable future.

But the sun began to set on the greyhound racing industry nearly ten years ago. GREY2K's ballot initiative in Massachusetts was a rallying cry for animal activists nationwide to help hasten the end of decades of horrendous cruelty and the wanton slaughter of greyhounds for a gambling industry.

*On May 23, 2001, several executive committee members of Grey2K announced the formation of a national organization call GREY2K USA. Its mission is to end dog racing in the United States through political means.*

# Part 2
# WILDLIFE

# 1: A Lion in Every Back Yard: The Mass Marketing of Exotic Animals

Jim Mason

WANT TO OWN your own tiger? They are nearly extinct in their native Asian habitat, but your neighbor might have one for sale. You may prefer an emu, serval, marmoset, sugar glider, or one of the hundreds of other out-of-the-ordinary animals available to everyday buyers on the Internet or at one of the hundred-and-some auctions around the country. Not very many years ago, I could have bought a tiger for only $350 at an exotic animal auction I attended in Ohio.

The buying and selling of rare and unusual animals is, according to some insider estimates, at least a $100 million-a-year business. Once the near-exclusive monopoly of zoos, circuses, and a network of dealer-suppliers, the traffic in exotic species has been rerouted into everyday cities and towns.

Helping to direct that flow are magazines like *Animal Finders' Guide*, *Rare Breeds Journal*, and dozens of other publications. The *Guide* alone reaches more than 10,000 pet shops and another 10,000 animal dealers around the United States.

Today, in most states, almost anyone can buy, breed, and sell just about any kind of animal. A whole new industry of importers, breeders, dealers, suppliers, veterinarians, auctions, trade associations, and lobby groups is hustling to cater to such buyers.

Auctions play a key role in the trade because they help to establish "fair market" prices on various species and to provide a good place for exotics fanciers to exchange business cards and hustle new recruits. There's a string of such auctions in states from Ohio to Texas, but the largest of them all is Lolli Brothers, held in Macon, Missouri. Lolli's holds several auctions each year, and at a typical one some 10,000 live exotic animals and 1,000 stuffed and mounted creatures are sold over a six-day period. Most trading, however, takes place through insider networks of big breeders, dealers, and industry leaders, all of

## Cruelties in the Exotic Pet Trade

Thanks to the expanded trade in exotic animals, people who lack the sense to care for dogs or cats are now able, throughout most of the country, to purchase, keep, breed, and sell just about any animal they fancy. Down-and-out farmers toiling in the shadows of agribusiness giants are hoping to meet the mortgage by raising ostriches, emus, and rare breeds of sheep, goats, cattle, and horses. Hustling animal trainers and profit-hungry operators of roadside zoos, drive-through game parks, canned hunts, trophy farms, and horn farms are stocking up on lions, tigers, camels, zebras, elk, deer, ibex, eland, and other large, spectacular mammals. Indeed, no form of life is sacred in the exotic animal business, where only two absolutes prevail—profit and the claim of a constitutional right to own whatever animal one pleases—and where every sort of animal is grist for the commercial mill: native and non-native wildlife, rare and endangered species, domesticates (especially unique breeds and oddities), and an assortment of freaks, novelties, and hybrids.

This is truly an animal slave trade, and it harms animals in many ways:

whom seem to have made each other's acquaintance. In addition, black-market trading in protected species constitutes a growing segment of the exotic animal business. Ironically, extending the hand of legal protection to a species drives up that species' price.

This traffic used to be confined to a small insider network of "game" ranchers, circuses, zoos, and animal trainers. But it went mainstream about 25 years ago after zoos began dumping their surplus animals into the private market. A few entrepreneurs organized breeders' associations and began stirring up

- *Isolation and Social Deprivation*: Highly social species such as wolves, primates, and herd animals need territory and group interactions that human owners cannot provide.
- *Unsuitable Climates*: Tropical and desert animals have special needs and do not thrive in pens, cages, and city apartments.
- *Inadequate Diets*: Nutritional needs and complex feeding behaviors are often ignored in favor of whatever is cheap and easy for owners.
- *Poor Environments*: Cages and pens, even if well designed, provide security for an owner's property, but little enrichment for the animals.
- *Improper Handling and Abuse*: Much of it occurs when an animal's behavior (natural or deranged) becomes inconvenient. Owners react by increasing restraint, declawing, pulling teeth, and using other manipulations that try to force docile, pet-like behavior. Leopard and bear cubs seen at auctions are usually declawed and often defanged.
- *General Deterioration*: Overall animal health deteriorates because of the aforementioned conditions and as a result of genetic health problems, like the unsound legs of Texas ranched ostriches.

demand for their species. Soon, thousands more got into the business. Through clever advertising and promotion, these animal breeders and dealers created a succession of trendy animal "pets." First it was llamas in the late 1970s; then in the 1980s pot-bellied pigs emerged; more recently, emus, ostriches, and other ratites or "big birds" have been hustled as novel meat and leather commodities. Lately the "in" animals are African pygmy hedgehogs, as well as servals, caracals, bengals (domestic and wild cat hybrids), and other small cats.

It's an animal-based pyramid scheme. Those who get in early make the big money selling breeding pairs to hobby breeders and others with dollar signs in their eyes. Once all of the suckers and dreamers have traded their money for animals, the breeders' market is spent, prices fall, and the fad is over. The crash in the "big bird" market is a case in point. When I attended auctions in the early 1990s, these were the hottest sellers. I saw "proven" breeding pairs of ostriches, for example, sell for up to $70,000 a pair. By 1993, the bubble was bursting; within years ostrich owners were lucky to get $1,000 for a mature bird. But the exotics industry insiders and entrepreneurs simply moved on to create the next "hot" animal. And so it goes, species after species.

Meanwhile, this greed and craziness generates tens of thousands of animals no longer wanted by the hobby breeders and no longer cared for by irate owners misled by promises of "the perfect pet." These animals fall into what has been called a cycle of hell. Many suffer and die of neglect in their owners' backyards; others perish in the shuffle from owner to owner. Some end up at auctions, roadside zoos, petting zoos, canned hunts, and taxidermists. When the big bird market crashed in the mid-nineties, many outraged ostrich and emu owners abandoned their animals to starve. Some owners turned them loose (there is a feral emu population in south central Missouri); others called in their friends and killed the birds with clubs and shotguns.

Even in the best of times, animals caught up in the exotic trade fare poorly. Members of tropical and desert-dwelling species languish and often die in environments that fail to match the special ecosystems in which they have evolved. Highly social animals such as wolves, primates, and herd animals, who need territory and group interactions, are kept in barren isolation instead. Their cages and pens may be clean and well designed in some cases, but cages meant to provide security for an owner's property confer little benefit on their occupants.

What's more, animals' needs and complex feeding behavior frequently are ignored because owners prefer using cheap and easy feed. Amusement is apt to turn into abuse when an animal's behavior—whether natural or deranged—becomes a problem. Some owners react to unwelcome behavior by declawing, pulling teeth, increasing restraint, and using other manipulations to try to force docile, pet-like behavior. Others send their exotic pets to canned hunts, petting zoos, taxidermists, auctions, and roadside zoos. Even Pat Hoctor, editor of *Animal Finders' Guide* and a breeder and ardent promoter of exotic animals, says his industry is "shaming itself."

The industry is largely unregulated; a person who sells or commercially exhibits an exotic animal protected under the Animal Welfare Act is required to obtain a license from the U.S. Department of Agriculture. However, an individual with a "pet" tiger in his backyard does not need a license, nor is a license required for animals not covered under the Act, such as birds and reptiles, who constitute the bulk of the trade in exotics. Because no organization or government agency tracks the trade in exotic animals, it is difficult (if not impossible) to ascertain the exact number of animals involved.

Although concerns about animal well-being are a priority for animal advocates, there are other issues that may help rouse the public and move policy makers to action. For example, many state and local public health officials are concerned about the craze for exotic animals because they see new threats to human health and safety. Large carnivores such as cougars and wolf hybrids can get loose and attack people. Other animals, especially primates, can carry diseases harmful to humans. Some 80 percent of adult macaques carry the herpes B virus, which causes fatal brain infections in humans. Some exotic species may spread diseases to horses, cattle, and other domestic animals.

Foremost in the minds of state fish and wildlife officials are concerns about impacts on native wildlife. Exotics can harm native species through disease, predation, competition for food and habitat, and hybridization. A few officials are willing to speak out about the dangers of creeping commercialization, a threat that is growing as the freewheeling exotics industry sends out all the wrong messages about where wildlife belongs. The cumulative effect puts higher prices on the heads of all wildlife and fosters wider commerce in animals—dead, alive, or in parts.

## Discover the Exotic Animal Industry

Thanks to investigative journalist Alan Green and the Center for Public Integrity, we have a thoroughly researched book that details the cruelty and carelessness of the exotic animal industry. *Animal Underworld* follows the trafficking in many species of animals as they move from zoos, laboratories, and theme parks into a black market of breeders, dealers, auctions, and hunting ranches.

According to the book, "This black market is seeming bottomless. At last count, for example, there were 250 or so tigers in the 180-plus zoos accredited by the American Zoo and Aquarium Association. But there are estimated to be as many as six or seven thousand pet tigers in the United States—some confined in windowless basements, others relegated to makeshift cages in backyards or back lots. Classified ads in

Ironically, people's fascination with and deep need for animals fuel this lamentable trade. Our long alienation from animals and our sense that wild nature is nearly gone stirs many people to want a last piece of it—a souvenir of sorts—embodied in a wild animal. Intelligent and responsible human beings have enough sense to know that cougars and monkeys belong in their native habitats, not in cages or on leashes. Then there are those who think it cute or cool to own an exotic—which practically guarantees that these beautiful, special beings fall into the hands of the least intelligent and responsible humans.

The least discussed concern with the exotics trade is its impact on culture and values. While part of society is trying to rebuild values based on the sanctity of the living world, the exotics trade is tearing them down. When bears and elephants are enslaved to dance in costumes before jeering crowds, the awe of nature is diminished. When zebras and lions are manipulated to produce "zorses," "ligers," and other hybrid freaks for

one specialty publication offer twenty-odd species of primates, including baby chimpanzees...; African lions, which in captivity are bred like beagles, go for as little as $200."

The centerpiece of the book is documentation that many of the nation's most prestigious zoos and scientists are key players in this dark trade. Animal advocates have known this all along, of course, but here is the documentation to use in your letters to the editor the next time your local newspapers publishes one of its periodic puff pieces about the local zoo and its valiant efforts to save endangered species.

For further gruesome enlightenment, see www.animalfindersguide.com and its links to related sites. Do a Google search using the words "exotic" and "animal" and you will have a huge window on the shadowy world of animal trafficking.

fun and profit, respect for nature is eroded. And when one wild species after another is captured, imported, confined, bred, bottle-raised, declawed, and otherwise processed for the pet trade, we dump the last remains of human respect and sensitivity toward other life in the world. In commodifying animals as pets and for other purposes, the exotics trade is sending out bad lessons about wildlife and nature. It is teaching that animals are separable from their communities, their ecosystems, and their evolution. It is teaching ignorance, disrespect, and callousness toward individual animals and, by extension, their species, their bio-communities, and the entire living world.

Better laws can check some of the excesses of the exotics trades (the number of wild-caught birds imported into the United States has dropped from 400,000 to 60,000 per year due to the Wild Bird Conservation Act of 1992), but there will always be limits on what laws can do. Advocates need to influence public opinion about companion animals, deciding which animals are appropriate and which animals are off limits. We also need to teach that circuses, petting zoos, drive-through zoos, and other such places are bad not only for the animals, but also for children in need of a sense of respect for themselves and for the living world around them. As captive wildlife expert Sue Pressman noted, these places "are to wildlife education what pornography is to sex education."

It is unconscionable that the tiger at the Ohio auction was sold cheaply because he was old and his coat was too shabby to make a good rug. Sadly, there may be more captives like him than there are tigers roaming free where they belong.

*This chapter was made possible by a grant from The Summerlee Foundation.*

*Author's note: I use the term "pet" throughout because it conveys the dominance and egoism that prevail in human-animal relations and that fuel the demand for exotic animals. The term "companion animal"* suggests ideals not yet achieved. I felt, therefore, that it would be inappropriate and misleading in this chapter.

# 2: The Trade in Drugs and Wildlife

ADAM M. ROBERTS

ASIDE FROM GUN running, drug and wildlife trafficking may be the two greatest moneymakers for international criminals—and some of these perpetrators capitalize on their cunning by combining the two. According to the International Police Organization, wildlife trafficking is second only to the drug trade as the largest illegal business in the world. Dick Smith, former deputy of the U.S. Fish and Wildlife Service (USFWS), ranks the animal trade as the world's third most lucrative contraband.

Animal-related drug smuggling has a large financial incentive. Smith estimates the profitability of wildlife smuggling at $5 billion a year (with many animals being worth more, ounce for ounce, than cocaine) while the World Wildlife Fund places the estimate at $20 billion annually. Combining the two forms of trafficking increases the already huge profits of the multibillion-dollar drug trade. According to Craig van Note, executive vice president of Monitor, an international ecological consortium, "Police agencies around the world are facing the fact that the drug smuggling goes hand-in-hand with wildlife smuggling and vice versa." The USFWS recognizes that smugglers often trade illegal drugs for endangered animals in cashless transfers.

The macabre list of examples of intermingled wildlife/drug smuggling provides a frightening insight into the creative and cruel mind of the smuggler: heroin hidden in snakes, snails, or elephant tusks, cannabis stuffed into antelope heads, cocaine surreptitiously inserted into gutted parrot carcasses, and heroin-filled pouches implanted into the stomachs of large, expensive goldfish. Domestic animals are also used as unsuspecting drug couriers. In December 1994, a debilitated English sheepdog named Cokey arrived from Colombia at New York's John F. Kennedy Airport with ten cocaine-filled balloons surgically implanted into her abdomen.

Two particularly egregious cases highlight how scheming smugglers continually develop innovative ways to use animals to transport drugs. In one case, dubbed Operation Cocaine Constrictor, more than 300 boa constrictors from Colombia were implanted with cocaine-filled condoms inserted into their rectums (which were then sewn shut), causing the deaths of all but 63 of the creatures. It may very well have been the assumption that few wildlife inspectors would want to examine closely a shipment of snakes that led the smugglers to devise such a cruel ploy.

In 1993, Operation Fishnet focused on a case in which liquid cocaine was carefully mixed into clear outer bags that were placed around inner bags containing valuable tropical fish. The shipments from Colombia were scrutinized only after some leaking bags emitted a strange odor, while others had a curious sediment buildup on the bottom of the bags. Bizarre cases like these point not only to the use of legal wildlife shipments to transport contraband, but also highlight the overwhelming need to increase funding for the Division of Law Enforcement in the USFWS. There is a "catch-22" in the current inspection system in which the Drug Enforcement Administration has the funds and expertise to pursue drug smugglers but has no reason to inspect wildlife shipments, while the USFWS, with heightened expertise in wildlife inspection, is woefully underfunded and understaffed and cannot possibly inspect all imported shipments, especially in cities such as Miami, which has become a hub for the importation of wildlife and drugs from Central and South America.

Latin America, known for its abundance of drug traffickers as well as magnificent wildlife, poses a double problem. *The Washington Times* reports that as leaders of the long-empowered Colombian Cali cartel are arrested, "drug agents now fear that newly powerful Mexican gangs may seize control of cocaine traffic" into the United States. This is further acknowledged in the startling "Crime Against Nature" report issued by the Endangered Species Project. The authors note, "Mexico's role as a major supplier for birds and reptiles is being increasingly characterized by the involvement of drug dealers."

The issue is compounded by the use of legal trade avenues, such as commercial fishing, to transport illegal drugs. This is especially important with trade between Mexico and the United States increasing in the post-NAFTA era, putting wildlife at greater risk because of more open borders with less control, making inspection and confiscation more difficult.

The link between drug smuggling and wildlife exploitation transcends the direct, physical use of animals to transport drugs. Jorge Hank Rhon, son of Mexico's former minister of agriculture, has been implicated in smuggling both drugs and wildlife. *The New York Times* reported in May 1995 that Rhon had been stopped at the Mexico City airport, where items made from ocelot fur and elephant ivory were found in his luggage. The *Times* stated that Rhon, a Tijuana racetrack owner, has been linked with drug traffickers in news reports but has never been charged with a related crime.

## Cartels and Traffickers

The drug/wildlife smuggling trade is highly organized, power-ful, and influential, and even has alleged ties to the Mafia. Investigative journalist Alexander Cockburn reports in the peri-odical *Counterpunch* that "[t]he Italian Mafia controls the Italian fishing business. Its boats and the canneries associated with them are the prime conduit for drug smuggling from Palermo and other Italian ports to the rest of Europe and the U.S."

The publication also reports that "investigations by the U.S. Drug Enforcement [Administration] and U.S. Customs Service have disclosed how fishing fleets and canneries south from Mexico, through Costa Rica, to Venezuela, Colombia and Peru have been deeply involved in drug smuggling." This is echoed by the *Los Angeles Times*, which stated that the Cali drug cartel uses regional fishing fleets "to smuggle both drugs and animals through the Caribbean to the United States and Europe."

"The Mexico Report," issued by Legal Research International in September 1996, asserts: "It is no coincidence that since the tuna industry was privatized in the late 1980s under Mexican President Carlos Salinas, most of the industry has fallen under the control of Mexico's most violent and notorious drug traffickers. Raul Salinas, the disgraced older brother of the former Mexican leader, is said to control one of the largest tuna canneries on the Pacific coast of Mexico." Furthermore, the Mexican newspaper *La Jornada* revealed that two drug kingpins, Mexican Manuel Rodriguez and Colombian José Castrillón, were partners in a tuna fishing company.

Stories linking tuna boat owners to drug smuggling rings are especially noteworthy because legislation passed in Congress in 1997 eviscerated dolphin protection, enabling a return to the days of fishing-related dolphin slaughter. As a result of the passage of legislation dubbed the "Dolphin Death Act," foreign fishing fleets (including those in Mexico) again are able to chase dolphins with noisy speedboats and helicopters, encircle them in mile-long purse-seine nets, and even kill them, yet still label the tuna "dolphin safe" on the U.S. market.

This legislation implemented an international agreement known as the Panama Declaration, which gutted tuna embargo provisions of the U.S. Marine Mammal Protection Act, allowed the sale of "dolphin unsafe" tuna in the United States, and corrupted the definition of the "dolphin safe" label. Legal challenges against the redefinition of "dolphin safe" are ongoing. Not surprisingly, signatories to this non-binding agreement (negotiated by the U.S. State Department, five environmental groups, and 11 other countries) include Panama, Mexico, Colombia, Costa Rica, and Venezuela. The irony is glaring.

Whether drug smugglers physically use wildlife to transport their illegal products or consolidate their shady business practices, the link between wildlife and drug smuggling must be exposed. For as long as it continues, smugglers will profit by exploiting both their victims and the worldwide system that cannot yet stop them.

# 3: Dying to Heal

ADAM M. ROBERTS, GRACE GE GABRIEL, AND JILL ROBINSON

IF ONE EXPERIENCES blood in one's feces, take two to three grams of a remedy called Gi-Wang daily with hot water. In addition to herbs, Gi-Wang contains bear bile, rhino horn, and elephant gallstone. For pain in the kidneys, hips, and lower intestines, a mixture called rGYA-RU 14 includes bear bile, rhino horn, mountain goat horn, and deer antlers. These and dozens of other animal-based remedies are found in the *Handbook of Traditional Tibetan Drugs*, compiled by T. I. Tsarong, and provide insight into the nature of the millennia-old pharmacopoeia of traditional Asian medicines.

Practiced throughout Asia and Asian communities across the globe, traditional medicine (TM) is based on harmoniously balancing the components of the body. Certain ailments are considered "hot" and are therefore treated with remedies considered "cold," and vice versa. Although most TMs are herbal, a small percentage contains animal parts; within that minor category, an even smaller percentage contains parts from threatened or endangered species. Regardless of how limited the use, it would clearly be better to employ herbal alternatives rather than harm sentient beings.

Some animals' parts used in traditional remedies are well known: tiger bone, rhino horn, seal penis, and bear gallbladder, for instance. Other less "charismatic" species are also used. Pangolin scales purportedly disperse congealed blood and reduce swelling; the head and shell of the elongated tortoise are utilized in postpartum tonics; the fat of the African python is applied to ease muscle fatigue and chest pains; and Reticulated python skin may be used to treat ringworm, warts, and rashes.

The negative welfare implications and conservation risks of using animals in TM are as important as in any other form of consumptive overutilization. Investigators for the International Fund for Animal Welfare (IFAW) and the Animals Asia Foundation (AAF) have seen and heard of cats, raccoons, and pangolins thrown into vats of boiling water and then skinned while still conscious; deer succumbing to broken and severed legs after being caught in steel-jaw leghold traps; and baby bears cringing in the back of tiny cages while waiting to be lowered into pots of boiling water.

Meanwhile, the wild populations of numerous species have declined dramatically, due in part to poaching for the supply of the trade in animal parts and products. Tiger, rhino, and some bear populations have all declined throughout most of their range as a result of this unsustainable pressure. According to its Ministry of Forestry, the Chinese government in 1984 proposed to reduce pressure on Asiatic black bears by establishing farms where caged bears could be housed and continually "milked" for their bile. This has been an unconditional failure. Wild animals are still captured to augment the captive stock, and the promotion of captive species' use in TM further stimulates market demand for bear products, resulting in increased poaching. Caged bears suffer endlessly from the often unsanitary steel catheter inserted into the gallbladder for easy bile extraction.

Some even have their feet cut off to supply the high-priced gourmet market for bear-paw soup.

This cruelty is particularly indefensible since there are alternatives to the use of animals in TM—not simply Western pills and tonics, but herbal alternatives that are cheaper, as effective, more humane, and still allow practitioners to engage in TM practices. An IFAW-funded report by EarthCare and the Chinese Association of Medicine and Philosophy concluded that there are at least 54 known herbal remedies to replace bear bile in its various medicinal applications.

Most importantly, the promotion of alternatives in large part comes from Chinese practitioners themselves. Dr. Sun Ji Xian of the Chinese Association of Preventative Medicine contends, "I choose not to use bear bile and go to the trouble of replacing it, because I believe that animals should not suffer." Dr. Ho Ka Cheong, president of the Hong Kong Chinese Herbalist Association, Ltd. adds, "Herbal alternatives have the same effect, so why use animals?"

A 1998 public opinion survey commissioned by IFAW and conducted in Beijing and Shanghai, China, found that 88 percent of the respondents found bear farming cruel and inhumane and just over 70 percent said they would refuse to use bear bile. Based on these poll results and the findings of a diminishing demand for bear bile by Traditional Chinese Medicine practitioners, IFAW started a public awareness campaign designed to educate international travelers about the products that might contain endangered species. Through this partnership with Chinese authorities of the Convention on International Trade in Endangered Species of Fauna and Flora (CITES), IFAW produced posters and brochures that were placed in various international airport departure lounges throughout China. In a survey commissioned by AAF and the Hong Kong SPCA later that same year, it was found that 93 percent of respondents found bear farming cruel, and, given that a plant could substitute for an animal product, an overwhelming 94 percent of the respondents would use a plant instead.

To ensure that those who wish to practice TM in Asia and elsewhere move away from using animals in their remedies, the global conservation and animal protection community must focus simultaneously on the simple economic law of supply and demand. Certain laws in the United States, for instance, address some of the issues regarding supply. In 1998 the U.S. Congress passed the Rhino and Tiger Product Labeling Act to prohibit sale of products that contain (or even claim to contain) parts or derivatives of rhinos or tigers. In 2002, Congress was again considering the Bear Protection Act to prohibit the import, export, and interstate commerce in bear gallbladders and bile. These and other legislative mechanisms attempt to cut off the flow of parts and products from threatened and endangered species.

At the same time, the humane and conservation communities must work with TM practitioners to promote use of alternatives to animal-based remedies. IFAW and AAF have begun the task of getting such Asian nations as China and South Korea to close their bear farms and begin transferring the bears to sanctuaries for long-term care. AAF has already started rescuing bears from Chinese bear farms and beginning the rehabilitation process under an agreement with the Chinese government that will ultimately see 500 bears retired peacefully to a sanctuary.

These groups also have engaged traditional medicine doctors, traders, and consumers to sign a pledge to move toward herbal alternatives.

Meanwhile, the 155 Parties to CITES have begun paying real attention to the use of threatened and endangered species in traditional medicines. In 1997, a resolution was passed on "Traditional Medicines" recognizing that "continued and uncontrolled use of several endangered species…[may present a] potential threat to the long term survival of these species…." The Parties have since agreed to compile a list of threatened and endangered species used in traditional medicines to educate government officials and provide an opportunity to explore the use of alternatives to each species on the list. The Animal Welfare Institute and IFAW have been urging the development of this list for some time, and IFAW presented a draft list at the CITES Animals Committee meeting in Hanoi, Vietnam in the summer of 2001. This aspect of the international education campaign continues.

It is hoped that this combination of legal advocacy and consumer activism will put a stranglehold on those who wish to supply animal parts for the TM trade, and will convince users to accept nonanimal alternatives. In the end, as with most issues, education is the key. For instance, while Viagra is all the rage these days, major media outlets such as NBC's *Dateline* have aired programs on "herbal" alternatives to the popular impotence drug. According to the March 15, 1999 program, "NuMan," the touted Chinese alternative to Viagra, "uses *natural* ingredients like ginseng and deer horn to help both impotency and *overall* sexual health" (emphasis added). Just as vegetarians read food labels to avoid consuming animal products, so must those who use "natural" or "herbal" traditional Asian medicines understand exactly what they consume.

# 4: Land Mines: Animal Casualties of the Underground War

ADAM M. ROBERTS AND KEVIN STEWART

IN HIS ACCEPTANCE speech for the Nobel Peace Prize on behalf of the International Campaign to Ban Landmines, Cambodian double-amputee Tun Channareth wrote: "My handicaps are quite visible. They can remind us of the invisible handicaps we all have...the 'land mines of the heart.' These land mines inside can lead us to war, to jealousy, to cruel power over others. If we ban the land mines of the heart along with the land mines in the earth, the needs of the poor will take priority over the wants of the rich, the freedom of the dominated over the liberty of the powerful.... Together we can stop a coward's war that makes victims of us all."

Animal activists fight daily to eliminate the death toll of the various "coward's wars" waged against other species. In the wilderness, they try to prevent bullets from reaching the targets of the hunt, and work to stop indiscriminate steel traps from inflicting unfathomable pain and suffering on their victims. It has become increasingly evident that such activists need to join the fight to ban forever the use of violent, indiscriminate land mines that destroy the lives of both humans and nonhumans with their devastating force.

In some instances, land mines directly threaten both people and animals. Reuters reporter Roger Atwood wrote in 1997 that roughly 20,000 land mines are strewn across the Falkland/Malvinas Islands, a remnant of Argentinean attempts to keep British soldiers off the land 15 years ago. According to Atwood, "No [human] has been killed by the mines since the war...but animals are regularly blown to pieces." The minefields are identified by fences and warning signs, but with "75,000 sheep, keeping the livestock from danger can be a struggle." Meanwhile, "birdwatchers, one of the biggest groups of tourists, are especially vulnerable as they walk in search of penguins, ducks, and songbirds."

In Sri Lanka, as many as 20 Asian elephants are killed by mines every year, according to zoologist Charles Santiapillai of the University of Peradeniya. Motala, an elephant working to help remove logs from the jungle along the Thailand-Myanmar border, was wounded by a land mine and has been slowly recovering after the surgical amputation of part of her left foot. The goal is to fit her with a prosthetic foot. Motala's plight drew international media attention and thousands of dollars in donations for her medical care.

Thousands of miles away, in Africa, land mines have ravaged wildlife, including threatened and highly endangered species. Mines reportedly have killed more than 100 elephants in Mozambique. Scott Nathanson, a Disarmament Campaign organizer, writes that elephants in the Gorongosa national game park "have been maimed because of anti-personnel land mines or killed because of anti-tank mines."

In Zimbabwe, Lt. Col. Martin Rupiah, a lecturer at the Center for Defense Studies at the University of Zimbabwe, claims that "every village near Chiredzi has lost at least one animal to land mines....In the Gonarezhou National Park, elephants and buffaloes have had to be killed after they were injured by land mines." In northwest Rwanda, one of the region's highly endangered mountain gorillas was killed by a land mine as a result of that country's civil war. According to the field staff of the International Gorilla Conservation Programme, the 20-year-old male silverback was named Mkono, which means "hand" in the Kiswahili language; he had already lost a hand to a poacher's snare.

In Croatia, Professor Djuro Huber of the University of Zagreb has documented wildlife fatalities due to land mines. His reports note the deaths of European brown bears, roe deer, lynxes, and foxes as a result of mines placed in the region from 1990 to 1996.

The placement of land mines also poses an indirect threat to wildlife. In many regions of the world, arable farmland is rendered useless when mines are placed in fields. This causes farmers to move into marginal adjoining regions otherwise inhabited by wildlife. As poverty increases because of farmland restrictions, hunting may increase to feed hungry families. Similarly, poaching wild animals may increase to fund arms purchases. Homemade land mines are used to kill tigers for their valuable pelts and bones. In 1995, Nick Rufford reported in the London *Sunday Times* that the Khmer Rouge in Cambodia used tiger skins and bones to purchase anti-tank land mines and guns.

Poachers in Angola similarly set land mines around elephant watering holes to slaughter them for their ivory, which is then sold on the black market.

Just as wildlife habitat and farmland are put in conflict as a result of land mine placement, mine explosions specifically harm livestock animals. Since herds are usually large, an explosion set off by one animal may kill many others. A study of the social and economic costs of mines in Afghanistan, Bosnia, Cambodia, and Mozambique concluded that more than 54,000 animals were lost to land mine detonations. Mines deployed during World War II killed more than 3,000 animals per year in Libya between 1940 and 1980.

A 1996 Reuters report by Jonathan Lyons in Iraq tells of a farmer named Sali Abdullah whose "horse stepped on a mine, sending fragments, dirt and rocks tearing through [Abdullah's] face and upper body. The animal was killed on the spot, but doctors remain hopeful they can save Abdullah's eyesight." Such livestock/land mine encounters are not strictly accidental. Lt. Col. Rupiah noted that land mines placed in Rhodesia (now Zimbabwe) back in the early 1960s still exist and that "[s]ince 1980, only 10 percent of the minefields have been cleared." He suggests that as much as 80 percent of these mines are placed in communal areas that should have been available for use by farmers in their villages after they won independence. Those farmers who chose to return to their lands "pushed their cattle ahead to detonate the mines."

In western Bosnia there are unconfirmed reports that residents of Sanski Most have developed their own method of demining, called "sheep-demining," in which they simply let sheep loose into unsecured areas. Sheep were also used to clear minefields during the 1980–1988 Iran-Iraq War.

A coordinated effort is under way to use well-trained dogs for mine verification and marking. Dogs trained at the Swedish Dog Academy are used at the Cambodian Mine Action Centre to find and identify mines, allowing human workers to fence off the surrounding area and eliminate the mine. The United States has supported the use of this new brand of "sniffer dog," which is apparently better at mine detection than mechanical detectors because many mines are now predominantly plastic and can be unearthed by the dogs.

Unfortunately, however, the United States has not been an enthusiastic supporter of recent global efforts to ban these dreadful devices and ensure their removal and worldwide destruction. The United States has refused to join more than 130 other nations in signing the historic Ottawa treaty (opened for signature in December 1997 and entered into force on March 1, 1999), the Convention on the Prohibition of the Use, Stockpiling, Production and Transfer of Anti-Personnel Mines and on Their Destruction. The Treaty simply establishes a schedule for all participating nations to stop using, developing, producing, acquiring, or stockpiling land mines, and delineates a commitment to ensure the destruction of anti-personnel mines. The United States was not alone in its refusal; other nations, including China, Egypt, the former Soviet Union, Israel, and Pakistan, also did not sign. Like the United States, these nations are among the world's leading producers and exporters of anti-personnel land mines. President Clinton used the excuse that land mines along the Korean demilitarized zone are an essential deterrent to an attack by North Korea. Meanwhile, approximately 26,000 people are killed or maimed every year by a fraction of the estimated 100 million mines spread throughout the world. No one knows for sure how many animals are killed, but it is clear that land mines are indiscriminate and devastating.

The 1997 treaty is an important step toward stopping the epidemic of mine casualties. However, every effort must be made to remove and destroy existing mines. A mine that costs as little as $3 to place may cost $300 to $1,000 to remove. Adequate funding is a vital component to the international land mine extraction effort. The United States committed $80 million to the effort in 1998, but the United Nations estimates that the entire effort may cost more than $30 billion to complete.

Some members of Congress are committed to the crusade to eliminate land mines. President Clinton signed the Land Mine Use Moratorium Act into law in early 1996, and Sen. Patrick Leahy (D-VT) and Rep. Lane Evans (D-IL) introduced legislation to bar American armed forces from using anti-personnel land mines for one year beginning in January 1999. Senator Leahy and Congressman Evans also introduced the Landmine Elimination and Victim Assistance Act of 2001 to promote alternatives to land mines, urge the United States to join the Ottawa Convention, and expand mine victim assistance.

There is now a historic opportunity to build on existing leadership in the quest for the cooperative global elimination of land mines. Animal activists need to enlist in the effort to win the coward's war for the sake of innocent beings everywhere.

*Editor's note: For more information on the campaign against land mines, go to www.heathermills.org and www.landmines.org.uk.*

# 5: Saving Sharks from the Jaws of Greed

SUSIE WATTS

LIKE A FIN rising above the water, the issue of shark conservation has, at last, broken the surface of public consciousness. Both feared and revered by different cultures, sharks worldwide face a whole range of serious threats. Despite this, only a handful of countries manage their sharks at all, no shark species are listed in any of the appendices of the Convention on International Trade in Endangered Species of Wild Fauna and Flora (CITES), and very few legally binding international agreements recognize shark species as being threatened or endangered.

The world has been slow to recognize the trouble that sharks are in. This is mainly because, until fairly recently, the economic value of sharks was relatively low and there was little incentive for governments to expend resources on monitoring them. The result is that compared with other species, there has been very little global information on the number of sharks killed deliberately, the number caught incidentally, the individual species that are most heavily utilized, or the volume of international trade in shark meat, cartilage, oil, skins, and fins.

Shark meat is traded in vast quantities around the world— 110,000 metric tons in 1994, according to the United Nations Food and Agriculture Organization (FAO). Shark meat is also a valuable source of protein in many parts of the developing world. Shark skins, too, are traded for use in making belts, watchbands, and (mostly in the United States) cowboy boots. Shark liver oil is used in the cosmetics industry and is also marketed as capsules for the medicinal trade. In India it is used by subsistence fishers as a wood preservative for their fishing boats. The increased worldwide market for shark cartilage is due to highly questionable claims that the substance can reduce the risk of cancer in humans.

Although the FAO attempts to gather shark catch data from around the world, some countries do not supply it. Others supply only sketchy data, or data relating just to recorded shark landings and not to discarded bycatch (sharks caught while fishing for other species).

The gathering of trade data is also problematic. More than 70 countries are involved in the international fin trade, either as importers, exporters, or both. Data collection is made very complex by the fact that Hong Kong, the center for the world's fin trade, exports fins to China for processing (labor is much cheaper) but then re-imports them for the retail trade. Shark meat is rarely, if ever, recorded by species when traded internationally.

Although almost all maritime countries have a shark fishery or snare sharks as bycatch, only a handful actually limit or regulate their shark fisheries in any way, despite increasing signs that all is not well. The accepted global figure for shark catches is 100 million per year, but this is thought by some experts to be a half to a third of the real figure. Some species, such as the Ganges shark and the Brazilian Guitarfish, are classified by the International Union for the Conservation of Nature (IUCN) as "critically endangered," and all species of sawfish are endangered. The great white shark and the huge, plankton-eating whale shark are now listed as vulnerable. Some species may have declined by as much as 80 percent in the past decade.

Sharks have always had bad press. They have been regarded as monsters of the deep—vicious, greedy predators lurking below the water's surface, waiting to rip apart the next innocent swimmer or surfer who comes along. Sharks are the megastars of people's worst nightmares, and there is a prevailing attitude of "good riddance."

The truth is that very few (perhaps ten) of the more than 400 species of shark have been known to attack humans. It is statistically more dangerous to ride in a car to the beach than it is to enter the water once there. On average, sharks kill about 15 people a year, a toll less than those killed by lightning or by slipping in the bath. But that doesn't stop people from hating and fearing them.

Another problem plaguing shark populations is the nature of sharks themselves. Unlike many fish who mature quickly and churn out hundreds of thousands of eggs at a time, sharks mature slowly. They have a long gestation period (one species is pregnant for two years) and produce only a few pups at a time in live births or as eggs. The age at which sharks reach maturity depends on the species and sex; the female dusky shark does not mature sexually until she is 21 years old. The majority of species studied do not reach maturity until they are at least six years old. As a result, there is no "quick fix" solution for the sharks. Even if governments acted immediately, it would take years to see the results of protective measures.

There is no simple answer to these problems, but a good place to start may be the international trade in shark fins and the widespread practice of shark "finning." The tradition of eating shark fin soup has existed for many hundreds of years, but in the mid-1980s there was a rapid escalation in the price of fins, mainly attributable to the liberalization of the Chinese economy. Suddenly shark fins became one of the most expensive fishery products in the world. The FAO estimated that there was a 100 percent increase in the volume of worldwide fin exports between 1980 and 1990. Today people in Taiwan and Hong Kong pay up to $100 for one bowl of shark fin soup.

## The Slice of Profit

On a recent trip to Spain, I saw 2,000 blue sharks being landed one morning at the "official" port, where catches are monitored and recorded. This volume of catch, a result of bycatch in the swordfish fishery, is brought in six days a week. However, I also discovered a "private" port that did not appear to be subject to any regulations or monitoring. Three tons of fins had arrived that day and a shark trader there told me that 400 to 600 metric tons of fins are exported from the town every month.

Shark meat has increased in value in recent years but is still far less economically attractive than meat from tuna or swordfish. The result is that when vessels fishing for these valuable species catch sharks (which they do by the millions), they keep the fins and throw away the rest of the shark, reserving space in the hold for the more valuable fish. Added to that already shameful waste is the fact that these sharks are frequently "finned" while still alive and are then thrown back into the water to be eaten by other fish, starve, or bleed to death.

Another alarming aspect of the international fin trade is that there is growing evidence that sharks of all kinds are being targeted specifically to supply the fin market. There are fishing communities in both eastern and western Africa where fin traders supply modern boats and other equipment to fishers in return for any fins they bring in. I have spoken to fishers in Asia, Africa, and the Middle East and have been alarmed by their constant references to targeting sharks for the fin market.

Attempts to protect some shark species internationally through CITES failed in April 2000. Proposals to limit international trade in the body parts of great white, basking, and whale sharks were all defeated by a strong, anti-protection lobby.

In 1999, the FAO agreed a voluntary International Plan of Action for sharks, giving a deadline of February 2001 for its members to assess their shark stocks and, if necessary, devise national plans of action. In February it was revealed that only 15 countries had even begun the process.

But there are also positive signs that the publicity generated about sharks in recent years is beginning to pay off.

As of October 2001, five countries have now banned the practice of finning: the United States, Brazil, Oman, Costa Rica, and South Africa. Most Australian states/territories now have finning bans in place, and the European Union is considering a ban. India and the Congo have banned shark fishing altogether, and more shark species and stocks are being protected at national level.

WildAid's consumer campaigns in eastern Asia are also showing early signs of success. The daughter of the Taiwanese president celebrated her engagement by giving a "shark-free" banquet, and a Singaporean megastar announced that she would not serve shark fin soup at her wedding reception. Movie stars, pop singers, politicians, multi-national corporations, and many individuals are signing a "no shark fin" pledge, and the media in eastern Asia are now regularly publicizing the plight of sharks.

Sharks have been around for 400 million years, more or less unchanged; but overfishing, excessive bycatch, inappropriate fishing methods, and the international shark trade have all taken their toll on sharks in the past half-century. The world is only now waking up to the realization that these animals need greater protection, and quickly. Let's hope we're not too late.

# 6: The Rocky Return of the Colorado Lynx

MARC BEKOFF

WHEN THE COLORADO Division of Wildlife (CDOW) began releasing Canadian lynx into the San Juan Mountains in February 2000, its aim was to return these animals to an area where trapping, government eradication programs, and human encroachment had erased their presence for almost 30 years. In March 2000, lynx were classified as a threatened species under the Endangered Species Act.

For this project, which was conceived by CDOW, 41 lynx were initially captured in padded leghold traps in Canada and Alaska, injuring some. They were then transported to Colorado where groups of them were released weeks apart. Another 55 individuals were released in April 2000, using new methods based partly on protests that I organized calling attention to the inadequacy of previous methods that led to the immediate starvation deaths of four of the released animals soon after they were freed. One lynx starved to death although her diet was supplemented in the field. One famished cat had to be recaptured. The pattern of starvation was clear and resulted from a lack of abundant prey compounded by the stress of capture and transport. As of March 2002, there were 40 known mortalities, including nine animals who starved to death, five who were

shot, and five who were hit by cars. There are 39 known survivors, and the whereabouts of 15 are a mystery because of
faulty or lost radio-collars, or because they are alive but have
disappeared or died. There is no indication of any successful
breeding, the absence of which spells doom for the Colorado
lynx.

There was strong resistance to Colorado's efforts by some
wildlife biologists, residents, activists, and trappers, whose concerns include poorly conducted habitat surveys, scarcity of
food, potential loss of control over land use, and the fact that
Colorado has banned trapping for the most part since 1996. But
such criticism, including that from biologist Richard Reading of
the Colorado lynx advisory team, was ignored. Commenting on
the starvation deaths, Reading told the *Daily Camera*, "I don't
think they [CDOW] did a thorough enough job analyzing those
[snowshoe hare density] data."

At a public meeting in October 1998, CDOW's John Seidel,
then lead biologist of the project, announced that lynx were
going to be "dumped" into southwestern Colorado. A mortality
rate of 50 percent was expected and permissible. Officials
claimed that it was acceptable to trap and move lynx even if
many would die in Colorado, because they could have been
killed for their fur in their homelands anyway. Mike Smith, the
Colorado Sierra Club's wildlife chair, recently echoed this sentiment. "They would have ended up on the back of somebody as
a fashion statement," he said. Dale Reed, a biologist with
CDOW (who once worked on the project), believed before the
releases that there wasn't enough food to support a sustainable
population. Proper habitat surveys hadn't been conducted, and
none of the major players within CDOW had extensive experience with lynx.

There are a number of reasons why CDOW might have
rushed into what Reed Noss, an eminent conservation biologist
who supports well-planned reintroductions, called a "pathetic"
project. First, there are the snowshoe hares who are the major

food source for lynx. Hares and lynx undergo regular ten-year population cycles, and some CDOW officials wanted to get lynx "on the ground" before the hare numbers fell. Unfortunately, the original estimates of food resources—which were marginal at best for sustaining lynx—were overestimated.

Second, CDOW may have rushed into the program to thwart efforts by Colorado ranchers to appeal an earlier lawsuit that failed to block the reintroduction. "We felt if lynx were on the ground, there would be less point for an appeal," Seidel told the *Rocky Mountain News*. The agency might also have released the lynx to preclude the species' federal listing. In 1998, Seidel stated, "If we don't begin work on this reintroduction, the federal government will take the lead within the next several years." If listed, Colorado would lose control of lynx habitat, including areas around the prized Vail ski area. Some critics of the program question the nature of the relationship between Vail and CDOW. Vail Associates, Inc. gave $200,000 to the project but also wants to expand the ski area into surrounding habitat; by promoting lynx reintroduction away from the resort area, it would divert land-use restrictions and not jeopardize development. The *Colorado Daily* recently cited a 1997 CDOW internal memo from biologist Rick Kahn in which he stated, "The rationale is if the reintroduction is successful, then there is less of a need to protect habitat to lynx adjacent to Vail. If the reintroduction fails then it will be an unequivocal demonstration that lynx populations cannot sustain themselves in Colorado habitats, and no amount of heroic effort to recover lynx will work...." Two USFWS biologists, one of whom believes that lynx still live in Colorado backcountry and views habitat fragmentation as a threat to lynx survival, report being discouraged from "seeking to stop projects that jeopardize lynx habitat." But CDOW spokesperson Todd Malmsbury said the agency is committed to the program's success and called any claims to the contrary "absurd."

**Redecorating Nature**

The poorly planned release of lynx into Colorado remains highly controversial. There are strange bedfellows in the resistance,
including zoologists, animal rights activists, conservation scientists, ranchers, woolgrowers, and trappers. Each group has very
different motivations, but they've come to the same conclusion:
the lynx should not have been released in Colorado. All wildlife
reintroduction programs demand close scrutiny. The interrela-
tionships among political agendas, economic factors, and biological and sociological variables (no public opinion surveys
were conducted) need to be studied carefully.

Patient, proactive planning is essential. This involves preserving critical habitat, assessing public attitudes toward the animals themselves, and protecting individuals from exploitation so
that sustainable populations can flourish. When animals are
translocated it's important to assess the psychological and physical impacts of stress and of breaking up or reforming social
(family) groups. Stress can influence survival and reproduction.
There also are cascading and unpredictable effects when ecosystems are changed. In Yellowstone National Park in Wyoming,
reintroduced wolves have killed about 50 percent of the resident
coyotes, the effects of which influence many other animals.

I raise the questions that I do not because I'm against all
reintroduction and translocation programs, but rather because
when we attempt to "redecorate nature" by moving animals
from place to place, there are many serious issues concerning
their well-being that need to be considered. Indeed, some well-
planned efforts seem to be on the road to yielding sustaining
populations (gray wolf recovery in Yellowstone National Park is
progressing faster than predicted, and red wolves are doing well
on the Alligator River National Wildlife Refuge in northeastern
North Carolina), and they can serve as models for future efforts.
I ask these questions because the issues are not as clear as some
people want them to be. The Yellowstone project was well moti-
vated and may be "successful" if it continues to proceed as it

has, whereas the Colorado project was more "decorative" in that the effect of the lynx on the ecosystem was not a motivating factor. While I deeply appreciate the good intentions and efforts of all involved, sometimes good intentions aren't enough. There is no room for failure, since these highly visible projects continually come under careful public scrutiny.

Emotions and passions run especially high in visible projects involving such charismatic species as wolves, grizzly bears, and black rhinoceroses. It's often because conservation issues become so personal that it is difficult to reach solutions that are readily agreeable to all human parties. What is important is that people agree that ethics is an essential element in any discussion of conservation and that ethical issues are not traded off against other agendas.


# 7: Wildlife Disservices

ELISABETH JENNINGS

ABUSES BY THE Wildlife Services program, formerly known as Animal Damage Control—the infamous U.S. Department of Agriculture operation that traps, poisons, shoots, burns, bludgeons, and maims millions of mammals and birds every year on public and private land—persist year after year. Spending more than $53 million in fiscal year 1999 in federal funds and other sources to commit such atrocities, the Wildlife Services shows a seemingly blatant disregard for environmental laws, relies on pseudo-science to justify its killing practices, and tries to circumvent public participation processes that could curtail its activities. But a vigilant examination of New Mexico's Wildlife Services has revealed that the agency is, as former Bureau of Land Management director Jim Baca put it, "an anachronism" that is accountable to no one but itself.

Wildlife Services' war on wildlife, allegedly to protect livestock, is being waged for the benefit of relatively few people who
are cashing in on a federal handout designed to buoy an ailing
animal agriculture industry. This subsidy is part of a pattern that
was established a century ago when ethics concerning land,
wildlife, and agriculture were virtually nonexistent. The benefi-
ciaries include millionaires as well as elected and appointed officials at the state and federal level who control the purse strings
for these and other similarly archaic agricultural programs.
What's more, Wildlife Services' policies don't require ranchers to
verify their livestock losses prior to implementing lethal predator control, so the very premise of predator control, lethal or otherwise, may very well be based more on greed than need.

### Catron County Coyotes, Sam Donaldson, and Other Dirty Deals

Years of watching and exposing New Mexico Wildlife Services'
activities have led activists in the state to the conclusion that the
program cannot be reformed—it must be abolished. In New
Mexico alone, Wildlife Services kills more than 12,000 birds
and mammals every year. Of the approximately 9,000 ranchers
in New Mexico, only 654 (seven percent) asked for Wildlife
Services assistance in fiscal year 1996. That seven percent rep-
resents a mere 0.04 percent of the entire state population.
Considering that the New Mexico program costs taxpayers
about $2.2 million annually, Wildlife Services represents politi-
cal "pork" at its worst.

In addition to wielding weapons at the behest of resident
ranchers, Wildlife Services also performs its grisly services for
millionaire absentee landowners such as Sam Donaldson of
ABC News. The agency visited Donaldson's Lincoln County
ranch 412 times over a five-year period, killing coyotes, bobcats, and foxes. Also, U.S. Representative Joe Skeen (R-NM),
chairman of the House Appropriations Subcommittee on the
Interior and Related Agencies, took advantage of Wildlife

Services' killing services 99 times between 1991 and 1996. He asked that black bears, cougars, bobcats, and coyotes be killed on his ranch.

Wildlife Services programs in New Mexico and other states have a history of failing to follow environmental, procedural, and regulatory policies. Wildlife Services has been operating in violation of the National Environmental Policy Act (NEPA) since the Act's inception in 1969. Even when Wildlife Services reluctantly prepares required Environmental Assessments (EAs) to evaluate its impact on the "human environment," it prefers to solicit required public input from members of state game departments, extension agents from state agriculture departments, ranchers, and others who it knows won't criticize agency practices. Wildlife Services' biologists regularly cite biased "scientific" studies that are self-serving and bolster Wildlife Services' long-standing practices of poisoning and killing. Wildlife Services ignores new biological research that suggests altering the status quo (for example, information that shows that killing coyotes most likely increases depredation by allowing younger, rogue coyotes who are more likely to kill livestock to move into the dead coyotes' territory). In 1999 in New Mexico, Wildlife Services was successfully sued by Animal Protection of New Mexico and Defenders of Wildlife for their inadequate and biased EAs, which relied on outdated and improperly interpreted scientific studies regarding cougars. The agency was ordered to conduct appropriate analysis of its predator damage management program in EAs that comply with federal law.

In its ongoing efforts to kill wildlife, Wildlife Services has allowed untrained and unlicensed trappers to use lethal M-44s, devices planted in the ground that inject sodium cyanide poison into the mouth of whatever animal pulls on the meat-baited top (whether that animal is an intended target or not). Wildlife Services trappers have endangered the public by improperly placing dangerous M-44s in forest areas used for public recreation. It has also failed to notify local medical facilities of the devices' presence, which could hamper prompt treatment for accidental poisonings.

In 1996, after only two days of field work, Animal Protection of New Mexico's investigation of New Mexico's Wildlife Services practices revealed more than ten violations of at least six EPA restrictions on the use of M-44s. As a result, the New Mexico Department of Agriculture fined the state Wildlife Services $1,000—the first such known fine in Wildlife Services history. Eight Wildlife Services employees and one supervisor had their public applicator licenses suspended until they were satisfactorily trained in the use of M-44s. At least 100 newspaper articles and radio and television reports covered the issue, reminding Wildlife Services officials that the public is watching.

## Audits and Accountability
The problems with New Mexico's Wildlife Services are part of a larger national picture that is no prettier: Wildlife Services has no rules and regulations by which to operate. There is no substantial or critical evaluation of its practices, except that which is demanded by the public. Created to eradicate wildlife in the West almost 100 years ago so that the land could be "tamed," Wildlife Services' work has not been substantially re-evaluated, even though values and priorities about land and wildlife have changed dramatically since that time.

A 1995 audit of Wildlife Services by the General Accounting Office (GAO) concluded that "Although written [Wildlife Services] program policies call for field personnel to give preference to non-lethal control methods when practical and effective, field personnel use lethal methods to control livestock predators."

The events in New Mexico have helped destroy the myths perpetuated by Wildlife Services that it follows the law, involves the public, and is accountable for its actions. Wildlife Services continues to be monitored by small organizations throughout the West, but much more help is needed to reduce and control the agency's own damage.

# 8: The Far Reach of the Fur Trade

KATHY BAUCH

NEWS THAT COATS and other products made of dog and cat fur are being sold around the world has shocked consumers in the United States and elsewhere. The revelations, announced on December 15, 1998, were the result of an 18-month undercover investigation conducted by the Humane Society of the United States (HSUS)/Humane Society International (HSI) and independent German journalist Manfred Karremann. A team of six investigators and three researchers documented the merciless slaughter of domestic dogs and cats in China, Thailand, and the Philippines. The investigators estimate that more than two million dogs and cats are killed for the fur trade each year.

Much of the enormous media attention—including major stories in *The Washington Post* and on NBC's *Dateline*—focused on the discovery of parkas with dog fur trim being sold by Burlington Coat Factory stores. At one such outlet in New Jersey, HSUS investigators found jackets trimmed with what the label described as "Mongolia dog fur," which DNA testing confirmed to be canine. When presented with that information, Burlington Coat Factory Warehouse Corporation expressed its dismay and ordered all the coats pulled from its stores. The company offered a refund or exchange to anyone who had already purchased one of the coats, and pledged to work with HSUS to ban the import of dog and cat fur into the United States.

Prompted by hundreds of print and broadcast reports, the public furor was understandable; what the investigation detailed was nothing less than horrifying. By establishing an identity as an officer of a fictitious U.S. company with an interest in importing fur, chief HSUS/HSI investigator Rick Swain gained access to fur facilities in China, making four trips to that country over a year and a half. Swain said that at the beginning of the effort, he expected to uncover a small, black-market trade in cat and dog skins abroad. But what the investigative group found is a multimillion-dollar, international industry. As he told *Dateline*, he saw hundreds of thousands of dog pelts in one warehouse. "I didn't believe it until I saw it," Swain said. "But I was there and I saw it. I felt it. I touched it."

The incentive is simple: dogs and cats are available, plentiful, and profitable. In China, investigators observed the killing firsthand. Some of these animals were bred on farms where anywhere from five to 300 dogs, or up to 70 cats, might be kept as breeding stock. Other animals may have been strays.

In Harbin, north of Beijing, investigators witnessed dogs shivering in a dark, unheated building in the midst of winter, tethered by wire nooses, without food or water. This particular place, investigators were told, generally killed 10 to 12 dogs a day, selling their flesh and fur. The investigator reports that he saw dogs being butchered who were still conscious as the skinning began. Undercover videotape shows a German shepherd blinking his eye as he was being skinned.

Cats suffer similarly awful fates. Investigators were told by people working at one Chinese fur market that the common method of killing is by hanging, sometimes with water hoses running into the cats' throats to drown them. Then a slit is made in the cat's stomach, the skin is opened, and the fur is pulled over the cat's head. The furriers say the cats may still be alive while they're being skinned.

Swain notes that while the death of any animal is a tragedy, there is something uniquely unsettling about the commercial slaughter of domestic cats and dogs. He explained, "Looking at these animals, I couldn't help thinking about the enormous trust that dogs and cats place in people. The magnitude of the betrayal of that trust was truly beyond belief. And all to satisfy a selfish desire for fur products."

Investigators traced the trade in dog and cat fur to factories and import/export companies in Asia and Europe. Cat and dog furs were quite openly displayed and offered for sale. At one Chinese company, a fur "plate" of six to eight cat pelts could be purchased for $21. (Two plates make a short jacket; three make a coat.) In Germany, drivers pulling into one gas station could buy cat pelts and cat fur products while filling their cars' tanks. Large orders appear to be no problem. A company in Beijing told investigators it could export 20,000 cat skins and 20,000 dog skins during a three-month period.

In the course of the investigation, it became clear that dog and cat fur is inextricably linked to the international fur industry as a whole, and that companies dealing in dog and cat fur also deal in the pelts of other species of "traditional" fur animals. In a showroom in China, for example, investigators saw full-length dog and cat fur coats hanging next to coats made of minks and foxes. At an auction house in Germany, 10,000 dressed dog furs from Korea were sold alongside those of foxes, minks, muskrats, bobcats, badgers, and nutrias.

Patricia Forkan, HSUS executive vice president, notes that "To the fur industry, dogs and cats are just more products to be bought and sold. The fur industry is a global entity and it's all connected. Dogs and cats may be killed in China or Korea, their pelts may be sold to countries like Germany, France, or Italy for processing and finishing, and they may end up as products sold anywhere in the world."

Including the United States. In addition to the "Mongolia dog fur" jackets, HSUS investigators found fur-covered figurines and toys that forensic testing confirmed were made from canine fur. These items were found at such shops as Fur and Furgery in New York City, The Purrfect Stamp in Gaithersburg,

Maryland, and The Bouvier Collection at Ronald Reagan National Airport in the nation's capital.

According to Forkan, the investigation not only draws further attention to the already callous fur industry, but it brings the issue of individual animal suffering closer to home for many consumers. Many fashion designers, retailers, and consumers have been able to distance themselves from the suffering of wild animals killed for fur. "That might not be so easy to do when the animals involved are dogs and cats. Maybe if people see Fluffy or Fido every time they look at a fur product, they'll turn their backs on the fur industry, once and for all. And that will be good news for millions and millions of animals of all species."

Almost two years after HSUS first exposed the horrors of the dog and cat fur trade, President Clinton signed a ban on dog and cat fur. It is now illegal to import, export, or sell products containing dog or cat fur in the United States. The Dog and Cat Protection Act of 2000 sets penalties of up to $10,000 for each item containing dog or cat fur and makes it possible to prohibit repeat offenders from selling any fur products. In addition, the law calls on the U.S. Customs Service to publish a list of businesses and individuals known to trade in dog and cat fur. It directs that agency to certify laboratories that are qualified to determine whether an item contains dog or cat fur, and attempts to ensure that such products won't be imported by requiring dog and cat fur products to be labeled.

Although the federal law bans dog and cat fur in the United States, illicit items may still make their way into the country. And anyone who thinks the way to avoid buying dog or cat fur products is to simply read the label is in for another shock. Current U.S. law exempts fur products (other than dog and cat fur products) under $150 from labeling, which effectively exempts most fur-trimmed or fur-lined garments, as well as such items as toys (including cat toys) and home accessories.

Further complicating the labeling issue is the fact that many companies and individuals involved in the trade of cat and dog fur use pseudonyms and mislabeling to disguise the true identity of their products. For example, "gae wolf" is a popular fur in the lower-end German fur market. But even many German consumers don't know that "gae wolf" is one of the fur industry's pseudonyms for domestic dog, usually German shepherd. Investigators also report that they were told that companies were willing to put any label in a garment that the customer wanted, effectively disguising the country of origin and the type of animal used.

It is unlikely that many consumers or even fashion industry workers could recognize dog or cat fur if they saw it. The president of a German company told investigators that when dyed, cat fur is not easily distinguishable from other fur. And while investigators saw many poor-quality fur pieces and garments, they also noted a growing number of high-quality items being put on the international market. Swain said he used to think that dog or cat fur would be easy to detect. "After more than a year of looking at this stuff, I was quite sure I could tell what I was handling. But I was shocked at the quality of some of the product I saw on my last trip to China. In fact, now every time I see a piece of fur trim, I have to wonder..."

The HSUS' published exposé was sent to those who have a direct impact on the use of fur: fashion designers, buyers, retailers, journalists, and consumers. HSUS also called upon all retailers to pull all fur-trimmed products from their stores, in light of the findings of the investigation. Predictably, some fur industry spokespersons quickly began a counter-campaign, suggesting that animal activists often fake film footage. But another spokesperson for the Fur Information Council of America told *The Washington Post* that dog and cat fur is "distasteful to think about," adding, "Who would want to buy that?" Indeed.

In the period since the initial investigation into dog and cat fur, publicity and action against the global trade in dog and cat fur has not stopped at U.S. borders. In conjunction with the Fur Free Alliance, an international coalition of anti-fur organizations, HSUS continues to work to raise awareness on this issue throughout the world and to further legislation that would prohibit the trade. And because illicit items may still make their way into the United States, the safest way for American consumers to be sure they aren't buying dog and cat fur is to buy no fur products at all.

# 9: The Ultimate Underdog

NICOLE ROSMARINO

EVERY WEEK THE calls come pouring in to Rocky Mountain Animal Defense (RMAD) and other prairie dog advocates: a 34-acre prairie dog colony is slated for development; shooters converge at the Top Dog Prairie Shoot for a weekend of live target practice; a municipality prepares to exterminate more than 90 percent of the prairie dogs on its open space; prairie dogs are getting run over by the dozen on a busy suburban street; the list goes on.

*Can you relocate them? Can you protect them on open space? Why are they shooting prairie dogs on public land? Can't you do something?*

The crisis is clear in the callers' voices, from the distressed neighbor who has just tearfully witnessed the bulldozing of the colony across the street, to the desperation of a prairie dog relocator pleading with a municipality to provide open space land for the victims of development, to the insistence of a biologist arguing for the need to conserve prairie dogs in urban and rural areas throughout their range, or a minister expounding on the need to move to a more compassionate mindset in which killing is not the answer to conflict.

Most of these voices go unheeded. Most of the time there is little change. Yet momentum is slowly building to save the prairie dog and the rich ecosystem this valuable creature sustains.

At the center of this conflict is the black-tailed prairie dog, a foot-long, one- to three-pound, sandy-colored mammal who lives in burrows and is native to the Great Plains. Prairie dogs are rodents who live in family groups called coteries, several of which form a colony or "town." A variety of wildlife species breed, feed, rest, and hide on the towns and within the burrows prairie dogs create.

The war over this unsuspecting creature is now reaching its pinnacle with the February 2000 decision by the U.S. Fish and Wildlife Service (USFWS) that the black-tailed prairie dog (BTPD) warrants a threatened listing under the Endangered Species Act (ESA). The agency has resisted finalizing the listing, citing higher priorities. That a species as controversial as the BTPD has not received formal listing is no surprise to wildlife advocates. Indeed, to understand how controversial the prairie dog is, a quick historical tour is in order.

## A History of Persecution

Perhaps prairie dog eradication was in the cards when Europeans first set foot on North America and began their colonial takeover of the land and its inhabitants. A pivotal event occurred in 1902, when C. H. Merriam, chief of the U.S. Biological Survey, charged that the prairie dog robbed cattle of 50 to 75 percent of their forage by supposedly overgrazing. In defense of cattle ranching and crop agriculture, the federal government wasted little time in instituting a campaign of prairie dog extermination that persists (though slightly modified) to this day.

This poisoning campaign employed up to 125,000 men per year in the 1920s. By 1938, the black-tailed prairie dog had been entirely exterminated in Arizona. A colony in Texas—

which turn-of-the-century reporters described as measuring 250 miles by 100 miles, with possibly 400 million inhabitants—was destroyed. As long ago as 1912, 91 percent of the prairie dog acres in Colorado were gone. Similar destruction rates occurred throughout the animal's extensive 11-state range.

The government eradication program was so successful that by 1960, only two percent of the original acres occupied by the black-tailed prairie dog (the most common of the five prairie dog species) remained. In 1998, that number dipped well below one percent, placing the prairie dog and the ecosystem this species sustains on the brink. The 100 to 700 million acres of prairie dog towns that existed in 1900 have been steadily reduced to less than 700,000 acres. Compounding the problem of severely reduced habitat, these few remaining acres usually take the form of small, isolated colonies that are unable to recover from losses due to sylvatic plague, poisoning, or shooting.

**What Was Lost**
The public is now beginning to appreciate what was lost in this frenzy of poison-soaked oats and gas cartridges. There remains only a trace of an ecosystem that once stretched across as much as one-third of the continental United States. As a result of drastic prairie dog reductions, other species have declined as well. The black-footed ferret, swift fox, and mountain plover are all closely tied to prairie dogs and their colonies and have all been recognized by the USFWS as biologically imperiled and in need of federal protection. In fact, more than 200 vertebrate species have been identified on or near prairie dog towns. It may well be that even more species were associated with the prairie dog historically, since all modern research on prairie dog-associated wildlife was conducted long after the animal's numbers had been reduced by 98 percent.

However, even in a highly reduced capacity, the prairie dog provides an essential prey base for a multitude of raptors as well as mammalian predators. Golden eagles and ferruginous hawks rely heavily on prairie dogs as food, while coyotes, foxes, weasels, badgers, and others hunt for them on the ground. In addition, the habitat alteration caused by prairie dog grazing and burrowing activities creates a variety of wildlife niches for highly specialized animals. The burrowing owl lives in prairie dog burrows and requires the colony's cropped grasses to hunt small mammals. The mountain plover is a grassland bird whose insect-foraging also requires such short vegetation, and actually nests on the ground in prairie dog colonies.

Prairie dog burrows are home to a variety of small mammals, including deer mice, 13-lined ground squirrels, cottontails and other rabbits, and voles. Burrows even provide refuge for such reptiles and amphibians as prairie rattlers, bullsnakes, and tiger salamanders.

The black-footed ferret and the prairie dog share one of the most fascinating relationships in the animal world. More than 90 percent of the ferret's diet is prairie dogs, and the ferret cannot survive outside of prairie dog colonies, requiring the burrows for shelter from the elements and other predators. As a result of prairie dog decline, the black-footed ferret is one of the most endangered animals in the world.

In addition, large ungulates (plant-eating hoofed animals) prefer the vegetation on prairie dog colonies. Buffalo, elk, pronghorn antelope, and mule deer were all historical members of the prairie dog community, enjoying the grasses and forbs found on dog towns.

Because of the ecological importance prairie dogs wield, they are described as a keystone species. Scientists increasingly recommend that protection for keystone species be prioritized, given the important role they play in ecosystem health.

Cattle have also shown a preference for grazing on colonies, and scientific research has repeatedly demonstrated that prairie dogs are not an economic threat to ranching, as their activities enrich the soil and vegetation. Prairie dogs may move into an area after it has already been overgrazed, attracted by the short vegetation. Consequently, many ranchers may be mistaking the overgrazing of their cattle as having been caused by prairie dogs.

In turn, as Mike Fox of the Intertribal Bison Cooperative in Fort Belknap, Montana, explains in the video documentary *Varmints*, "The rancher looks at [the short-clipped grass] as 'those prairie dogs are stealing from my cows,' and it's just the opposite—those prairie dogs are creating ideal conditions that attract those cows to their prairie dog colonies." University of Wyoming biologist Scott Seville puts it another way: "If prairie dogs are directly competing with cattle...how could the Plains have supported so many bison when prairie dogs were so numerous and widely distributed before European settlement?"

Curiously, the "lowly" rodent at the foundation of this ecosystem has been found by Northern Arizona University researcher Con Slobodchikoff to possess one of the most sophisticated languages in the nonhuman world. Their yips and cries encode complex statements that allow prairie dogs to discern the difference between the color of shirts worn by people and whether a human carried a rifle when previously seen at the colony. It was the animals' bark-like communicating that inspired early explorers Lewis and Clark to call them "little dogs of the prairie."

**The Continued War**
Yet the war against the prairie dog continues. Although those seeking to eradicate prairie dogs are many, ranchers continue to be the most adamant, despite the fact that scientific research (much of which was carried out in the name of range science, not wildlife advocacy) has repeatedly shown Merriam's 1902 decree to be false. Prairie dogs are not a problem for cattle ranching and actually benefit rangeland health. Their digging, urinating, and defecating enriches and fertilizes the soil; their burrows channel precipitation to the water table; and their digging and clipping improves the ability of soil and plants to

absorb and store water. In fact, the nutrient quality of the vege-tation on the colonies is increased by the animals' activities.

Despite the many reasons for ending prairie dog persecu-tion, prairie dog eradication continues, taking several forms. The most common is poisoning, which commonly involves the use of aluminum phosphide gas. Tablets or cartridges of this toxic and flammable chemical are deposited in each prairie dog burrow, followed by crumpled-up newspaper and well-com-pacted dirt to seal each entrance. Trapped with no hope of escape, prairie dogs and any other animals in their burrows suf-fer for hours or even up to three days before dying. The death of each creature entails implosion: the circulatory system bursts, and the victims literally drown in their own blood.

An additional threat to prairie dogs is the sylvatic plague (the rodent variety of the bubonic plague), which was intro-duced to North America in 1899 by sailors from Europe and Asia. Prairie dogs have no immunity to the disease, and whole colonies can be eliminated by the plague overnight. The plague is primarily transmitted by fleas and has been working its way across the continent, hitting Colorado in 1945. Deer mice and other rodents can carry the disease, and transmit it to others.

Despite the elimination of 98 to 99 percent of prairie dog-occupied acreage, government agencies and private parties con-tinue to eliminate these animals from the land. Urban develop-ment is skyrocketing in Colorado, and cattle markets are plum-meting. In the case of urban development, prairie dogs are elim-inated as new settlers move in. In the case of ranching, prairie dogs are blamed for some of the problems of a dying industry. Part of the original (and current) mission of the U.S. Department of Agriculture's Wildlife Services division (previ-ously called Animal Damage Control) is to eradicate prairie dogs. The program still provides an enormous flow of poisons to private interests for prairie dog extermination from its supply depot in Pocatello, Idaho. The Forest Service, which adminis-ters the National Grasslands, manages those Great Plains areas—more than three million acres of which are prime black-tailed prairie dog habitat—for less than a bare minimum of prairie dogs. Because of ranchers' intolerance for native wildlife, prairie dogs exist on less than one percent of suitable areas of National Grasslands. Similarly, the Bureau of Land Management manages less than one percent of its holdings for prairie dogs.

Local and state government agencies, with few exceptions, are also complicit in prairie dog persecution. State wildlife and agriculture departments throughout the Great Plains continue to allow and/or encourage prairie dog killing. Municipal and county governments in this region often encourage prairie dog extermination and habitat destruction out of intolerance for native wildlife and as a result of unchecked urban development and agriculture.

The most extreme form of slaughter is prairie dog shooting. During these private events, shooters sit at tables near or within a prairie dog colony and aim their high-powered rifles at animals emerging from their burrows. The accuracy of these rifles is staggering, with killing power at more than 400 yards. Always intent on maximizing the number of direct hits, shooters usually leave wounded and dismembered prairie dogs to writhe in agony on the killing fields. According to the June 1998 issue of *American Hunter* (a publication of the National Rifle Association), "What draws most people into the sport is the fact that you get to do a lot of shooting....It's not uncommon in varmint-hunting situations to shoot from 200 to 1,000 rounds in a single day!"

Curiosities like the "triple," in which one bullet hits three prairie dogs who are on a mound hugging each other, the "flipper," where the force of a bullet flips a prairie dog backward on impact, or the "red mist," where a prairie dog is literally exploded by the force of a bullet, are rewarded with cheers from onlookers and prizes from contest organizers. And, as Mark Mason of the Varmint Militia enthusiastically points out in *Varmints*, there's also the "4-, 5-, and 6-pup club" when one bullet strikes more than one prairie dog at once. He adds, "We love to see 'em blow up." In the same film, an elderly female participant at one shoot declares, "It was fun to go out and shoot prairie dogs...and you can appreciate God's handiwork out here."

On the Buffalo Gap National Grasslands, one of the last remaining healthy prairie dog complexes (a group of neighboring colonies) was subjected to massive shooting pressure in 1998. Calculations based on government documents indicate that some 162,000 of the approximately 216,000 prairie dogs there were killed in just a couple of months. The Forest Service consequently closed some areas to shooting, in the first closure to prairie dog shooting on its land. Shooting has been prohibited on federal lands in Colorado, and FWS has determined that shooting can detrimentally impact prairie dogs on the local level.

**Confronting Myths**

Important obstacles to prairie dog protection are the multiple, enduring myths that provide rationales for continued persecution of this important keystone species. These myths should be confronted and debunked wherever they are encountered.

*Myth #1: Prairie dogs are everywhere.* Fact: Less than one percent of historic prairie dog acreage still exists. This minuscule remnant often takes the form of isolated and fragmented colonies that are unable to sustain prairie dogs in the long term. Few healthy prairie dog complexes (multiple colonies living near each other) remain, and these are essential for sustaining the multitude of wildlife associated with prairie dogs.

*Myth #2: Prairie dogs multiply like rabbits.* Fact: Prairie dogs have a very low reproduction rate compared to other small mammals. They breed once a year, with an average litter size of three to four pups. Also, when confronted with physical barriers to expansion, prairie dogs practice infanticide, sometimes reaching 50 percent destruction of litters.

*Myth #3: Prairie dogs spread the plague.* Fact: Infected prairie dogs do not spread the plague, because they are too busy dying from it. They lack immunity to plague, and nearly all die quickly after contact. Other mammals, such as mice, cats, and dogs, carry the plague. However, plague in humans is easily treatable with standard antibiotics.

*Myth #4: Prairie dogs and cattle can't coexist.* Fact: Prairie dogs and cattle have a mutually beneficial relationship. Prairie dogs improve the forage for cattle, and cattle grazing allows prairie dog colonies to expand in midgrass prairie. Cattle and prairie dogs have demonstrated a preference for grazing together, just as bison and prairie dogs did historically. There is no evidence that cows break their legs by stepping in prairie dog burrows. Rather than focusing on the myth that prairie dogs are a threat to the livestock industry, public policy should focus on the ecological damage caused by the livestock industry.

*Myth #5: No one will miss the prairie dogs when they're gone.* Fact: Dozens of vertebrate species are dependent to some degree on prairie dogs and the rich habitat they create. More than 200 wildlife species have been found on or near prairie dog colonies. The black-footed ferret is now endangered as a direct result of losing prairie dogs as a main source of food and habitat. A whole community of prairie life will miss the prairie dogs if we let them disappear.

**Fighting for the Underdog**

Globally, grasslands are in ecological crisis. In North America, the prairies of the Great Plains are recognized by scientists as severely imperiled. As noted in *Prairie Conservation: Conserving America's Most Endangered Ecosystem*, "Today, no piece of prairie exists that has not been impacted by humans in one way or another. The plant and animal communities that have occupied the Great Plains for thousands of years have been completely restructured by humans in the last two centuries." Consequently, according to the edited volume, in terms of natural resource conservation in North America, "prairies are a priority, perhaps the highest priority." The magnificent thundering herds of bison and antelope that used to bring the prairie to life are no longer. Plains gullies are bereft of the haunting presence of plains wolves or grizzly bears. The rich mosaic of prairie dog colonies, thickly vegetated uncolonized areas, and healthy streamside zones is a rare find.

The unique and mesmerizing prairie dog ecosystem has been almost entirely replaced by wheat fields, devastated pastureland, and urban asphalt. With every prairie dog shoot, every application of poison gas, every plague outbreak, and every strip mall erected on prairie dog towns, this irreplaceable ecosystem becomes just a memory and the Great Plains just a wasteland.

As a result of this lethal onslaught, the prairie dog is in dire straits. Fortunately, animal rights groups and other environmental advocates have recognized the prairie dogs' plight and are working on private ecosystem preservation efforts combined with policy reform at all levels of government.

Ecosystemic preservation on private land is one of the most effective strategies for protecting prairie dogs in rural areas. It is generally not feasible in urban areas with a high demand for new houses, office buildings, strip malls and the like, given the prohibitive land prices that accompany high consumer demand. Conveniently, given the human depopulation of rural areas throughout the Great Plains, there is significant potential for this ecosystem to flourish once again. The Southern Plains Land Trust (SPLT) is attempting to acquire land on which to bring back prairie dogs and the wildlife associated with their towns. The SPLT vision includes reforming policy on public lands in order to create a true shortgrass prairie preserve where, with some hard work and imagination, the bison and prairie dog will once again graze together. "Prairie dogs continue to be persecuted, even on public lands," explains SPLT President Lauren McCain. "By acquiring private land, we will provide a safe harbor for prairie dogs, and will fully restore the rich ecosystem they create." The Great Plains Restoration Council (GPRC) shares that vision, and is working with SPLT toward the long-term goal of a Buffalo Commons series of preserves from Mexico to Canada.

However, prairie dogs also need to be protected where they currently exist, whether in rural areas, where they are at the mercy of ranchers, or in urban areas, where they are at risk of being crushed and suffocated by bulldozers. Recognizing the inherent value of the prairie dog and its associate wildlife, RMAD has worked for policy change throughout Colorado, going after developers, ranchers, shooters, and government agencies. As a result, prairie dogs have been protected on open space areas in the city of Lakewood (while strides have been made in Boulder and Fort Collins), a statewide restriction on contest killings (including prairie dog shoots) has been adopted, and awareness of the need to protect prairie dogs and their colonies has spread. Grassroots and national organizations have joined together under the Prairie Dog Coalition, whose mission is to support education and advocacy efforts to protect all species of prairie dogs and their ecosystems throughout the United States.

The work conducted on the regional, state, and local levels by groups like SPLT and RMAD has been accompanied by a concerted effort to gain federal protection for the black-tailed prairie dog under the Endangered Species Act. Leading that program is the Biodiversity Legal Foundation (BLF), Predator Conservation Alliance, and the National Wildlife Federation, who petitioned the USFWS to list the black-tailed prairie dog as threatened in 1998. While the agency declined listing, it did agree with the organizations that the black-tailed prairie dog warrants a threatened designation. This prairie dog species is now a candidate for listing under the ESA.

It is apparent that ESA listing is required to obtain meaningful protection for black-tailed prairie dogs. Ranchers show no sign of letting up in their war against wildlife in general and the prairie dog in particular. Developers show little tolerance for this creature and perhaps even less restraint in their mission to convert natural areas into cash flow. As a rule, elected officials and administrators have shown their inclination to support ranching and development interests. Money talks.

Increasingly, citizens in the Great Plains are talking, too. They're talking to their city council members and mayors about the need to provide protection for prairie dogs now. They're talking with each other about the need to build a community movement throughout the region to support native wildlife.

They're debunking the myths that have allowed prairie dog eradication to continue. These true prairie citizens—humans who recognize that prairie dogs, like any other animals, are not ours to gun down or poison, but must be regarded with respect—are calling for nationwide support in their quest to guard and restore a much-forgotten national treasure. The fate of one of its most humble inhabitants, the prairie dog, will determine whether that sea of grass known as the Great Plains can once again be called the Serengeti of North America.

# Part 3
# HUNTING

# 1: Sport Hunting: The Mayhem in Our Woods

MICHAEL MARKARIAN

HUNTING, IT IS true, is an American tradition—a tradition of killing, crippling, extinction, and ecological destruction. In the 19th and 20th centuries, hunters have helped wipe out dozens of species, including the passenger pigeon, the Great auk, and the heath hen. They have brought a long list of others, including the bison and the grizzly bear, to the brink of extinction. In its report on the Endangered Species Act of 1973, the U.S. Senate's Commerce Committee stated, "Hunting and habitat destruction are the two major causes of extinction."

With an arsenal of rifles, shotguns, muzzleloaders, handguns, and bows and arrows, hunters kill more than 135 million animals yearly. They cripple, orphan, and harass millions more. The annual death toll in the United States includes 35 million mourning doves, 27 million squirrels, 17 million ducks, 13 million rabbits, 12 million grouse, quail, and partridges, six million deer, and thousands of bears, moose, elk, swans, cougars, turkeys, wolves, and other creatures.

**The Seven Deadly Sins**
Although the American public has increasingly questioned the appropriateness of killing animals for recreation, some especially egregious hunting practices have come under widespread attack. And the hunting community, despite its repeated rheto-

ric of "hunting ethics," has refused to end repugnant practices that go above and beyond the realm of cruelty. Here are a few examples:

- Some state wildlife agencies set hunting seasons on bears, squirrels, and other animals during the crucial months when they give birth and nurse their young. When a mother is killed by a hunter, her orphaned babies are certain to die of starvation or predation.

- From African lions to European boars, exotic animals—surplus zoo animals or those purchased from auctions—are unfair game for fee-paying hunters at private shooting preserves. These "canned hunts" offer guaranteed kills, giving the animals not only a prison sentence on a fenced-in preserve, but also a firing squad.

- Hunters in 38 states lure mourning doves to sunflower fields and blast the birds of peace into pieces. Hunters often use the birds as nothing more than target practice or to train young hunters, referring to the activity as "wing shooting." They leave at least 20 to 30 percent of the birds they shoot crippled and unretrieved.

- From pigeon shoots in Pennsylvania to coyote "body count" hunts in the West, contestants use live animals as targets while competing for money and prizes.

- In many states, trophy hunters litter our public lands with piles of rotten food so they can attract unwitting bears or deer and shoot the feeding animals at point-blank range (nine states allow bear baiting and 17 allow deer baiting). Similarly, many states allow trophy hunters to unleash packs of radio-collared dogs to track and chase bears, cougars, raccoons, foxes, bobcats, and other animals in a high-tech search-and-destroy mission. Once a frightened animal flees to a tree, the hunter follows the radio signal on a handheld receptor and shoots the trapped animal off the tree branch.

- Bowhunters use archery equipment to wound more animals than they kill. Dozens of scientific studies indicate that bowhunting yields a more than 50 percent crippling rate. Thus, for every animal dragged from the woods, at least one animal is left to suffer.
- Hunters shoot nonnative ring-necked pheasants who are hand-fed and raised in pens, then released into the wild just before hunting season. Even if the pheasants (native to China) survive the hunters' onslaught, they are certain to die of exposure or starvation in the alien environment. It is interesting to note that while hunters often defend their sport by claiming they save overpopulated animals from starvation, in the case of pheasants and other species, hunters intentionally breed them knowing they may starve to death.

## A Dying Tradition

Every year the number of sport hunters decreases. According to the U.S. Fish and Wildlife Service (USFWS), 10 percent of Americans purchased hunting licenses in 1975, seven percent in 1991, and only five percent in 1996. Leading researchers in hunting demographics indicate that if current social trends continue, sport hunting itself could be extinct by the year 2050.

To fight these trends, the USFWS and 49 state wildlife agencies sponsor youth recruitment hunts on public land, some for children as young as five years old. Similarly, most agencies have adopted the "Becoming an Outdoors Woman" program in an effort to entice a segment of the population that traditionally has not been welcomed by the hunting fraternity, and thus to increase sales of hunting licenses, firearms, and outdoor clothing.

## Wildlife Mismanagement

Because they make money from the sale of hunting licenses, wildlife agencies aim not to protect individual animals or biological diversity but to propagate "game" species for hunters to shoot. State agencies spend millions of dollars manipulating habitat for such species by burning and clearcutting forests. They build roads through wilderness to facilitate hunter access, and they spend millions for law enforcement and hunter education. They are out to conserve sport hunting, not wildlife.

Because of widespread hunting, nonconsumptive wildlife enthusiasts cannot safely walk in the woods during hunting season. They get fewer opportunities to view wild animals, who become skittish or nocturnal for fear of being shot. Most importantly, nonhunters are denied an equal voice in determining how wildlife is treated. A mere five percent minority of the public—the hunters—have nearly 100 percent control of the wildlife. It is no exaggeration to say that wildlife, wild lands, and wildlife agencies are being held at gunpoint.

Times are changing, however, and some state agencies are beginning to realize they have a growing constituency, other than hunters, to which they must answer. Several recent studies indicate that 51 to 73 percent of Americans oppose sport hunting. As state residents, individuals have a voice in how their wildlife is treated. It is essential that animal advocates become educated about hunting, attend state wildlife meetings, and get involved in the decision-making process to ensure that their voice is heard.

# 2: White-Tailed Deer: The Phantom Menace

David J. Cantor

TO HEAR SOME people tell it, white-tailed deer have become the new "killer bees": a sinister and ever-encroaching biological threat to the health and safety of suburban

America. The proliferation and/or increased visibility of *Odocoileus virginianus*, particularly in the Northeast, has many members of the public, local officials, and media clamoring for drastic actions that often fail to solve the perceived conflicts and instead result in widespread slaughter and cruelty.

Specifically, deer are being blamed for invading residential areas and devouring large amounts of ornamental vegetation, preventing forest regeneration, eating large quantities of farm crops, causing dangerous collisions with vehicles, and spreading Lyme disease. Too often, the response to these concerns is to kill the deer in large numbers.

Yet hunting typically fails to reduce white-tail populations or eliminate complaints about the deer. Allen T. Rutberg, Ph.D., an ecologist and former vice president for wildlife issues at The Humane Society of the United States, writes in *The Science of Overabundance: Deer Ecology and Population Management* that "[t]he most visible weakness in the assertion that hunting is necessary to control deer populations is that it has largely failed to do so over the last two decades....Just because deer are being killed doesn't mean that deer populations are being controlled." Likewise, author, biology professor, and outdoors columnist Thomas Eveland, Ph.D., noted at a 1998 public presentation in Philadelphia that "[a] quick surge in a deer population can occur if hunting is implemented where it hasn't been before," since surviving deer have far more food per animal and food supply is a key factor determining reproduction and fawn survival rates.

There are both biological and political factors at work in these situations. In terms of sheer numbers, there are an estimated 15 million white-tailed deer in North America, compared with 500,000 at the turn of the century. Too much hunting nearly wiped them out. Deer management programs designed to boost populations for hunters have resulted in much larger deer numbers. With a rapid increase in suburban sprawl occurring in the same decades and providing enormous amounts of low-growing vegetation for deer to eat, complaints about deer were inevitable. Unfortunately, uninformed officials have often been willing to accept the "deer problem" label for the situation rather than understand the root causes as being sprawl and management for hunters.

Deer are intelligent, sensitive animals who live in family and larger groups. Herbivorous mammals who eat an estimated 600 different foods, deer find shelter and protection in mature forest. They eat the new growth that is usually abundant at the forest's edge, as well as low-growing vegetation within the forest, to provide the approximately 4,000 calories each needs per day. When necessary, deer will stand on their hind legs to reach higher tree leaves. They feed particularly at dawn and dusk, positioning themselves so that at least one group member is likely to spot approaching danger from a good vantage point. Their white tails serve as warning flags, easily seen when they flee. They communicate through a variety of sounds and physical gestures, including snorts, grunts, bleats, hoof stomping, rearing up, and nuzzling. Their evolved survival skills are not based on such human considerations as property and plant ownership, automobile speed or right of way, or the distribution of parasites.

The decision to use deer kills to resolve various situations comes after some predictable actions. Four main parties are usually involved in instigating a deer kill: members of the public, the local government, the state wildlife agency, and the news media. Each has its own functions, concerns, incentives, and methods that must be understood in order to prevent needless killing.

## Community Complicity

Only a small minority of Americans have hunting licenses, and surveys show that increasing majorities of people consider sport hunting unethical. But even some who might oppose sport hunting can be quick to condemn deer when they perceive deer as the cause of inconvenience or danger. Far from being paragons of responsibility prepared to make tough decisions (as some portray themselves), many civic groups avoid responsibility for learning critical information and defining problems accurately so that humane long-term solutions can be found, as opposed to killing, a quick fix that fails to address root causes and so is typically repeated year after year. Officials and lay deer-kill promoters often portray deer kills as "working" even when the slaughter in a park or residential area has continued for 15 or more consecutive years, sometimes with more deer being killed each year than in the preceding year.

In 1999 in Montgomery County, Maryland, residents surrounding an arboretum near a large wooded park helped arboretum managers instigate a deer kill by complaining about car-deer collisions, Lyme disease, and flower damage. In Philadelphia, Friends of the Wissahickon, a nonprofit organization that has worked for decades to maintain the world's largest city park, paid a consultant $40,000 to evaluate "deer impact." All of the most important claims by this man, who was already well known for never recommending nonlethal options, were disputed based on reliable information. The park commission nevertheless used his report as the basis for a deer kill.

Even after repeatedly being shown major problems with the report, which was recommended as a basis for action despite the fundamental scientific principle that all such reports be evaluated with the utmost skepticism, Philadelphia's park commission hired shooters to kill deer. They claimed to have killed well over 400 in January 2001, and the commission and others quickly began promoting the killing as a "success" despite the facts that no particular number of deer killed indicates the animals' future numbers in the same area, and that the health of vegetation in the park is a long-term matter that cannot be determined by the killing of any animals. The commission has long failed to respond to repeated requests that it work to prevent access to large deer-food supplies outside of the park.

These are the key food supplies that enable large numbers of deer to live in the area that includes the park the commission claims to protect by killing deer.

Local governments—town councils, township boards, park commissions, public safety committees, and others—often receive complaints about deer from members of the public. Some officials are predisposed to agree that "something must be done" to reduce the deer population. Like their constituents, many have read deer-bashing articles, which have proliferated in the last decade. Like the members of the park commission in Philadelphia, most officials in a position to decide the fate of deer are not required to demonstrate knowledge of basic ecological concepts such as the tendency of increased food supplies to bring increases in deer numbers.

In Tredyffrin Township, Pennsylvania, dozens of local residents assembled at a Township Board meeting wearing large buttons reading "Say Yes to Less" (meaning fewer deer). Organized by a resident who had already spent years promoting bow hunting throughout the area, many railed against the deer and warned the board members that if they did not vote to allow bow hunting on public property, they would be failing to act in the public interest. Not previously having become informed about the root causes of the complaints about deer, board members predictably found it difficult to accept that they were not facing a "deer problem" but a situation in which widely accepted land-use practices amounted to feeding deer for many years so that their population naturally had grown. They also had difficulty accepting that practical humane measures could remedy the situation. The typical poorly reasoned thinking in these situations goes: If it's a deer problem, then kill the deer.

Local officials need to appear responsive to residents' concerns, lest they lose cooperation in other matters or fail to be re-elected. They are usually far better versed in local sports, zoning, chamber of commerce activities, and parade routes than in wildlife management.

When residents voice a concern loudly and consistently, local officials are inclined to accede to their demands if they can do so lawfully and without being seen as creating a more serious problem than the one they are asked to solve. As long as a locality complies with state wildlife regulations, it can have deer killed.

Some states have "sunshine" laws requiring local governing bodies to hold public meetings on a range of matters they may take up. The fact that officials profess a desire to hear all sides or to gather all of the facts is no indication that their minds are not already made up. A group of animal activists in Maryland were outraged upon finding that a meeting publicized as officials' wanting to hear residents' views turned out to be a question-and-answer session about the deer kill the officials had already approved.

One or more members of a governing body may believe animals have rights, or hold other humane values; the vote to kill deer often is not unanimous. However, deer-kill proposals almost always pass. Those officials who are opposed rarely fight hard for the deer, choosing instead to remain silent or try to raise doubts without jeopardizing their council seats.

Often invited by local officials or residents pushing for a deer kill, the state wildlife agency frequently sends an agent to public meetings. These agencies exist mainly to facilitate hunting, and their policies aim to manipulate deer herd sizes through killing and food and habitat "management."

Nonlethal methods for preventing the problems blamed on deer have not proven effective or ineffective for herd management, because they are not used for herd management—"herd" being the term used by wildlife agencies to denote the entire population within their jurisdiction, not the relatively small number of deer in possible deer-kill areas. But many measures have proven effective for preventing car-deer collisions, Lyme disease, and plant damage. Likewise, the wildlife contraceptive

PZP (porcine zona pellucida) has proven effective for preventing pregnancy in does.

So why mislead the public by implying that so few options exist? Unlike most state agencies, the agencies charged with overseeing wildlife and administering hunting, fishing, and trapping are not usually maintained by the state's general fund revenues from taxes and other sources. They operate on hunting license fees, voluntary contributions, sales of timber from "game lands," and federal funding under the 52-year-old Pittman-Robertson Act (PRA). To receive PRA funds, each state long ago passed legislation stipulating that such revenue received by the state can only be used by the wildlife agency. These federal funds go to the agencies based on each state's land area and the number of hunting licenses issued. That is a key reason "scientific herd management" through hunting is the agencies' bread and butter. They manage herds not to prevent problems in residential areas, but to serve themselves and their hunter constituents.

More licenses must be purchased for a controlled hunt in which the state specifies a number of hunters allowed to shoot deer in a particular area than for a lone sharpshooter hired by the local government. But, as the Pennsylvania Game Commission (PGC) did in Philadelphia in 1999, wildlife agencies may stipulate that a locality may hire a sharpshooter the first year but must consider involving a multitude of hunters in subsequent years.

Promoting deer kills also serves wildlife agencies' interests by masking the agencies' own responsibility for deer population growth. As the director of the PGC's Bureau of Wildlife Management editorialized in the December 1998 issue of *Pennsylvania Game News*, "Over the past decade (1988-97), Pennsylvania hunters have harvested 3.9 million deer, more than any other decade....In terms of deer harvest, these are the good old days! In addition to harvest data and population estimates, there is ample evidence deer populations in many areas of the state are higher than we should responsibly maintain them." In other words, killing more deer than ever before ultimately produced more deer than ever before.

**The Media**
News reporters usually repeat wildlife officials' distortions without showing any expressed or implied skepticism. Rarely do reporters covering deer-related disputes possess prior understanding of deer, the factors that affect their populations, or the many options for controlling populations and behavior. Nor are they typically versed in animal rights or wildlife, ecology, horticulture, land use, health, or safety issues. They typically treat conflicts over deer as one more "he said, she said" dispute rather than as a life-and-death matter worthy of thorough investigation. No matter how much information reporters receive, articles follow the same pattern: complaints from residents, promises of action from local officials, hunting support from state officials, objections from activists, and downplaying the well-researched claims of pro-animal scientists and advocates. There exists in the news media a peculiar differentiation between the suffering of one animal and the suffering of many; the same newspaper that would characterize the killing of a kitten as a cruel and shameful act can turn around and treat the mass slaughter of dozens or hundreds of deer as a valuable service that only hysterical "Bambi-lovers" could object to. Newspaper editorial boards often voice approval of deer-kill proposals without bothering to learn the full range of relevant facts—an unacknowledged manifestation of speciesist prejudice. If editors applied similar prejudice to matters of sex- or race-based discrimination, they would endure advertising withdrawals and subscription cancellations.

The basic charge that deer are overpopulating is simplistic. Studies meant to determine carrying capacity—the number of animals who can live sustainably on a certain amount of land—are conducted on "game lands," not in residential areas with gardens, arboretums, parks, roads, golf courses, and other places cleared of forest and providing edge lands with enormous deer food supplies.

No data exist to show how many deer can live sustainably in a human environment, so claims made about "optimal" numbers have no relevance to the communities where deer kills are proposed. If the local vegetation were not sufficient to nourish the deer, the deer would not be there, or their numbers would decline without human interference, due to lower rates of fawn survival and reproduction.

## Loss of Predators

There is also the erroneous claim used by deer-kill advocates that, because human settlement and development have eliminated predators who previously controlled the deer population, we humans must now fulfill that "natural role" using bullets and arrows. However, the elimination of predators does not account for larger herds or complaints about deer in residential areas. According to Ron Baker, author of *The American Hunting Myth*, "Hunting, whether in the presence or absence of large predators, is no guaranteed annual 'check' on deer populations." Deer-kill supporters must be reminded that natural predators kill mostly the sick, old, or weak individuals in a herd, not the random (and often large and healthy) animals most often targeted by hunters. This is a major distinction that greatly affects herd size and viability. Also, natural predators eat many other animals also present where deer live, and thus would not be likely to significantly reduce urban and suburban deer populations boosted and maintained by vast human-provided deer food supplies.

"We often think predators control prey, but that is rarely the case," says Eveland. "Prey controls predators; predators diminish as prey declines. It is not the case that removing wolves, cougars, and other predators causes deer to increase." Rutberg agrees: "Game managers rely on a few specious ecological arguments to justify hunts and other lethal deer reductions. Probably the most widely used of these myths is that presettlement populations of deer were controlled by predators, removal of predators ended natural control, and, consequently, hunters are needed to control deer populations....[Deer] populations are regulated through a complex interaction of food availability, predators, and other variables."

Some measures people can take to prevent deer from eating gardens—fencing, stringing nylon cord, using repellents, and planting only plants that deer do not favor—may over time have the added effect of lowering the local deer population or causing emigration. Humane approaches also by definition teach respect for animals and promote tolerance and coexistence.

**Car-Deer Collisions**
When it comes to car-deer collisions, which number about 500,000 per year according to the National Safety Council, such accidents are part of a much larger problem. Suburban sprawl, facilitated and perpetuated by society's dependence on cars, is a major factor in perceived conflicts with deer. Widespread clearing of forests for roads, housing developments, schools, malls, office and industrial parks, and other structures creates edge lands with enormous amounts of low-growing vegetation, increasing deer food supplies and thus reproduction and survival rates.

It is also important to note that hunting increases car-deer collisions. Dominant does—the deer most likely to keep others from entering roadways with cars approaching—are sometimes killed, and other herd disruptions by hunters may also contribute to accidents. A 1998 report by Erie Insurance, the country's twelfth largest insurer of private passenger vehicles, showed that the daily number of deer-related collision claims in Pennsylvania increased during mating season (late October to early November) and hunting season (late November to early December). In 1997, Erie Insurance received an average of 34 deer claims a day; that number increased fivefold on the first day of buck season and doe season for 157 and 160 losses, respectively.

One way to decrease collisions is for more people to drive less; another is to drive more slowly in areas known for abundant deer. Activists in Hudson, Ohio, successfully averted a proposed deer kill by convincing officials and the public that slowing down for deer would mean slowing down for human beings, too. They persuaded authorities to enforce speed limits more strictly and consistently and to install deer warning signs on the main road in and out of town. They also got roadside reflectors installed. Specially designed to prevent deer from entering the road between dawn and dusk, when most collisions occur, the devices reflect car headlights in a way that deer perceive as a physical barrier between themselves and the road. Car-deer collisions in Hudson have since declined dramatically.

So-called "deer whistles," the bullet-shaped plastic devices mounted on car bumpers and designed to alert deer to auto danger through ultrasonic sound, have received poor reviews. According to the Insurance Institute for Highway Safety, "Georgia's Game and Fish Department found that in hundreds of observations from vehicles equipped with deer whistles, deer didn't respond....According to wildlife biologists at the University of Georgia, deer cannot hear ultrasonic sound. Whistles blown by mouth near captive deer produce no response."

## Lyme Disease
The spread of Lyme disease is also unfairly blamed solely on deer. Although transmitted by a parasite known as a deer tick, Lyme disease is carried by members of many animal species. Human vigilance, not deer kills, can prevent and mitigate the illness through the use of repellents and prompt treatments. Even if deer are killed, ticks can find other hosts, including companion animals. Like deer, many of the other animals that

carry ticks are herbivores; removing the deer may increase the amount of food available for smaller animals, causing them to proliferate and provide even more potential disease hosts. Even the American Lyme Disease Foundation has stated that it does not recommend killing deer as a way to control Lyme disease. Killing deer may even encourage human residents to indulge a false belief that disease-carrying ticks (these arachnids carry many serious diseases besides Lyme disease) have been significantly reduced; as a result, many people may fail to take appropriate precautions.

The matter of urban and suburban deer is a complex one with different answers for different locations and circumstances. It is critical that those wishing to protect deer from harm become familiar with the facts and see to it that other citizens and decision-makers are also educated. It is in everyone's best interest to find reasonable, effective ways to prevent problems before they occur and to protect the well-being of humans and deer alike.

# 3: Canned Hunts

RICHARD FARINATO

TEXAS, 1991. A declawed black leopard is released from a cage in the back of a pick-up truck. He is set upon at once by a pack of hounds. Several people watch the dogs tear at the cat, until one person finally shoots the leopard and poses with the kill.

Pennsylvania, 1994. A man armed with a bow, dressed in camouflage clothing, stands in a field, selecting his quarry from a flock of exotic sheep herded toward him. One of the sheep, after being hit by several arrows, collapses along the fence line, only to be hit by more arrows and then by a bullet.

These scenes appear in videos that are part of The Humane Society of the United States' campaign against canned hunts, in which hunters pay a fee to stalk and kill an animal in an enclosure. There are hundreds of canned hunts across the United States, from bare-bones, mom-and-pop setups lacking amenities to elaborate resorts that provide food, lodging, entertainment, transportation, guides, dogs, and weapons—and, of course, trophy-handling services. Depending on the scale of the operation, the shooting menu may include deer, elk, bison, cattle, swine, big cats, bears, zebras, several species of exotic goats and sheep, Asian and African antelope, and other large mammals. Yet although the setting and the species may vary, the animal is always confined, always helpless, and always the victim of someone's ego-driven notion of recreation.

Shooting a confined animal at virtually point-blank range is the most reprehensible form of sport hunting. There is, in fact, no sport involved, no fair chase, and no skill either. Hunters ordinarily claim they are pitting their ability as predators against a wild animal whose instincts for survival are highly developed and constantly in use on his own turf. However, in the shabby confines of an enclosure, an animal is reduced to a live target in a shooting gallery for people who are frequently unskilled with firearms and unable to make a quick kill.

The animal targets in canned hunts often are trained, conditioned, or bred for their fates. They may be tame or hand-reared, fed at regular times at feeding stations, and moved through a system of corrals and paddocks. Such training eliminates the animals' natural fear or flight response elicited by the presence of human beings, and ensures an easy target for canned-hunt clients. Animals may be set up for the kill as they gather at a regular feeding area or move toward a familiar vehicle or person in anticipation of being fed. Once a pattern is well established, even the most wary species of antelope or deer can be manipulated effectively, guaranteeing a kill.

Unfortunately, any time wild animals are bought, sold, traded, or exhibited, there is the risk of a connection, either direct or indirect, to canned hunts. Whenever animals are bred—in a zoo or in a hobbyist's backyard—too many offspring are invariably produced. Breeders dispose of their surplus animals by selling or trading them to brokers, dealers, game ranches, or other individuals. Go-betweens often supply game ranches with animals directly or deliver animals to auctions, where they may be purchased by game ranches for hunts.

In addition to the exotic animals who are bred to be killed, canned hunt victims are acquired from several other sources: animal dealers, brokers, animal auctions, private breeders, wild-animal ranches, and zoos. Although few people would associate zoos with canned hunts, animal protection groups have documented connections between zoos and canned hunt operators. These connections are usually traced through a middleman or dealer who gets animals from a zoo, and then disposes of them to hunts or to suppliers of hunts. The American Zoo and Aquarium Association (AZA), a membership organization that accredits roughly 200 zoos in the United States, until recently did not prohibit the disposition of animals from member zoos to hunt operations provided that the zoo animals themselves were not shot or hunted. Such a policy simply allowed such animals to be used as breeders for future hunting stock. It was only in the new de-accession guidelines adopted and recommended as of March 2001 that the AZA stated that "animals shall not be disposed of to organizations or individuals that allow the hunting of these animals or their offspring." The AZA has no regulatory or enforcement power over member zoos; there is no penalty to pay for ignoring these guidelines, aside from loss of membership in the AZA. And animals are liable to end up in hunt operations through the actions of middlemen like dealers or brokers.

## Cruelty and Disease

Despite hunt operators' precautions, animals inevitably escape from ranches and hunts because of human carelessness and natural disasters. Thus, besides the obvious cruelty they inflict on the target animals they produce, canned hunts impose burdens on other animals, society, and the environment. Some animals who escape from hunt pens displace native wildlife, disrupt natural communities, and spread disease to livestock, wildlife, and people. Diseases of wildlife, both native and exotic, are much more difficult to control than are livestock diseases. Diagnostic tests and vaccines developed for livestock often prove unreliable or ineffective when applied to other species. What's more, exotic animals may carry diseases largely unknown to domestic stock. In 1991 an epidemic of bovine tuberculosis—whose origin had been traced by the Wyoming Fish and Game Department to a Montana game ranch—devastated elk ranches in western Canada. Wyoming Fish and Game officials estimated that 80 percent of the 4,200 elk on private ranches in Alberta had been exposed to TB. In the fall of 1991, bovine TB also appeared on a game farm in New York and an elk ranch in Colorado. Now the spotlight is focusing on chronic wasting disease in deer and elk, with the United States Department of Agriculture earmarking $26 million to combat the spread of the disease to wild animals and livestock from elk and deer shipped from state to state for hunts and farming.

Thanks to the canned-hunt industry and the trade in exotic animals of which it is a part, there are now free-ranging populations of blackbuck antelope, sika deer, fallow deer, mouflon, sheep, and wild boars in the United States. Native white-tail deer dwindle where sika and fallow deer are present. Mouflon sheep interbreed with native bighorn sheep, compromising the genetic integrity of the native species. Wyoming Fish and Game reports that wild elk from Yellowstone National Park have mixed with the TB-exposed elk on the Montana ranch that initiated the Alberta epidemic.

Game ranches and hunts, which are legal in most states, were once most commonly found in Texas, where exotic game ranches appeared some 40 years ago. Such ranches now have spread throughout the continental United States and Hawaii. The Animal Welfare Act does not regulate game preserves, hunting preserves, or hunts. The Endangered Species Act affords some protection to listed endangered or threatened species, but it does not prohibit private ownership of endangered animals, and it may even allow canned hunts of endangered species under certain conditions. California, Wisconsin, Indiana, Virginia, Montana, and Oregon have laws that prohibit or restrict canned hunts. Additional states have acted to restrict or prohibit certain activities. In Texas, for example, a "canned hunt" bill was enacted that prohibits the shooting of carnivores (lions, tigers, leopards) and large mammals (elephants, rhinos, hippos). Although that seems beneficial on the surface, these are animals who rarely feature in the canned hunt setting. It still allows the basic species (wild and exotic hoofstock from around the world) to be hunted, but makes Texas look like it has addressed the issue of canned hunts. In New York, hunt ranches of fewer than 10 acres in size are banned. Critics feel that this is not seriously addressing the problem.

In addition, a federal bill to outlaw the use of exotic animals in hunts has been proposed in Congress each session since 1994. These and additional laws are desperately needed, for canned hunts are nothing more than a form of commercial slaughter. They evoke outrage from animal protection groups, indignation from ethical sportspersons, and horror from the public. We hope these feelings will translate into ever-building support for legislation on the state or federal level that will ban or regulate this leisure-time butchery. To do anything less is to allow people to operate shooting galleries that perpetuate the abuse of animals in order to satisfy the egos of "hunters" who do not possess the dignity of the trophies they seek.

# 4: Hunters Set their Sights on Children

MICHAEL MARKARIAN AND NORM PHELPS

IN 1996, THE hunting industry raked in $21 billion, more than double its $10 billion in 1985. But the manufacturers and sellers of firearms, ammunition, and archery equipment— as well as the hunting lodges, outfitters, and guides who share this bonanza—are not celebrating. High-cost, high-tech equipment may be swelling the industry's coffers, but federal reports and surveys show a declining customer base. Not only are America's hunters becoming scarcer, but they are growing older, as fewer young people take up killing animals for sport.

When asked why he robbed banks, career criminal Willie Sutton replied, "Because that's where the money is." For the hunting industry, the money is where the children are, in the schools—and that's where hunting groups are going with a campaign to teach America's children that shooting animals from ambush is good, wholesome fun.

Using $330,000 in grant money from the U.S. Fish and Wildlife Service (USFWS), the Council for Wildlife Conservation and Education, Inc., an arm of the National Shooting Sports Foundation (NSSF), produced three pro-hunting videos for distribution to schools: "Wildlife for Tomorrow," aimed at grades 4 through 7, and "The Unendangered Species" and "What They Say about Hunting," for grades 7 through 12. All three credit hunters with saving many species of wildlife from extinction, and portray animal advocates as emotional, uninformed city-dwellers. The NSSF's announced goal is to place these videos in 100,000 schools, where they will be viewed by 18 million children. When The Fund for Animals asked the USFWS for $142,000 to produce and distribute materials presenting the other side of the hunting debate, it declined.

A different approach to inhumane education has been taken by the deceptively named American Animal Welfare

Foundation, which created a role-playing exercise for secondary schools called "People, Animals, and the Environment" with the goal of teaching "the many benefits of responsible animal use," including sport hunting. In 1995, the Illinois Department of Natural Resources placed "People, Animals, and the Environment" in all of the state's 4,300 public secondary schools. Teachers were paid a $90 stipend to attend workshops on how to present the program effectively.

But private industry is not alone in taking hunting into the classroom. State wildlife agencies, whose budgets and salaries depend on the sale of hunting licenses, are also getting into the act. Most states require new hunters to pass a hunter education class typically consisting of 12 hours of instruction on such topics as handling firearms and field dressing dead animals. In at least 19 states, hunter education classes are conducted in public high schools on school time. In at least 14 of these states, firearms are brought into the classroom.

Going one step further, the Wyoming Game and Fish Department is taking an ambitious outreach effort into public schools under the banner of the famous OREO cookie logo, which it uses with permission from Nabisco. In addition to the traditional hunter education class, the Outdoor Recreation and Education Opportunities (OREO) curriculum includes hunting modules such as "Hunter Skills" (including falconry and fur trapping), and "Shooting Sports," which includes "hunting with rifles, shotguns, pistols, black powder, and archery."

The Wisconsin Department of Natural Resources has allocated $150,000 "to promote the learning of hunting, fishing and trapping skills" in Wisconsin's public schools. The Missouri Department of Conservation distributes a comic book to Missouri's public schools titled "Chris' First Hunting Adventure." The comic portrays young Chris killing his first deer, then slicing through the deer's stomach with a knife while thinking, "Wow, what a privilege it is to be able to hunt and enjoy the beauties of nature and to have the education to take care of this deer in the right way."

In response, animal rights groups have worked to get a more honest portrayal of hunting into schools. For example, The Fund for Animals created "Project Respect," featuring a video titled "What's Wrong with Hunting," and a curriculum unit called "Critical Perspectives on Hunting." The Fund also publishes two periodicals, *Animal Free Press* for secondary schools and *Animal Crusaders* for elementary schools, both of which often take on the issue of hunting. The Humane Society of the United States sponsors "Earth/Animal-Protection" clubs in secondary schools around the country and supports them with fact sheets and tips on getting started, raising funds, selecting projects, and conducting campaigns.

These and similar humane education programs often sponsored by grassroots organizations are springing up all around the country, but they need community support in order for schools to include in their curricula a humane education program that speaks to the needs of all nonhuman animals.

But it's not just in the schools where hunters are taking aim at children. On a Saturday morning early in the fall, for example, most children are watching cartoons, begging their parents to take them to the mall, or tying up the phone. But today state wildlife agencies are luring groups of youngsters to state parks and other recreational lands for a different kind of recreation: hunting.

While their grinning parents look on approvingly at a youth pheasant hunt in California, youngsters struggle to load their weapons correctly. Then a state-hired driver arrives with several hundred pheasants cramped in tiny crates. The pheasants are released, and one 10-year-old girl, dressed from head to toe in camouflage and wielding a shotgun one size too large, approaches a pheasant. The bird was raised in captivity and was hand-fed until this day and has no knowledge of the wild or fear of humans. The bird stands still. The young girl takes aim, squinches her eyes nearly closed, and squeezes the trigger.

Most state and federal wildlife agencies hold special youth hunts as part of a proactive campaign—often at taxpayers' expense—to recruit children into hunting. Currently, 49 state wildlife agencies sponsor children's hunts in which participants as young as eight years old—and with no minimum age in some states—can learn to kill mourning doves, rabbits, pheasants, squirrels, deer, elk, Canada geese, and other animals.

This youth recruitment plot is no scattershot effort. Officials from Cornell University and the New York Department of Environmental Conservation determined that one hunter education class or a single hunting experience does not turn a child into a lifelong hunter. Thus, New York offers a mentorship program that pairs young recruits with experienced hunters, who lead the children through more than a year of hunting-related activities, including a hunter education course, the purchase of firearms and outdoor clothing, and a series of hunts. Because children have a natural affinity toward animals and often become upset at the sight of a dying animal, mentors are trained to teach recruits that an animal's death is not bad and that sport hunting is a legitimate activity.

This is critical because studies conducted by pro-hunting researchers in 1993 show that 83 percent of hunters start before they turn 19. The same research shows that if people are not taught to kill animals at an early age, most of them will be unwilling to do so throughout their lives. Therefore, the younger the recruit, the better. In *Sports Afield* (December 1994), Guy Martin, the self-proclaimed "Sporting Dr. Spock," describes teaching his two-year-old daughter to hook a fish and dress a deer. "You have to start them as soon as is practicable," says Martin, "before any fairy tale-based fears or prejudices about the natural world have had a chance to settle."

Most youth hunts are held in September before the regular hunting season opens and the weather turns cold. If they are not competing with other hunters, children have a better chance to kill animals and gain a feeling of accomplishment. Squirrels are a favorite target for youth hunts, because they are easy to find and the hunting equipment needed is minimal.

When The Fund for Animals learned about the special deer hunt for youths aged 11 and older sponsored by the Missouri Department of Conservation, The Fund sent a letter to the department's director, Jerry J. Presley, asking that the hunt be canceled. Presley replied that The Fund's "criticisms of hunters are self-righteous, self-serving, and grossly exaggerated," but some members of the department disagreed. One department insider wrote that a state agency should not be in the business of recruiting hunters, "just as the Missouri Boat Patrol should not recruit boaters [and] just as the Missouri Department of Revenue should not recruit adherents to a welfare existence."

It is not only state agencies, however, that act as recruiting firms for the sport-hunting community. The USFWS, which is charged with the protection of endangered species and migratory birds, has hosted several youth hunts on federal land, but it should not be in the business of recruiting hunters—especially at the expense of U.S. taxpayers, more than 95 percent of whom do not hunt.

The hunting community's scheme of youth recruitment subverts the purpose of our national wildlife refuges, our national forests, and even our national parks. Refuges and other federal lands should be sanctuaries for America's wildlife, not havens for hunters who want to indoctrinate unwitting children into a dying bloodsport. State and federal agencies should represent the views of the entire public, not just the tiny minority that enjoys killing animals for recreation. There is no justification for peddling hunting propaganda in the guise of comic books to schoolchildren. The majority of Americans oppose sport hunting, and it is high time we took back our public schools, our public funds, and our public lands—for the good of our wildlife and our children.

# 5: Nailed to the Wall

Wayne Pacelle

TROPHY HUNTING IS a billion-dollar-a-year industry, centered on the U.S.-based Safari Club International. The industry has its familiar players: guides and outfitters, arms and ammunitions manufacturers, taxidermists and, of course, trophy hunters. But it also has some unexpected players, such as some of the world's most prestigious natural history museums, including the Smithsonian.

**Ambassadors or Assassins?**
It was billed as a mission to help the Cabo Delgado province of Mozambique, a country rich in wildlife but stricken with poverty. It was fertile terrain for Safari Club International (SCI) to sow the seeds of its central doctrine: helping people by hunting wildlife. The opening of Cabo Delgado's borders to foreign hunters would generate revenue for local peoples and give them a reason to conserve wildlife, assuring that animals would have tangible value for those who might otherwise resort to indiscriminate poaching. The visiting SCI leaders—then-president Skip Donau, past president Lance Norris, Kenneth Behring, and others—were prepared to offer more than just an abstract principle to cement a future arrangement. They made a donation of $20,000 to a local hospital and conducted a "survey" of big-game populations in the province (despite being ill equipped for a true biological assessment).

Not surprisingly, they were treated like heads of state on a humanitarian mission. But schmoozing with local government officials, lavishing gifts, and counting animals were not the principal purposes of the trip—they wanted to hunt. After all, as Norris allegedly told Niassa Game Reserve manager Mark Jenkins, "Hunting is what SCI is all about."

And hunt they did, if that's what it can be called. More accurately, they engaged in a wildlife killing spree. According to Jenkins and field personnel at the Niassa Game Reserve, the SCI delegation exhibited highly unsportsmanlike hunting techniques, leaving a number of wounded animals to suffer and die, and killing elephants, allegedly in violation of national law.

Highlights of the July 1998 expedition were enthusiastically noted in the pages of *The Hunting Report*, a small but influential newsletter read by a few thousand of the world's elite trophy hunters. Editor Don Causey wrote, "A delegation from Safari Club International on a special invitation safari has taken three elephants....The largest of the three weighed a mind-boggling 92 pounds [the weight of a single tusk] and is thus one of the largest takes in Africa in recent years." Although SCI claimed that it received government authorization for the elephant hunts, a declaration signed by the national director for Forestry and Wildlife stated, "It is hereby declared that, in terms of Ministerial Diploma No. 60/90 of 4th July 1990, the trophy hunting of elephants in Mozambique is forbidden, and also the export of ivory."

According to a report by Jenkins, a "helicopter had dropped off the hunters and then drove the elephant into their guns." The reserve manager also noted that the SCI delegation shot "3 lion, 5 buffalo, 1 eland, 3 kudu and 6 impala." He added, "The Reserve Game guards also heard reports from throughout the area that wounded animals were dying along the river. Specifically, 1 impala and 2 kudu were found with gunshot wounds, and an eland with gunshots in its chest had been found alive in the river, struggling to avoid being eaten by crocodiles."

These were the elected leaders of the world's most acclaimed trophy hunting organization. Businessmen. Community leaders. Wildlife enthusiasts.

**Quarry Quotas**

Although the U.S. Fish and Wildlife Service (USFWS) reports a gradual but steady decline in U.S. hunting, the ranks of international trophy hunters continue to grow. The Humane Society of the United States, in its report "Big Game, Big Bucks," has documented a startling surge in recent years in the number of sport-hunted trophies imported into America.

SCI, founded in 1972 by C. J. McElroy, serves as the hub for the worldwide trophy hunting industry, boasting 32,000 members, 140 chapters, and a museum at its headquarters in Tucson. Its monthly *Safari* magazine is full of first-hand accounts of members' hunting excursions, plus advertisements for taxidermists, hunting guides and outfitters, and exotic hunting ranches. SCI's national convention—held in either Reno or Las Vegas—draws crowds in excess of 10,000. The convention's exhibit hall features more than 1,000 guides and outfitters, who sell their services for up to tens of thousands of dollars.

SCI's programs include 29 hunting achievement awards, labeled as either "Grand Slams" or "Inner Circles," that appeal to the wealthy hunters' zest for one-upmanship and keep the industry well financed. For example, to achieve the "Africa Big Five Grand Slam," a hunter must kill an African lion, a leopard, an elephant, a rhinoceros, and a Cape buffalo. To achieve a "Bears of the World" Grand Slam, a hunter must kill at least four different kinds of bears, such as polar bears, Alaska brown bears, grizzly bears, Eurasian brown bears, Siberian brown bears, and others. The Inner Circles are even more difficult to achieve, and have five levels. To claim the highest, "Diamond" level, a hunter must kill 76 different species. For a hunter to collect all of the SCI's 29 hunting awards, he or she would have to kill a minimum of 322 different species or subspecies.

In his book *Blood Ties*, author Ted Kerasote (a columnist for *Sports Afield*) describes the creation of the Grand Slam for the world's sheep. He quotes Jack O'Connor, one-time shooting editor of *Outdoor Life* and only the fifth person to achieve this award, as saying, "They're after glory...and the sooner they can get the tiresome business over with and slap those ram heads on the wall, the better they like it." O'Connor alleged that the desire to complete a Grand Slam had created "a tremendous amount of lying, poaching, and cheating."

In addition to the quantity of trophies collected, there is also a quality issue. SCI publishes an awards book in which it lists the biggest specimens killed. On his trip to Siberia, Kerasote asked Bob Kubick (whose trophy room is 42 by 34 feet), "What happens when the record book pushes people into blasting sheep from helicopters?" Kubick, whose personal wealth once reached $700 million, said, "I don't think the record book does it so much as the thought of the money you've paid, and that you've got to take something home."

During a trip with top SCI hunters, Kerasote documented that Donald Cox, one of SCI's most accomplished hunters and president of Specialty Steel Treating, shot a rare sheep with the aid of a helicopter. One month after returning from Siberia, Cox was given the Weatherby Award, presented annually by the firearms company of the same name to the hunter who collects "the greatest number of average as well as record game animals throughout the entire world...and [is] a person who has contributed greatly to conservation and hunting education, and one whose character and sportsmanship are beyond reproach."

Though SCI purports to operate by a code of ethics— including a tenet that demands that SCI members honor the laws of the country they hunt in—its members have been nabbed again and again by the thin ranks of game cops who enforce wildlife laws. Take, for instance, its former Louisiana chapter president, Sonny Milstead, M.D., who shot an endangered Bengal tiger on a private hunting ranch in Texas. Or Paul Asper, who illegally killed and imported a Jentiink's duiker from Liberia, a black-faced impala from Namibia, two gorals and two serows from Nepal, and two northern huemuls from Peru—all endangered species. Or Dave Samuel, who paid a $100,000 fine and spent 30 days in jail for his endangered species-killing escapades.

But while illegal conduct by prominent SCI hunters has been well documented, the group's lawful conduct is highly questionable, too. Few laws exist to protect wildlife throughout the world, and species not protected by international treaties are at the mercy of the consciences of SCI members. And, sadly, there's not much mercy in this gang. Take this firsthand account of hunting in the high arctic by SCI member J. Y. Jones in the July/August 1996 issue of *Safari*:

> Musk ox hunting is like a frontal assault on an enemy position, and we simply marched toward the herd in full view...By the time we neared the herd, we could see the German and Italian hunters already in prone position to shoot. Both apparently are excellent marksmen, because two bulls went down immediately. At their shots, the other animals began milling and mixing, making the choosing of an animal very difficult for Alberto and me....
>
> I settled the cross hairs on what appeared to be the largest bull in the herd and squeezed off the shot....The bull collapsed immediately, rolling only slightly down the gently inclined slope. My peripheral vision caught sight of a second animal struggling in the snow so I knew Alberto also had connected!

Musk oxen, when facing a threat, typically form an outward-facing circle that shields the young in the center. Walking up to these frightened animals and gunning them down with high-powered rifles is about as cowardly and unsportsmanlike as it gets. But it's not much different or more difficult than shooting elephants, rhinos, and a number of other species whose evolutionary hard-wiring teaches them to confront a threat rather than flee. And what's the sport in being ushered around by a professional guide whose fee is tied to the ultimate success of the hunt?

## Political Trophies

In addition to promoting practical services needed by the international trophy hunter, SCI also provides political services, opening up hunting opportunities in foreign nations and, most importantly, assuring that U.S. laws don't prevent hunters from displaying their all-important trophies. With its enormously wealthy and influential constituency, SCI has substantial power on Capitol Hill. Its lobbying efforts are led by two former congressmen, Ron Marlenee of Montana and Bill Brewster of Oklahoma, both of whom had abysmal ratings on conservation issues while in office.

SCI has mounted major campaigns to weaken the Endangered Species Act (ESA) and the Marine Mammal Protection Act (MMPA), and has worked to secure appropriations funds for trophy hunting programs while also beating back attempts to cut off trophy hunting subsidies or to outlaw canned hunts. In 1994, SCI achieved one of its major victories by successfully amending the MMPA to sanction the import of sport-hunted polar bear trophies from Canada, the only country that allows non-nationals to hunt the bears. Since that time, SCI members have imported dozens of trophies from Canada, some of which had been in storage for more than two decades.

In 1998, SCI led the fight to maintain funding for Zimbabwe's much-hyped Communal Areas Management Program for Indigenous Resources (CAMPFIRE) program. CAMPFIRE is the SCI's model program of "sustainable utilization," in which rural communities allegedly benefit by selling hunting concessions for big-game species such as elephants and leopards. While SCI claims it's a tremendous working model, CAMPFIRE implementers have taken $28 million from U.S. tax revenues to keep the program afloat. Independent evaluators hired by the U.S. Agency for International Development concluded that the program would not be self-sustaining without continuing foreign aid investments.

With its allies in Congress, including most of the 200 members of the Congressional Sportsmen's Caucus, SCI also puts considerable pressure on the U.S. Fish and Wildlife Service. It is now pressing the agency to reverse its longstanding decision not to allow private citizens to import sport-hunted trophies from endangered species. SCI's immediate goal is to win approval for the import of cheetah trophies from Namibia.

SCI has also pressured the USFWS not to upgrade protections for certain populations of argali sheep, who are listed as endangered across most of their range and listed under the ESA as threatened in three countries. Ron Nowak, a top USFWS biologist, urged the agency to classify all argali populations as endangered, but it has delayed a final decision for more than four years. What's more, Nowak wrote that the USFWS has granted import permits for sport-hunted trophies from the threatened argali populations that clearly do not meet the standards that it is supposed to observe in reviewing permit applications. In 1997, Nowak wrote to the USFWS Office of Management Authority, "Do not allow a back-room scheme, developed to circumvent the law on behalf of special interest, [to] drag FWS through a long legal struggle, in which it will throw away its limited resources and the public's money to back a dubious and demeaning position."

Two years later, the agency still had not listed all argalis as endangered, and continues to award dozens of import permits for threatened populations, even though the conservation standard for the granting of such permits is not being met. In fact, at the 1995 SCI convention, Interior Secretary Bruce Babbitt presided over the auctioning of a permit to kill a threatened argali sheep. In May 2001, The Fund for Animals and other animal protection organizations and wildlife scientists sued the USFWS in federal court to compel the agency to list all argali populations as "endangered" throughout their range and to bar the import of any sport-hunted trophies of the sheep.

Amazingly, SCI gets taxpayer monies from the USFWS through the auspices of the African Elephant Conservation Act, which was created to support conservation projects to benefit elephants. SCI has been awarded nearly a half dozen Interior Department grants, which it uses to promote its trophy hunting programs in Tanzania and several southern African countries.

In addition to being active in Congress, SCI sends a sizable delegation to the Convention on the International Trade in Endangered Species of Wild Fauna and Flora (CITES), whose 140 signatory nations set rules regarding the global trade in threatened and endangered species. SCI has won battles to facilitate the killing and importing of dozens of imperiled species, most notably leopards, African elephants, wild sheep, goats, and antelopes. It is pushing to win export allowances for jaguars, the western hemisphere's largest cat.

SCI also actively promotes the doctrine of sustainable utilization to developing countries. Its view is that "wildlife must pay its way," and that placing a value on animals in a crowded world gives locals a reason to conserve species. It has used this doctrine—and its members' cash—to open Ethiopia to sport hunting and to expand hunting opportunities elsewhere. It now wants to establish sport hunting in Kenya, where the practice has been banned since 1977.

But while SCI's muscle and money are formidable, the group is touting a central practice—the killing of rare animals for their heads—that is anathema to most Americans. A 1997 survey by Penn & Schoen revealed that 86 percent of Americans oppose the trophy hunting of elephants. A 1999 survey by Yale researcher Steven Kellert showed similar levels of opposition to polar bear hunting.

It's a perverse subculture, to be sure. And it's also a destructive one. Hundreds of thousands of animals suffer and die for the amusement of wealthy elites who have the means to pursue any hobby, but choose one that doesn't just require bloodshed, but flaunts it as well. There's no societal value to the exercise, just a selfish, all-consuming mentality of killing and collecting. It's a mindset where the participants know the price of every animal, but the value of none.

# 6: National Wildlife Refuges: Sanctuaries or Killing Fields?

CAMILLA H. FOX

O N NOVEMBER 13, 1995, a golden retriever named Bandit went for a fall afternoon walk with his caregiver along a road in Wisconsin's Trempealeau National Wildlife Refuge. In the air was a mouth-watering scent that Bandit could not resist. The aroma came from the bait placed in a Conibear trap set to catch a raccoon. Instead, the trap caught Bandit. The frantic caregiver could not loosen the trap's death grip on Bandit's head, and the dog suffocated in his arms. The trap was perfectly legal; the refuge annually sells permits to trap muskrats, beavers, and raccoons in certain areas. But neither Bandit nor his caregiver had any warning, and Bandit paid the ultimate price.

**Tragedies Abound**
This horror story is hardly an isolated incident. Across the National Wildlife Refuge System (NWRS) such tragedies are all too frequent. Traps are left unattended to catch whatever unlucky creature comes along—often taking hours or days to finally cause death. Many non-target animals, like Bandit, other family companions, and even endangered species, fall victim to body-gripping traps, a problem that has raised increasing concern and outcry among animal advocates and the public. Incredibly, when stories like Bandit's arise, the blame is usually

placed not on the trapper but on the companion animal's guardian. Reporters quoted the Trempealeau trapper as saying, "Dog owners [must] be vigilant around their animals during trapping seasons no matter where they are." Such reasoning raises the question of why the 99.9 percent of the population that doesn't trap must go to such lengths to guard against the minute percentage that does, particularly on public property.

By law National Wildlife Refuges and the wildlife within them belong to all U.S. citizens equally. U.S. Fish and Wildlife Service (USFWS) statistics show that of the 27.1 million refuge visitors in 1995, 81.5 percent came to view and photograph wildlife, for environmental education, and for similar nonconsumptive recreational pursuit; only 4.5 percent of refuge visitors went there to hunt or trap. Out of 535 national wildlife refuges, 302 allowed hunting, 268 allowed fishing, and an unknown number allowed trapping (although the number is presumed to be no less than 280, the number that allowed trapping in 1997). Unfortunately, the number of wildlife-killing "sport" programs in the refuge system are increasing due to the 1997 National Wildlife Refuge Improvement Act (also known as the NWR Organic Act), which designates hunting and fishing as "priority uses" and stipulates that they "shall receive enhanced consideration" by refuge managers. Backers of the bill pushed the Act through Congress with claims of an overarching "conservation" mission for the refuge system. Yet, while the new law makes it more difficult for such secondary uses as grazing, mining, and logging to take place on refuges, it does nothing to stop or lessen the recreational killing of wildlife. Instead, the Act has boosted the status of bloodsports, mandating that refuge managers allow hunting and fishing unless they can provide justification for not allowing them. Had one of the primary sponsors of the new law, Rep. Don Young (R-AK), had his way, the bill would have elevated hunting and fishing to priority "purposes" of the System instead of priority "uses." No wonder that some of the heaviest lobbyists turned out to be such pro-hunting and trapping organizations as the National Rifle Association, Safari Club International, Ducks Unlimited, and the Wildlife Legislative Fund of America.

## What Went Wrong?

The first national wildlife refuges were established under the direction of President Theodore Roosevelt, to "preserve wildlife and habitat for people today, and for generations to come." Hunting, trapping, and other activities inimical to preserving wildlife were prohibited in most refuges until the 1950s, when amendments to the Duck Stamp Act resulted in many refuges allowing hunting and trapping. Consumptive wildlife users argued that their monetary contribution to "conservation" gave them the right to kill wildlife on public lands. More than 3,000 Waterfowl Production Areas (WPAs), mostly in the Midwest, are part of the refuge system. Under the guise of "avian conservation," these areas cater to waterfowl hunters and trappers, with "management" focused on eliminating bird- and egg-eating predators such as foxes, coyotes, raccoons, and skunks. To accomplish this task, a national Predation Avian Recruitment Team has been developed under the auspices of the International Association of Fish and Wildlife Agencies. Their mission is to increase the number of pheasants, quail, turkeys, and waterfowl within the refuge system by "surgically removing" predators. Trappers may kill predators on WPAs without the permit required on other refuge units. That the traps sometimes kill the very species they are intended to protect doesn't appear to concern the USFWS, the agency charged with managing the refuge system.

Since its inception, the NWRS has been administered under a collection of presidential proclamations, executive orders, administrative orders, and laws. The Refuge Recreation Act of 1962 authorized "recreational uses" of NWRs, further expanding hunting, trapping, grazing, mining, and other activities harmful to wildlife. In 1966, the National Wildlife Refuge

System Administrative Act established a "compatibility standard" for allowing public uses on refuges. The USFWS defines "compatible use" as "a wildlife-dependent recreational use or any other use of a refuge that, in the sound professional judgment of the Director, will not materially interfere with or detract from the fulfillment of the Mission of the System or the purposes of the refuge. The action must also be in accordance with the principles of sound fish and wildlife management and administration, and otherwise must be in the public interest." Today, before a refuge is opened up to hunting or fishing, the USFWS must go through the National Environmental Policy Act process and allow the public to comment on the issue. However, no public comment is required before a refuge can allow trapping; it is up to refuge managers to decide if trapping is "compatible" with the purpose of the individual refuge.

**Public Outcry**
Over the past 20 years, animal advocates have brought the issue of trapping-related cruelty to the forefront of public consciousness, and efforts to ban or restrict trapping have been successful in a number of states and local jurisdictions. Public outcry prompted Congress to include language in the 1997 Appropriations Bill directing the USFWS to convene a task force to "study the use of animal traps in the National Wildlife Refuge system...[and to] consider the humaneness of various trapping methods...and other relevant issues." It stipulated that the task force include "interested outside parties." However, the USFWS, arguing that a task force could not be convened in the allotted time, convinced Congress to allow it instead to conduct a survey of every refuge unit manager. The intent of the survey, which requested specific information pertaining to all refuge trapping programs, was never fully clear. In its final 87-page report to Congress, the USFWS offered a glowing and self-serving account of the benefits of trapping, concluding that it is "a professional wildlife management tool" that provides "impor-

tant benefits for public health and safety and recreational, commercial, and subsistence opportunities for the public." This report argued that trapping on refuges is conducted primarily for "facilities protection" and for the protection of migratory birds and threatened and endangered species; trapping for "recreation/commerce/subsistence" is listed as the last of 11 reasons for trapping in refuges. However, a copy of the survey data obtained by the Animal Protection Institute (API) through the Freedom of Information Act revealed that the USFWS' official conclusions did not accurately reflect the information submitted by the refuge managers. API's analysis of the questionnaire data found that the most common purpose cited by refuge managers for trapping was for "recreation/commerce/subsistence." The USFWS not only twisted information to form a particular conclusion (trapping is necessary and a good "wildlife management tool") but excluded vital data, such as the types of traps used and the incidents of non-target species being killed.

**Ending the Cruelty**
API and many other groups believe that commercial and recreational trapping and the use of body-gripping traps should be prohibited on all refuges. Humane concerns aside, the use of such traps is not compatible with the preservation of threatened and endangered species that inhabit refuges. In fact, leghold traps, neck snares, and other body-gripping devices pose a serious hazard to many of these species and may actually hinder their recovery. As lands specifically set aside to provide animals a safe home, refuges should be maintained as inviolate sanctuaries, not as playgrounds for trappers and other consumptive wildlife users.

# Part 4

# ANIMALS IN ENTERTAINMENT

# 1: The Elephants' Graveyard: Life in Captivity

JILL HOWARD CHURCH

EIGHTY-SEVEN BULLETS didn't kill Tyke the elephant—life in the circus did. On August 20, 1994, Tyke was scheduled to perform in the final act of Circus International's Saturday matinee in Honolulu. Just before entering the ring, the 21-year-old, 9,000-pound African elephant charged William Beckwith, a circus groom, and slammed him to the ground. When Allen Campbell, Tyke's trainer, attempted to save Beckwith, Tyke crushed Campbell to death.

Leaving the injured Beckwith and a stunned circus audience behind, Tyke bolted from the arena. She was chased for several blocks by city police, who fired scores of bullets into her. When the police had cornered the wounded Tyke, workers from the Honolulu Zoo arrived to give her a lethal injection. Afterward, as a horrified crowd looked on, Tyke absorbed three final bullets.

Beckwith the groom, who had been hired by the circus five weeks earlier after being picked up at a truck stop, survived his injuries. Tyke's owner, John Cuneo of the Hawthorne Corporation, said that Beckwith probably had startled Tyke by walking behind her, but Tyke's rampage was not an isolated incident at Circus International. Earlier in the week another elephant had rammed the fence during a performance, knocking one circus patron into the next row of seats and pinning his wife and eight children beneath the fence. Thirteen months earlier

Tyke had trampled a circus worker in North Dakota, breaking his ribs.

There are an estimated 200 elephants currently being used in U.S. circuses and traveling shows. Since 1983, captive elephants have killed more than 30 people during either performances or rides. Dozens more have been injured, including keeper and handlers as well as spectators (see "Elephant Attack Cases"). Conversely, between 1994 and 2000, more than 30 circus elephants have died from illness or injury; at least three (including Tyke) were shot to death following violent behavior. An elephant in Florida was poisoned, apparently in retribution for killing one of her handlers.

These incidents are caused by a volatile combination: keeping powerful, intelligent animals in nonfamily groups, in small spaces, and then subjecting them to abuse and deprivation. The abuse comes in the form of chains, whips, electric prods, and a device called an ankus or bullhook—a three-foot wooden pole with a sharp metal hook at the end. Trainers and handlers use bullhooks to prod elephants behind the ears, inside the mouth, behind the knees, and in other sensitive areas to get them to perform. Bullhooks are also used to subdue and punish the elephants.

When they are not being subjected to such "discipline," circus elephants are kept virtually immobile by chains attached to one front leg and one rear leg, preventing them from taking more than one or two steps in any direction. Elephants are forced to stand in place for hours on end, often in their own urine and feces. As a result, their feet are vulnerable to injury and infection, and their joints become arthritic from lack of use. To relieve the stress of standing in one place for so long—sometimes up to 20 hours a day—chained elephants often rock back and forth almost continuously. Elephants are also susceptible to tuberculosis, which can be passed on to humans who come into contact with them.

In its booklet *Everything You Should Know About Elephants*, the Performing Animal Welfare Society (PAWS) argues that "if more institutions made a commitment to improving their housing for these animals, the need for discipline would be minimized, the mental health and stability of the elephants would greatly improve, and headline such as 'Circus elephant goes on rampage, trainer killed' would, in all probability, no longer be commonplace."

PAWS founder Pat Derby is a former animal trainer who has worked with elephants for more than 30 years. In her autobiography, *The Lady and Her Tiger*, Derby wrote, "Elephants bring out a fury in many men as no other creature does: a rage to dominate and to hurt." Derby also contends that elephants are not aggressive by nature. "The way you create aggression in an elephant is through abusive training."

Derby, whose California refuge is home to six "retired" elephants, is somewhat more tolerant of zoos that try to improve their elephants' conditions; but, she says, "We are at war with circuses." She insists that it is impossible to travel with elephants and to treat them humanely at the same time.

In 1990 PAWS helped to pass an elephant protection bill in California. That bill—which outlawed training methods that break the skin, the use of electrical devices in training, and withholding food, water, or rest—was passed largely in response to the abuse of a female elephant named Dunda at the San Diego Wild Animal Park.

**Dunda**

In 1988, Dunda was transferred from the San Diego Zoo to the wild animal park to become part of a breeding program. Elephant keeper Lisa Landres, who had cared for Dunda for 10 years at the zoo, says that Dunda was drugged before being put into a crate for the 60-mile trip from the zoo to the park. There, against the advice of Landres and other zoo handlers, Dunda was chained alone in a barn. Frightened by her unfamiliar surroundings, she became volatile and was then chained to the floor. She was beaten over the head repeatedly with bullhooks and axe handles for two days by half a dozen trainers. After suffering the blows and urinating blood, Dunda reportedly rolled over, moaned, and gave up, her spirit finally broken.

Landres did not hear about the incident for three weeks. When she went to the park and saw Dunda's swollen head and gaping wounds, Landres did not recognize her. A veterinarian told Landres the beating was the worst he had ever seen.

The San Diego Wild Animal Park defended its trainers, saying Dunda was "difficult." The charge enraged Landres, who says Dunda was never aggressive and that the park had lied to cover up its abuse. Landres says Dunda acted out of fear, "and you cannot beat the fear out of an animal." After Dunda's story was made public, Landres says, she and another keeper were continually harassed by the San Diego Zoo management. "They made our lives miserable."

Alan Roocroft, manager of elephant programs at the wild animal park, supervised Dunda's "discipline." He claims that reports of the incident were exaggerated.

"If elephants had been 'abused,' " says Roocroft, "then the people who inflicted the injuries didn't know what they were doing. Or the people [who witnessed it] didn't know what they were looking at....Just because you use a stick with a metal hook on the end doesn't, to me, mean brutality."

Landres had known about the abuse of other elephants for years. "When you're in the elephant 'biz,' it's like you're in a secret club," she explains. "We all know each other's dirty little secrets." With few exceptions, she has harsh words for trainers. "The training of elephants attracts the absolute scum of the earth."

Landres wrote her master's thesis on the abnormal behavior of captive elephants, and has studied wild elephants in Africa. Eventually she left the San Diego Zoo to become a field investigator for The Humane Society of the United States (HSUS).

Later she worked for Friends of Animals. She spent several years visiting zoos and circuses across the country, documenting abuse and neglect. She concluded that "circus elephants are totally, neurotically insane," especially those used for rides. Circus elephants, she says, "have no life. Every natural behavior they have is thwarted."

Landres found her work as an investigator extremely frustrating because of inadequate animal protection laws and abysmal law enforcement. "I was seeing these incredibly intelligent animals suffering so much in captivity," she says. "[But officials] don't believe you unless you document it." She investigated one case in which signed affidavits from witnesses and video footage of abuse could not convince a Wisconsin district attorney to bring charges against a zoo. The frustration of animal protection work became so overwhelming that Landres left the profession in 1992; Dunda now lives at the Oakland Zoo.

The U.S. Department of Agriculture (USDA) is primarily to blame for the lack of sanctions against elephant abusers. Although the Animal Welfare Act (AWA), which the USDA is responsible for enforcing, governs zoos and circuses, the provisions of the act are weak and vague, and the USDA conducts site inspections only once a year. As a result, says Richard Farinato, director of captive wildlife protection for HSUS, "Elephant owners do what they damn well please with their elephants.

"It's a bad situation," Farinato continues. Cruelty prosecutions are rare because witnesses will not come forward, state laws vary, and traveling acts like circuses cannot be forced to stay in one location while an investigation is pending. Law enforcement officials, he says, "honestly believe that these are accidents—isolated incidents." Farinato, who spent 15 years as an assistant zoo director, says the benign image of circuses and zoos contributes to public apathy. Landres agrees. "[People] give the benefit of the doubt to the animals' owners, not to the animals," she says.

Nevertheless, not every abuse goes unnoticed. On September 17, 1994, when the King Royal Big Top Circus appeared in Lebanon, Oregon, trainer Bela Tabak was arrested by local police after witnesses said he had beaten a baby elephant named Mickey with a sharpened bullhook. Spectators heard Mickey's screams as he was gouged over and over after not performing correctly. In May 1995, Tabak pleaded no contest to second-degree animal abuse charges and was fined $500; his USDA license was revoked. An $8,000 civil penalty was levied against King Royal.

Beating young elephants like Mickey "sets them up to be another Tyke," says Derby. "There is no hope for this elephant. He's going to be a killer by the time he's a 10-year-old." According to PAWS, Mickey is now at the Carson & Barnes Circus.

Florence Lambert, president of The Elephant Alliance, a California-based group that monitors and speaks out against elephant abuse, believes that "the majority of the paying public is just unaware" of the way elephants are treated. "By education, we're going to change the majority." Lambert also monitors trade publications and notes that cruelty issues are now being discussed there. The mainstream media is also picking up on the state of the circus and the appeal of newer acts that don't rely on animals. In April 2001 *Time* magazine observed, "Mixing hokum with the perception of brutality, the traditional circus seems uncomfortably out of place in today's entertainment market. It's the interspecies version of a minstrel show."

Because the death rate of captive elephants still exceeds their birth rate, America's elephant population is growing smaller and older. But innovations in artificial insemination have resulted in many more elephants being impregnated, so the population may stabilize. However, after only a few years, male elephants become too unruly for use in performing and are often relegated to a life of isolation and confinement. The females are used until they literally can't continue any longer.

Tracing captive elephants can be difficult, since they are routinely sold among zoos and circuses and their names are sometimes changed in the process.

Farinato claims that many zoos are re-evaluating their elephant exhibits and are either upgrading or eliminating them. Numerous zoos have stopped chaining their elephants at night, and, says Farinato, "more small facilities are choosing not to keep elephants because they know they can't devote the time and funds to maintain them properly." Still, he says, many zoos "don't want to give up their marketing gags" of elephant rides and shows. They may be forced to, however. Growing numbers of municipalities have enacted bans or specific restrictions on circuses and similar exotic animal attractions. As of 2001, 13 U.S. cities had banned animal acts outright; five others prohibit any training method that causes pain or discomfort; and Cedarburg, Wisconsin, requires criminal background checks for all circus employees. Delaware, Georgia, and Tennessee prohibit elephant rides. A proposed ban on the use of exotic animals for entertainment in Seattle, Washington, was fiercely debated in 2000 and failed by only one vote.

The treatment of elephants is also getting national attention in Congress. In 2000, Rep. Sam Farr (D-CA) introduced the Captive Elephant Accident Prevention Act, which would have criminalized the use of elephants in traveling shows or for rides. The measure was also strongly supported by Sen. Robert Smith (R-NH), who tried in vain to prevent Ringling Bros. from bringing its elephants to perform at the U.S. Capitol. During testimony for the bill, former Ringling trainer Tom Rider said, "After my three years working with elephants in the circus, I can tell you that they live in confinement and they are beaten all the time when they don't perform properly." As for government oversight, he said, "Whenever the USDA inspected the circus, the circus always knew in advance that they were coming. We were always told to clean up [and] don't hit the elephants when they come around. I know for a fact that any attempt by the

USDA to regulate the circus or to enforce laws is a joke." However, the circus industry—led by Feld Entertainment, Ringling's parent company—lobbied heavily against the bill, and it was ultimately tabled. However, the congressional testimony shed more light on circus abuses, and the legislation may very well be reintroduced.

Ringling Bros. has had its share of elephant-related incidents. In January 1998, a three-year-old elephant named Kenny was used in performances despite being ill with an infection. When he collapsed and died after a show, the circus was charged with Animal Welfare Act violations that it settled with the USDA for $20,000. In 1999, a four-year-old named Benjamin drowned in a pond under unusual circumstances (former trainer Rider testified that Benjamin had been subjected to beatings). In all, the Elephant Alliance reports that 14 of Ringling's elephants died between 1992 and 1999 at an average age of only 32.

Ringling operates a "conservation center" in Florida to breed elephants, not with the intention of returning any to the wild, but to replenish its performance stock. Ringling even stated in a 2002 full-page newspaper ad aimed at its critics that "[i]t's disingenuous at best to suggest that endangered animals should be put back into the wild, and very destructive to the cause of conservation at worst. They are dying out there. A wild environment is far from peaceful for endangered species." As if circus-train boxcars and tractor-trailers are an elephant's natural habitat.

## Abuse

In 1999 at the Ringling breeding center, USDA inspectors found that two 18-month-old elephants (Doc and Angelica) had scars and lesions on their legs as a result of rope burns inflicted while the babies were being forcibly separated from their mothers. In a letter to Ringling, the USDA said, "We believe there is sufficient evidence that the handling of these animals caused trauma, behavioral stress, physical harm and unnecessary discomfort."

In August 2001, Ringling elephant trainer Mark Oliver Gebel, son of the late trainer Gunther Gebel-Williams, was charged with striking and wounding an elephant with a bull-hook just before a performance in California. Due to what the jury considered insufficient evidence, he was acquitted.

The Clyde Beatty-Cole Bros. Circus has also been repeatedly cited for Animal Welfare Act violations related to "the abusive use of an ankus," among a long list of other charges.

In early 2002, People for the Ethical Treatment of Animals (PETA) released an undercover videotape of Carson & Barnes Circus trainer Tim Frisco teaching other handlers how to use bullhooks and electric prods on several elephants during a training session. On the tape, Frisco is seen telling the others that "[i]f you're scared to hurt 'em, don't come in the barn...Make 'em scream...When you hear that screaming, then you know you've got their attention." When hit, the elephants do indeed scream. Frisco makes sure to note that the private training is important because "I'm not gonna touch 'em in front of a thousand people."

Former elephant trainer Carol Buckley says that little has changed in the elephant-training industry since she experienced it years ago. With traditional training—which she says is practiced by all circuses and half of all zoos—"you develop a dominance and you maintain that dominance." Although she admits to once using such techniques, Buckley now supports only positive reinforcement training methods, but knows that the use of bullhooks, electric prods, and beatings is common. "An adult elephant has a life of her own, and there are things that she's not going to want to do." Buckley says circus elephants are forced to live together "whether they like each other or not," and that trainers deliberately discourage friendships among the elephants, who in the wild live in close-knit, matriarchal groups.

In 1995, after years of working with her own elephant, Tarra, Buckley co-founded The Elephant Sanctuary in

Hohenwald, Tennessee, to provide a haven for old or injured female Asian elephants. The 800-acre facility is now home to six former zoo and circus elephants, including two who suffered permanent crippling injuries as a result of their mistreatment. In her experience, Buckley asserts, "there is not a single captive elephant who has not sustained either physical or emotional injury." To be happy and healthy, she explains, elephants need three basic things: room to roam, compatible elephant companions, and live vegetation—necessities they seldom receive in captivity.

In the best interests of the elephant residents, her site is not open to the public, but serves both as a sanctuary and an educational forum to promote the humane treatment of captive elephants. It can now accommodate up to a dozen animals, and with the pending acquisition of more land, might eventually take in as many as 100 elephants—if the circuses and zoos would let them go.

Buckley laments the fact that "zoos and circuses are equally determined to keep elephants on exhibit" because of the animals' popularity with the public. But she also believes that most people would not support the poor treatment of elephants if they knew the facts and persuaded the businesses involved to either improve conditions or, ideally, stop using elephants as attractions altogether.

"This is such a traditional industry," she says of the entertainment world. "To expect change to come from the inside—it won't happen. The pressure has got to come from the outside."

Still, as PETA president Ingrid Newkirk wrote soon after Tyke's death, "How much human blood and misery will mingle with that of the elephants before their struggle for freedom is successful?"

# Elephant Attack Cases (1985-2001)

**1985**
Woman killed at Clyde Beatty-Cole Bros. Circus grounds, New London, Connecticut[3]

**1987**
Handler killed at Fort Worth Zoo, Texas[3]
Two children injured during ride in Pensacola, Florida

**1989**
Trainer killed, Busch Gardens, Tampa, Florida
Trainer injured, San Diego Wild Animal Park, California
Keeper injured, Oakland Zoo, California
Keeper injured, Pittsburgh Zoo, Pennsylvania
Circus employee injured, Champlain County Fair, Vermont

**1990**
Trainer killed, Hanneford Family Circus, Fort Lauderdale, Florida
Handler killed, Lion Country Safari, Loxahatchee, Florida
Handler killed, Oakland Zoo, California
Keeper killed, Cunna Safari Park, Japan
Keeper injured, San Francisco Zoo, California
Trainer and spectator injured, Great American Circus, Reading, Pennsylvania

Several people injured, Marine World-Africa USA event, Oakdale, California

**1991**
Worker killed, Knowland Park Zoo, San Diego, California
Keeper killed, San Diego Wild Animal Park, California
Handler killed, Oakland Zoo, California
Keeper killed, Kiryu Zoo, Tokyo, Japan
Keeper killed, Twycross Zoo, Leicestershire, England
Spectator killed, Bangkok, Thailand
Circus worker killed, Windsor, Ontario
Circus worker killed, Tarragona, Spain
Trainer injured, Houston Zoo, Texas
Trainer injured, Metro Washington Park Zoo, Portland, Oregon

**1992**
Keeper killed, San Antonio Zoo, Texas
Keeper killed, National Zoo, El Salvador
Keeper killed, Moscow Zoo, Russia
Twelve people injured, Great American Circus, Palm Bay, Florida[1]
Nine people injured, Lafayette, Indiana
Handler injured, Shrine Circus, Bloomington, Minnesota
Child injured, Indianapolis, Indiana

**1993**

Man killed, Clyde Beatty Cole Brothers Circus grounds, Fishkill, New York

Keeper killed, Lowry Park Zoo, Tampa, Florida

Trainer killed, Ringling Bros. Circus breeding compound, Williston, Florida

Worker injured, Circus International, Minot, North Dakota[2]

Child injured, Great American Circus, Altoona, Pennsylvania[2]

Keeper gored, Toronto, Canada

Spectator injured, Vallejo, California

**1994**

Trainer killed, several people injured, Circus Benneweis, Nyborg, Denmark[1]

Child injured, King Royal Circus, Riley County, Kansas

Visitor injured, Louisville Zoological Gardens, Kentucky

Two trainers injured, Jordan Circus, Salt Lake City, Utah

Three children injured, Shriner-sponsored circus, Muskegon, Michigan

Family injured, Surabaya Zoo, Indonesia

Trainer injured, Lincoln Park Zoo, Chicago, Illinois

Keeper injured, Cleveland Metro Park Zoo, Ohio

Woman injured, Moscow Circus event, New York City

Family injured, Circus International, Honolulu, Hawaii

Trainer killed, groom injured, Circus International, Honolulu, Hawaii[1,2]

**1995**

Keeper killed, wildlife park, Brussels, Belgium

Trainer killed, Togni Circus, Rome, Italy

Keeper killed, Cairo Zoo, Egypt

Owner killed, Thailand[1]

Twelve people injured, Clyde Beatty Cole Brothers Circus, Queens, New York

Mall stores damaged in rampage, Hanover, Pennsylvania[3]

Employee injured, Tarzan Zerbini Circus, Fort Wayne, Indiana

Keeper injured, Zurich Zoo, Switzerland[1]

**1996**

Child killed, Iquique, Chile

Two keepers killed, Bangkok, Thailand[1]

Trainer killed, National Zoological Gardens, Colombo, Sri Lanka[4]

Assistant trainer injured, Los Angeles Zoo, California

Trainer attacked, Quebec, Canada

Trainer injured, Jordan World Circus, Casper, Wyoming

Rider injured, King Royal Circus, Comfort, Texas

**1997**

Handler killed, Frank Buck Zoo, Gainesville, Texas

Tourist killed, Bangkok, Thailand

Eight people killed, trainer injured, Bangkok, Thailand

Owner killed, New Delhi, India[1]

Trainer killed, National Zoological Gardens, Colombo, Sri Lanka[4]
Handler injured, Shrine Circus, Alberta, Canada
Man injured, Seagoville, Texas

**1998**
Keeper killed, Hrodno Zoo, Belarus
Trainer killed, Kathmandu, Nepal[1]
Keeper injured, Henry Vilas Zoo, Madison, Wisconsin[5]
Child, trainer injured, Commerford & Sons petting zoo, Syracuse, New York
Keeper injured, Indianapolis Zoo, Indiana

**1999**
Worker killed, Leonardo Circus, Ontario, Canada
Keeper killed, Bangkok, Thailand
Trainer killed, Modelo Circus, Valledupar, Colombia
Handler injured, Tarzan Zerbini Circus, Duluth, Minnesota
Trainer injured, Bethune, South Carolina
Tourists injured, Syed Zarir, Africa
Two keepers injured, Henry Vilas Zoo, Madison, Wisconsin[5]

**2000**
Trainer killed, Ramos Family Circus, Riverview, Florida[1]
Keeper killed, London, England
Man killed, another injured, Thailand
Visitor killed, two injured, Bangkok, Thailand
Bystander killed, others injured, Thodupuzha, India

Worker injured, Culpepper & Merriweather Circus, Yucca Valley, California
Child injured, Sorocaba Zoo, Sao Paulo, Brazil
Tourist killed, Bangkok, Thailand
Three people injured, Bangkok, Thailand

**2001**
Handler killed, Brian Boswell Circus, Broederstroom, South Africa
Woman killed, Kathmandu, Nepal
Keeper killed, Chester Zoo, London, England
Keeper killed, London Zoo, England
Trainer killed, Moscow, Russia
Keeper killed, Dvur Kralove nad Labem Zoo, Czech Republic
Two handlers injured, Knoxville Zoo, Tennessee
Spectators injured, Circus Vasquez, Charlotte, North Carolina
Trainer injured, Kuala Lumpur, Malaysia
Keeper injured, Singapore, Philippines

1 Cases in which the elephant was killed.
2 Same elephant involved
3 Same elephant involved
4 Same elephant involved
5 Same elephant involved

# 2: Marine Mammals in Captivity

NAOMI A. ROSE

KEEPING MARINE MAMMALS in captivity has become increasingly controversial. Through such movies as *Free Willy* and *Flipper*, the public has been exposed to the message that whales, dolphins, seals, and sea otters all are served best when they are allowed to remain free in the ocean, the only environment that can truly satisfy their special needs.

The National Marine Fisheries Service (NMFS) regularly updates and publishes the Marine Mammal Inventory Report, which documents the number of marine mammals in all U.S. marine parks and aquaria (it also includes those foreign facilities that trade with the United States). Based on these reports, there are approximately 385 bottlenose dolphins, 21 orcas, five pseudorcas ("false killer whales"), 32 beluga whales, two pilot whales, 21 Pacific white-sided dolphins, and a handful of other species, along with thousands of seals and sea lions, kept in U.S. facilities. When taking into consideration all marine parks and aquaria worldwide, the number of bottlenose dolphins in captivity jumps to an estimated 1,000.

To understand why so many people (including a growing number of scientists) believe that marine mammals are unsuited to captivity, several things should be considered. First, marine parks and aquaria emphasize the educational benefit of captive display, but this "benefit" does not withstand scrutiny, nor does it address the animals' quality of life. Also, a growing body of evidence indicates that certain species suffer greater mortality in captivity than in the wild. Finally, holding marine mammals in confinement raises serious ethical concerns.

The education provided by most, if not all, marine parks concerning marine mammal biology is minimal and often poor. Notably lacking in almost every marine park show is information concerning natural behaviors, ecology, habitat, social structure, and population demographics. Marine parks do inform the public about captive behaviors, which usually differ substantially from the natural state. The public is led to believe that what they see in marine parks is in some sense "normal." This is a blatantly self-serving message and is counter-educational.

For example, in the wild, whales and dolphins (cetaceans) spend little time motionless, and are under water 80 to 90 percent of the time. Yet in captivity, individuals frequently are observed floating motionless at their pools' surface. It is undoubtedly this unnatural inactivity and lack of below-surface time that cause the gradual and permanent (full or partial) dorsal fin collapse of all captive male orcas (including Keiko of *Free Willy* fame) and many female orcas, as well as many dolphins.

The industry's educational literature propagates more misinformation by claiming that captive marine mammals get "adequate exercise." Captive marine mammals are obviously unable to exercise as much as they could in their natural environment. Cetaceans travel 50 to 100 miles in a day, and seals and sea lions (pinnipeds) migrate thousands of miles annually. In their small sea pens or concrete tanks, captive animals are denied this natural activity level. It would take more than 500 circuits around a typical aquarium tank for a dolphin to cover 50 miles.

Captive social groups are wholly artificial. Marine facilities mix unrelated animals, different stocks, and species that are never seen together in the wild. Sexes may be segregated, natural territoriality can rarely be accommodated, and calves typically are taken from their mothers and moved to separate quarters long before they would disperse under natural conditions. Yet marine park literature frequently states that captive marine mammals are maintained in healthy social groups, a conclusion that defies rational support.

Marine parks also suggest that captivity provides safety for the animals. Natural habitats are often portrayed as hostile, dangerous places, where wildlife is imperiled by pollution, predation, and parasites. Not only is this a heavily biased, misleading, and negative representation of natural conditions, it is an implicitly anti-conservation message that will hardly encourage people to protect the marine environment.

Regarding mortality, recent studies indicate that certain cetacean species continue to demonstrate higher annual mortality rates in captivity than in the wild. For example, a 1997 International Marine Mammal Association report confirms this conclusion for orcas, as does a 1995 paper published in *Marine Mammal Science* by two U.S. government scientists. Various analyses have demonstrated that age-specific annual mortality rates for captive orcas are two to six times higher than for wild orcas. Seventeen orcas have died at SeaWorld parks since 1986, most in their teens and twenties and none older than 30. Since captivity purportedly relieves the pressures of foraging and natural hazards, and provides veterinary care, captive animals should (theoretically) experience lower mortality rates than their wild counterparts. However, this is clearly not the case with orcas. These whales, and cetaceans in general, simply cannot adapt to confinement.

As for longevity, a 1993 SeaWorld brochure states unequivocally that the maximum life span for orcas, whether in the wild or in captivity, is 25 to 35 years. A 2001 newspaper article quotes a SeaWorld representative asserting the same. This is simply untrue. Since no captive orca has lived beyond age 30 (and most don't live past 25), this may be an appropriate statistic for orcas in marine parks, but clearly it is not for those in the wild. In 1973, scientists observed a group of about two dozen adult northeastern Pacific orcas at least 15 years old. Many of these animals were still alive in 2001 and thus were at least 43 years of age, and several females in this group, given the number of offspring and the offspring's estimated ages, were well into their fifties and sixties. In addition, a 1990 report published by the International Whaling Commission estimates maximum longevity for northeastern Pacific orcas at 70 to 80 years for females and 50 to 60 years for males.

## Ethical Considerations

Because marine mammals perform in shows, the dolphin is depicted as an intelligent, gentle human companion, and the sea lion is seen as a congenial clown. These images have become cultural icons; one does not think of tigers or bears or even adult chimpanzees in this way. But regardless of how often these species are held in zoos, they are still wild animals, and potentially dangerous ones at that. Orcas, dolphins, and sea lions are wild and carnivorous predators, too. They are tamed and trained when in captivity, but they are not domestic animals.

A frequent industry argument in favor of captivity is that these animals are friends with their trainers and veterinarians. However, there have been many accidents and injuries to trainers and even to visitors with these animals. In 1991, a trainer was killed by a male orca, and a private citizen drowned in a tank with the same orca several years later. These incidents are the fault of the unnatural proximity to humans forced on these animals, not of the animals themselves. Further, human presence can never substitute for the companionship of others of these wild and social animals' own kind. Their intelligence may allow marine mammals to adjust to our manipulations, but their adaptations do not make these manipulations beneficial or ethical.

Marine mammals' natural habitats cannot be simulated in captivity, because the tanks are often chemically or otherwise treated and filtered to prevent the animals from swimming in their own wastes. Nothing is farther in composition from the vast ocean's sand, rocks, currents, storms, and diverse flora and fauna than the small, smooth-sided, empty, chlorinated tanks of most marine parks and aquaria. Many pinnipeds and polar bears are provided only fresh water, a situation without any justification beyond industry convenience and cost. The natural activity levels, the sociality, the hunting behaviors, the acoustic perceptions, the intelligence—indeed, the very texture of the natural environment of these creatures—are all severely compromised by the circumstances of captivity.

The captive display of marine mammals provides poor or even false education. Certain species never adjust to confinement, contrary to the claims of the captive display industry. It is extremely difficult to justify keeping marine mammals, particularly the wholly aquatic cetacean species, in sterile tanks that do not even remotely resemble their natural habitat. Wild marine mammals belong in only one place: the ocean.

## 3: Crush Videos

ADAM M. ROBERTS

SCENE OPENS: SINGLE *guinea pig restrained, each leg spread outward and taped to the floor. Enter woman, filmed from the knees down, wearing jeans and high-heeled red shoes. "Well little man, I've been waiting for this for quite some time...You are my little victim...That's it, squirm for mistress. Oh, I can take you now. I feel your heart beating against my toes." She laughs. "Are you frightened, little man, hmm? You know that your destiny is under my heel. Squirm for me...No, you're mine, little man, to torment and torture." Slowly, she walks around the terrified creature, meticulously stepping on each leg. Unmistakable sounds of bones shattering. Shrieking squeals of agony and terror. She painstakingly demolishes each leg, viciously flattens the back, and pierces her victim's head with her sharp stiletto heel. "Oh, how sweet it is to crush his little skull....Beg. Beg for mercy."*

This is the multimillion-dollar business of torturous, pornographic animal cruelty films called "crush" videos. It is estimated that there are as many as 2,000 titles in print to supply the global demand, which reportedly extends to Mexico, Brazil, Japan, Dubai, and throughout Europe. These videos feature the crushing of insects, mice, rats, guinea pigs, hamsters, birds, cats, dogs, and monkeys. Many of these videos are sold or offered through crush web sites. On the "Original Crush Message Board" appears this interaction: "Hi, I would love pics or any sites of turtle or tortoise crushing. Could anyone help me out? Thank you, Crushtatic." The first of many replies includes the following offer: "I have the Japanese crush video, with two of the sexiest Asian girls crushing the hell out of turtles. Both are totally cruel...."

Getsmart productions features the $40 Frog Stomp, "A 90-minute video of Vanessa crushing over 100 tree frogs beneath her high-heel sandals." Steponit, another distributor, includes the $100 "Mistress Di, Princess of Death" series, where in one video she crushes mice by sitting on them on a box top with a Plexiglas lid: "There is a mirror under the Plexiglas so you can see both sides of the action." One undercover investigator with the Ventura County, California, district attorney's office, posing as a film participant, was asked to crush a dog. She "was instructed on how to torture a dog on video, step by step" and "to make the crushing incident last ninety minutes before the animal actually died."

While doing undercover research on the Internet in foot-fetish chat rooms, the investigator discovered that viewers fantasize being crushed to death under a dominating woman's foot. Since in reality this could only happen once, these men are sexually stimulated by imagining that they are being trampled instead of the animals.

District attorneys attempting to prosecute those involved with these films often run into substantial roadblocks. Although the act of stomping an animal to death violates state anti-cruelty statutes, the identities of the "performers" are often concealed and the date and location of the film's production is often unknown, all of which make prosecution difficult. Tom Connors, deputy district attorney for Ventura County, California, told a congressional subcommittee that "the ability to prosecute the production of these 'Crush Videos' requires either a policeman or interested citizen stumbling onto the production of one of these videos while it was occurring and making an arrest, an actual participant coming forward with the necessary information [who is] willing to testify about what has happened...or by the police conducting an undercover operation."

On May 20, 1999, to remedy this legislative loophole, Rep. Elton Gallegly (R-CA) introduced H.R. 1887, a bill to prohibit the creation, sale, or possession of a depiction of animal cruelty with the intention of placing that depiction in interstate or foreign commerce for commercial gain. Convicted violators could be fined and/or imprisoned for not more than five years. The bill defines such cruelty as a visual or auditory depiction "in which a living animal is intentionally maimed, mutilated, tortured, wounded, or killed, if such conduct is illegal under Federal law or the law of the State in which the creation, sale, or possession takes place." An example of the need for this legislation is the case of one Long Island man, Thomas Capriola, who was arrested in 1998 for his part in creating and selling crush videos. He marketed them on a web site called "Crush Goddess." He was charged under the state's animal cruelty law and ultimately was sentenced minimally to probation and community service. Had he been prosecuted under the federal law, he would have faced the stricter federal penalties.

Said Gallegly, "In all my years of pushing legislation to protect animals, this is clearly one of the sickest forms of animal cruelty I have ever heard of." The bill passed the House of Representatives on October 19, 1999, by an overwhelming vote of 372 to 42. Senators Jon Kyl (R-AZ) and Bob Smith (R-NH) shepherded the bill through the Senate, where it was passed unanimously on November 19, 1999.

Bill opponents mistakenly claimed that it would ban hunting videos or Spanish history films showing bullfights, but if hunting or bullfighting is legal, the sale of videos depicting those acts would remain legal. Others assert that however abhorrent crush videos may be, banning them violates the First Amendment. Actress Loretta Swit, representing Actors and Others for Animals, responded, "Well, if that's true, we would have to extend the same kind of protection to rapists, child molesters and murderers, because they're just expressing themselves. But we don't, of course, because these acts are fundamentally wrong and we have agreed, as a nation, to condemn these crimes. We should just as strongly condemn these crush videos." President Clinton signed the bill into law on December 9, 1999, calling it a ban on "wanton cruelty to animals designed to appeal to a prurient interest in sex."

An advertisement for Mistress Di includes the teaser, "You will see her dance; you will see her body; you will see her kill." Now, we hope, we won't see her or her fiendish friends ever again.

# 4: The Venom over Rattlesnake Roundups

TERESA M. TELECKY

CONCERNS ABOUT ANIMALS killed for sport or entertainment often focus on more familiar, furry faces, but help is also sorely needed for the thousands of snakes victimized by "rattlesnake roundups," which are among the most deliberately cruel public events existing in the United States today.

"The Truth Behind Rattlesnake Roundups," a report published by The Humane Society of the United States (HSUS), demonstrates that rattlesnake roundups are not only grossly inhumane, but are also environmentally destructive and a public health hazard. These annual events occur about 30 times a year in rural parts of Alabama, Georgia, Kansas, New Mexico, Pennsylvania, Oklahoma, and Texas. They have been held since the 1920s, when the original misguided intention apparently was to rid farming or ranching areas of as many rattlesnakes as possible, ostensibly to protect livestock and humans from bites. But we now know that the number of livestock deaths from rattlesnake bites is very low. Roundups actually cause more people to be bitten by rattlesnakes than would occur by accident, because the events bring people in closer contact with the snakes.

Today's rattlesnake roundups are principally profit-generating entertainment events that are sponsored by local clubs, chambers of commerce, volunteer fire departments, and occasionally by private businesses. Sponsors often claim that money earned from the events is donated to worthy causes that include small local charities but also involve such large organizations as the Muscular Dystrophy Association, the American Heart Association, the American Cancer Society, and Special Olympics. Local franchises of Coca Cola, Anheuser-Busch, Hardee's, and other corporations sponsor roundups and/or advertise their products at them.

**The Torturous Toll**
Of the 15 rattlesnake species in North America, four are usually found in roundups: the eastern diamondback, the western diamondback, the timber, and the western or prairie rattlesnake. Rattlesnakes are well known for their highly specialized attributes and behaviors, which are adaptations for capturing, killing, and ingesting warm-blooded animals, usually small to medium-sized mammals and birds. Heat-sensitive "pits" on the sides of their heads can detect prey; their retractable, tubular fangs discharge venom into animals who are paralyzed and then swallowed whole. Their rattles are made of a horn-like substance and are used to warn away predators. Rattlesnakes are generally nocturnal and share communal resting areas known as dens or burrows.

Rattlesnakes use the same dens year after year, never venturing too far afield. Dens are also used during the winter, when rattlesnakes undergo a type of hibernation. Unlike most reptiles, rattlesnakes do not lay eggs but instead bear living young. Some species become sexually mature at four to five years of age and give birth to up to 17 young every other year. The snakes' late sexual maturation and slow reproductive rate, combined with low survivorship of young, make them highly susceptible to exploitation.

Many thousands of rattlesnakes are collected from the wild each year to supply roundups. Collectors drive the snakes from their resting areas either through the use of toxic chemicals or by outright destruction of the den or burrow. The most common chemical used is gasoline, which is sprayed or poured into the den through a plastic tube. Rattlesnakes and other animals occupying these areas suffer both long- and short-term effects from exposure to these chemicals. Rattlesnakes are roughly handled during collection and are held for weeks or months without food or water in crowded and unsanitary conditions while the collector increases his stockpile. Many snakes arrive at roundups crushed to death, dehydrated, or starved.

No states officially monitor populations of eastern diamondback rattlesnakes, but the consensus among herpetologists and snake hunters is that the species is absent from large areas where it was once found. One organizer of the Opp, Alabama, roundup said, "When I started we just hunted in the woods around here. We used to get 15 a day. You won't get none today."

The events vary greatly in size, and anywhere from as few as ten to as many as several thousands of rattlesnakes are used in a variety of contests and exhibitions that cause and promote cruelty. In "sacking contests," people compete to see who can shove a certain number of rattlesnakes into a bag in the shortest period of time. "Sacking" snakes are often used repeatedly, and are so roughly handled that their ribs and jaws are broken.

In "daredevil shows," snakes are harassed into defensive coils and then placed on people's heads; harassed into striking balloons or the soles of shoes; and put into sleeping bags with a person, after which the bag is repeatedly stomped. They are kicked and otherwise beaten. Some snakes have their mouths sewn shut with wire or fishing line so they can be used as photo props.

At some events, rattlesnakes are publicly slaughtered by decapitation; this is an unacceptable killing method for reptiles because their slow metabolism allows the head and body to "live" and respond to pain for more than an hour afterwards. Snake handlers at some roundups capitalize on this by torturing the severed heads of rattlesnakes to show the public that the head will still try to bite the handler. After decapitation, the snakes' bodies are attached to a string or wire and hung vertically before the public while handlers skin the still-writhing bodies. Regarding Texas roundups, one state biologist commented, "Unfortunately, there are many individuals here who get their jollies from torturing animals."

**Health and Habitat**

Rattlesnake meat from these public slaughters is sold at the roundup, as are skins, other body parts, and curios made from rattlesnakes. Roundups have become intimately tied with the complex and unmonitored interstate and international trade in rattlesnake parts. Snakes collected for roundups constitute only about 15 percent of all rattlesnakes taken from the wild for domestic and international trade; no other wild animal in the United States is as extensively exploited without regulation or oversight.

Roundups are environmentally harmful. Wild populations of the timber and eastern diamondback rattlesnakes are known to be declining in part due to hunting pressures; the timber rattlesnake is considered endangered or threatened in eight states. The toxic chemicals used to collect rattlesnakes contaminate groundwater and are detrimental to other wildlife, including the threatened gopher tortoise, burrowing owls, indigo snakes, box turtles, and raccoons. The destruction of dens and burrows prevents the use of these important areas—which are limited in the natural environment—for many years. Some roundups import non-native rattlesnakes from other states, causing them to become established in areas where they did not previously exist, and where they threaten local species.

Rattlesnake roundups also pose a significant risk to public health and safety. They bring members of the public into close contact with the snakes and encourage reckless behavior. Rattlesnake meat sold at roundups is obtained from snakes killed under unsanitary conditions and may contain harmful bacteria and parasites as well as residues from the toxic chemicals used during collection. Communities that host roundups may bear significant costs for medical treatment for any bites that occur. Treatment of such non-accidental bites reduces the local anti-venom supply.

Roundup organizers and rattlesnake handlers negatively influence public perceptions about snakes with misinformation in their displays and materials. They quote erroneous figures of up to 4,000 human deaths per year from rattlesnake bites, when actually fewer than 15 people die each year in the United States from the bites of all venomous snakes combined. Another oft-repeated fallacy is that venom collected at roundups has important medical applications; however, techniques used to collect and store venom at roundups does not conform with strict Food and Drug Administration standards for production of anti-venom.

Roundup organizers are becoming increasingly adept at presenting a falsely pro-environment face and providing insincere words of respect for the animals used in their events. Claims that snakes are returned to the wild, that gassing is no longer a capture method, and that snakes are respected and admired are now common in roundup promotional materials. Many roundups use schools to promote their "educational" events. The participation of children in rattlesnake roundups is particularly troubling; such events not only teach children and other spectators how to behave inappropriately and unsafely around rattlesnakes, they also expose them to and encourage callous behavior toward animals.

There are some signs that organizers are willing to transform roundups into events that can raise money while not harming snakes, humans, or their environments. A roundup in San Antonio, Florida, was progressively transformed into a festival that promotes understanding of reptiles. The change in focus did not reduce the amount of money earned; the two-day event raised $30,000 in 1998.

It is clear that rattlesnake roundups, as traditionally conducted, must end. Socially responsible citizens and organizations should understand the cruelty and destructiveness of such roundups and the implications they have for society. As this understanding progresses, these events will cease, to the benefit of people and wildlife alike.


# 5: Risky Business

Naomi A. Rose

FROM EARLIEST WRITTEN history, stories abound of humans swimming with dolphins. Greek urns depict sailors being rescued by these creatures, who were believed to be gods or transformed men, benign and altruistic. Today people pay for the privilege of swimming with these graceful denizens of the sea, with their eternal smiles and gentle manner. The only problem is, believing all dolphins are beneficent beings who seek our company as eagerly as we seek theirs is as much based on myth as believing in Poseidon.

Captive "swim with the dolphin" (SWTD) programs have become very popular. People are powerfully drawn to the charismatic yet mysterious dolphin, popularized in modern media and ancient myth. There are now at least 14 marine parks and aquaria in the United States that offer SWTD programs, ranging from a full in-water experience, where snorkeling or scuba gear is used, to wading, where participants stand in shallow water, pet the animals, and give them commands. In the Caribbean Sea, these programs are proliferating at an astounding rate—in the past few years, seven Caribbean countries have opened new SWTD facilities, while six more are proposing to open them. At SeaWorld in San Diego, people can even wade with orcas, the most powerful predators in the sea. SWTD programs present whales and dolphins as friendly companions who desire to interact with humans as much as we do with them; unfortunately, this image is false and even dangerous.

Captive dolphins (both wild-caught and captive-bred) are usually strictly trained to interact with people. They must be controlled to minimize the risk of injury to human participants. Ranging in size from six to eight feet long and weighing up to 450 pounds, dolphins can inflict bites, lacerations, and bruises, and even break bones (all have occurred in SWTD programs). Their level of aggression can vary based on gender, age, and species. They are strong, agile predators who can indeed kill humans: three people are known to have been killed by close encounters with whales and dolphins in the past decade. In 1991 at Sealand of the Pacific (a Victoria, British Columbia, facility that has since closed), trainer Keltie Byrne fell into the orca pool by accident and the three adult whales there drowned her. In July 1999, at SeaWorld Orlando, a man who snuck into the park after hours was found dead in the orca tank, believed drowned by one of the same whales who drowned Byrne. Several years ago, a swimmer severely provoked a friendly male dolphin he was swimming with in the waters off a Brazilian beach. After the swimmer shoved objects into the dolphin's blowhole, the dolphin retaliated by ramming the man, inflicting fatal internal injuries.

SWTD programs are also harmful from the dolphins' point of view. Captivity itself is stressful, placing the animals in confined spaces, depriving them of natural foraging opportunities, and strictly controlling their social and behavioral environment. With few or no choices about what to eat, where to go, or what to do, these highly intelligent, social creatures can become bored, stressed, and in some cases mentally disturbed. SWTD programs add another level of stress by exposing the dolphins—evolved to exist in relatively stable social groups—to a parade of strange people. The encounters, which all seem spontaneous and voluntary to the human participants, are in fact largely staged and manipulated, as the dolphins are strictly trained to perform certain kinds of interactions. A 1994 U.S. government study found that programs that allowed spontaneous interactions between people and dolphins resulted in more injuries to people and more submissive behaviors from dolphins (and submissive behaviors are associated with stress in social mammals). Therefore, the researchers who conducted the study recommended that only supervised, controlled interactions be allowed. There is little that is voluntary about an SWTD dolphin's behavior toward swimmers: he or she is being told what to do virtually all the time.

Before April 1994, the U.S. Department of Commerce's National Marine Fisheries Service (NMFS) closely regulated captive SWTD programs through the Marine Mammal Protection Act (MMPA). The NMFS considered these programs to be experimental. However, when the MMPA was amended, regulatory authority over all captive marine mammals was transferred to the Department of Agriculture's Animal and Plant Health Inspection Service (APHIS). APHIS lifted the experimental designation on SWTD programs and proposed to issue standard regulations under the Animal Welfare Act. Unfortunately, from April 1994 until September 1998, APHIS' ponderous bureaucracy held up publication of any regulations at all. During this period, SWTD programs proliferated, expanding from four to at least 14. If there were any injuries to people during this period, the government did not hear of them, since the previous NMFS requirement to submit injury reports was no longer enforced. Between 1989 (when the NMFS began monitoring SWTD programs) and 1994, the NMFS recorded almost two dozen serious injuries.

Finally, in September 1998, APHIS published final regulations that set standards for how many attendants a facility must provide per customer; set the maximum swimmer-to-dolphin ratio; defined how large enclosures must be; instituted the requirement to have a "refuge" and a "buffer" area within the enclosure, where swimmers cannot go and from which dolphins cannot be recalled; set the maximum number of encounters in which a dolphin will participate each day and each week; noted veterinary requirements; mandated experience requirements for other staff; and made record-keeping requirements. But in March 1999, the Washington, D.C. *Legal Times* published a notice stating that a dolphin facility in Las Vegas had hired a powerful D.C. lobbying firm to seek nullification of these final regulations, apparently because the facility, which may develop a SWTD program, could not comply with the rules. One month later, APHIS suspended enforcement of the regulations, claiming that facilities operating new "wading" programs were unaware that they would have to abide by "swim-with" regulations and therefore had not taken the opportunity to participate in the public process of formulating them. But such reasoning did not justify suspending "swim-with" regulations as well; APHIS had exempted wading programs from regulation within one month of implementing the final regulations so it could examine the special circumstances of such programs.

Now, once again, SWTD programs in the United States are unregulated, and APHIS has given no indication of how long it might take to re-establish regulatory enforcement. So however tempting it may be for curious, well-meaning people to want to frolic with "Flipper," the public should regard whales and dolphins as the complex, wild predators that they are, and accord these amazing animals the respect they deserve by enjoying them from a safe distance in their natural habitat.

# 6: Tatters in the Big Top

Marianne R. Merritt

THE IMAGE OF the circus as a vestige of an honorable American entertainment tradition is falling to shreds. Through the work of dedicated activists, as well as individuals who have worked in the circus industry, the inherent cruelty of animal-based circuses is not only being criticized, but is increasingly no longer being tolerated. Ringling Bros. and Barnum & Bailey Circus touts itself as "The Greatest Show on Earth," but its show, and others of its ilk, have been under growing attack by animal advocates, local legislators, and even members of Congress. Legislative initiatives and grassroots activities challenging the use of exotic animals in circuses are proliferating and gaining momentum.

Animals in circuses suffer horribly under deplorable conditions. They are forced to live in dirty, crowded quarters; are not provided with consistent veterinary care (many circuses don't travel with veterinarians); and are trained and kept under control through the use of such devices as bullhooks (sticks with sharpened hooks at one end), clubs, whips, chains, electric "hotshot" prods, food and water deprivation, and other forms of what is unemotionally labeled "negative reinforcement." Elephants are kept in chains up to 95 percent of the time, and exotic cats and other animals are housed in small cages where they are barely given room to stand up, move around, or stretch.

Baby elephants are torn from their mothers at unnaturally young ages to be trained. One (literally) shocking training method entails hosing down elephants prior to applying a hot-shot, thereby making their sensitive skin even more vulnerable to pain. Performing animals are hauled from town to town, day in and day out, in boxcars or trucks, without any ability to exercise the full range of their natural behaviors. They are never left alone for any substantial period of time without being poked, prodded, and trotted out before the masses. Once they outlive their commercial usefulness, they are frequently sold to captive hunting ranches, sent to roadside zoos, auctioned off to private animal collectors, or sentenced to other dismal fates. A lucky few animals find homes at sanctuaries such as those operated by the Fund for Animals, the Performing Animal Welfare Society (PAWS), and The Elephant Sanctuary in Hohenwald (Tennessee).

Activists all over the world have taken steps to expose and prevent the abuses that occur regularly in circuses. Many U.S. animal protection groups have extensive anti-circus campaigns, and more and more state and local governments have passed or considered banning circuses with exotic animals. To counter these measures, Ringling Bros. and other circuses have launched well-financed public-relations and lobbying counter-strikes. Feld Entertainment, Ringling's parent company, was estimated by *Fortune* magazine in 1999 to have generated more than $500 million that year from its various business ventures. A 1995 *New York Times* article estimated Ringling's advertising budget at $25 million, a figure that has likely grown in the face of court challenges and legislative hearings aimed at restricting circus activity.

## A Record of Mistreatment

Ringling Bros., with its formidable pocketbook and impetus to protect its profit margin and reputation, has formed a defense based on offense. For example, it has resorted to passing out

glossy pamphlets to circus patrons, claiming that its relationship with its animals is "based on constant contact, daily rou-
tines and nurturing, which foster trust and affection. Training
involves a system of repetition and reward that build on respect
and reinforces the trust between animal and trainer." However,
documentation provided by government inspection documents
and by individuals who have worked at Ringling Bros. reveals a
far grimmer picture. For example, Ringling touts its purported
success at its Center for Elephant Conservation (CEC), where it
has bred ten Asian elephants.

Of those offspring, however, two babies are dead: Kenny,
whose death resulted in the imposition of Animal Welfare Act
charges that Ringling settled in 1998 for $20,000; and
Benjamin, who drowned in 1999 under suspicious circumstances and who reportedly was beaten by his handlers. Of the
remaining eight, two were found during a 1999 U.S.
Department of Agriculture (USDA) inspection to have "large
visible lesions on [their] rear legs." According to two trainers
interviewed during the routine inspection, the young elephants—Doc and Angelica—suffered rope burns while being
forcibly separated from their mothers. One inspection memo
noted that Bill Lindsay, Ringling's chief veterinarian, attempted
to downplay the seriousness of the lesions found on the babies:
"Dr. Lindsay was very upset and asked repeatedly why we could
not be more collegial and call him before we came. I explained
to him that all our inspections are unannounced. We also asked
at that time to take pictures of Doc and Angelica. All Ringling
personnel were very reluctant to let us take pictures..."

The inspectors returned to the CEC the next day to take
photographs, and it was noted that the babies "appeared
'cleaned up.' " The inspectors also noticed that there were additional scars on the babies' front legs. The memo notes that
Lindsay "was upset that we had even written a note about the
scars and stated that we were 'silly' for making such a big issue
over a little thing." Ringling Bros. called the separation method

"standard industry practice," but the USDA consulted with six elephant experts about the inspection and thereafter communicated to Feld Entertainment that "we consider the handling of these two elephants as reported on our inspection report of February 9 to 10 to be noncompliant with the Animal Welfare Act regulations....[W]e believe there is sufficient evidence that the handling of these animals caused unnecessary trauma, behavioral stress, physical harm, and discomfort to these two elephants..."

In addition to information from government inspections, more has been learned from three former Ringling employees who have come forward with stories about the company's animal-handling practices. A complaint filed on behalf of PAWS with the USDA in April 2000 identifies Tom Rider, a former Ringling elephant handler, as an eyewitness to abuse. The complaint charges that "Mr. Rider has identified several handlers and trainers by name who he personally witnessed repeatedly beat the elephants in the Blue Unit, including the babies. Mr. Rider also traveled with the elephants on tour, and said that they live on cramped stock cars, are chained for more than 23 hours per day, and exposed to extreme temperatures, and left to stand in their own waste for hours at a time."

In January 1999, another former Ringling employee, Glenn Ewell, stated in an affidavit: "[A]fter one of the performances in Denver, one of the adult females by the name of Nicole was severely beaten by Randy and Adam because she performed poorly. The elephants were taken back to the holding area and after the other elephants were chained in place, Randy took Nicole and tried to get her to do the routine she refused to do during the performance. When Nicole refused to do the movements as instructed Randy took a bull hook and began beating Nicole in the head, on the trunk and behind the front feet. The beating continued until the handle of the bull hook shattered. While Randy was beating Nicole in the head and trunk area, Adam began beating her on the lumbar and hindquarter area on the right hand side. One of the strikes by Adam to the lumbar area resulted in the metal hook penetrating the skin and causing an open wound from which blood began flowing. After the beating was over a person by the name of Sonny doctored the wound with some type of powder to stop the bleeding. No other veterinary care was provided to my knowledge. All of the animal crew previously identified were present and witnessed the beating."

Since 1992, 14 Ringling Bros. elephants have died, and other animals in the circus haven't fared much better. In February 1999, a 15-year-old horse who performed for Ringling collapsed and died shortly after being unloaded from his train car. In January 1998, a tiger confined to his cage was shot to death by a Ringling employee, apparently as payback shortly after the tiger mauled the employee's brother, the cat's trainer. The USDA issued a "serious warning" to Ringling about the incident.

In September 2001, Mark Oliver Gebel, the son of Ringling's longtime (and now deceased) animal trainer, Gunther Gebel Williams, was charged in California with violating its animal cruelty laws. These charges stem from his apparent striking of female Asian elephant, which left an open wound in her shoulder, when the elephant hesitated while entering a performance ring. He was later acquitted, but the trial testimony helped renew the issue of circus abuses.

The Feld Entertainment organization, which owns Ringling Bros., apparently was so concerned with the actions of the animal protection community that it hired individuals—including Clair George, former deputy director of the Central Intelligence Agency—to obtain information about and/or infiltrate animal protection groups, including PAWS and PETA. In an affidavit filed by George in litigation in Virginia, he admitted that as part of his "consulting work for Feld Entertainment" he reviewed reports by investigators "based on their surveillance of, and efforts to counter, the activities of various animal rights groups." Two lawsuits filed by PETA and PAWS arose out of this surveillance by Feld Entertainment. In apparent partial response to the PAWS litigation, the parties reach a settlement in which Feld Entertainment agreed to turn over a number of its retired elephants to PAWS. Although the remainder of the settlement will not be publicly disclosed by PAWS nor Feld Entertainment, at least some of the elephants previously used in this circus will have an opportunity to live out the remainder of their lives in PAWS' animal sanctuary.

Other circuses have similarly dismal track records. In 1999, the Clyde Beatty-Cole Brothers Circus was charged with, and later settled, a complaint filed by the USDA under the auspices of the Animal Welfare Act for the "abusive use of an ankus" (bullhook) on several of its elephants. In February 2000, Clyde Beatty again was cited by the USDA for bullhook scars on two of its elephants. Indeed, the circus had been cited in January 1999 for failing to provide the USDA with access to records pertaining to the health of its elephants. The Sterling & Reid Circus was cited in April 1999 for poking and prodding exotic cats with poles and for striking a lion across the face, as well as for leaving camels tethered in direct sunlight for a lengthy period without any shelter. The same circus, while under investigation by the USDA, turned over three of its tigers to the Oakland Zoo in 1999. Sterling & Reid also featured in its acts a trainer named Brian Franzen, who was convicted of animal cruelty charges after eight ponies in his care were seized after being found dehydrated, malnourished, and living in substandard conditions. In 1997 in Britain, Mary Chipperfield—once considered the grand dame of the circus industry—was convicted of beating a chimpanzee with a riding crop. This is just a sampling of the recently documented abuses occurring behind the scenes.

**Recent Legislative Initiatives**

Because of animal abuse and the inherent dangers of bringing wild animals into close contact with the public, many jurisdictions and lawmakers are working to get rid of animal-based circus "entertainment" once and for all. Initiatives have come before city councils and on up to the U.S. Congress.

At the national level, the most recent congressional action was the introduction in 1999 of the Captive Elephant Accident Prevention Act (H.R. 2929), which would criminalize the use of elephants in traveling shows or for riding purposes. As noted by the bill's sponsor, Rep. Sam Farr (D-CA), "Since 1983, at least 28 people have been killed by captive elephants performing in circuses and elephant ride exhibits. More than 70 others have been seriously injured, including at least 50 members of the general public who were spectators at circuses and other elephant exhibits. More than a dozen children have been injured, many of them hospitalized, due to elephant ride accidents." Although hearings were held on the bill in July 2000—prompting strong debates between animal advocates and circus promoters—the bill did not pass, but it is anticipated that a similar bill will be re-introduced into Congress in the future.

At the state level, the Rhode Island House of Representatives passed a bill in June 2000 that would have prohibited elephants, bears, tigers, and lions from being used in circuses, carnivals, and parades that perform in the state. This is the first time such a bill has been passed by a component of a state legislature, and approved despite heavy lobbying by the circus industry. The bill was not introduced into the state Senate before it recessed, but, like the federal bill, it will likely be reintroduced in the future.

In Maryland, a bill that would have restricted the use of elephants in performances narrowly failed to pass a committee vote in 2000, but it too will probably be reintroduced. The state of Maine also has taken action to protect elephants in circuses through the introduction of legislation. Elsewhere, thanks to local ordinances, exotic animal acts are currently banned or tightly restricted in many jurisdictions around the United States. The most recent jurisdictions to pass such legislation include Orange County, North Carolina; Boulder, Colorado; and Pasadena, California. In one of the most hotly contested debates, and one that received national media coverage, the Seattle city council in 2000 nearly passed an ordinance that would have made it illegal to use exotic animals for entertainment. The circus industry lobbied heavily against the ban, and the measure failed by only one vote.

Such anti-circus activism occurring all over the country has been taking its toll on the industry. As noted in the May/June 2000 edition of *White Tops*, a circus trade periodical, "[t]here were a noticeable number of cities and towns not wanting to sponsor circuses...." One sign that animal circuses—particularly Ringling Bros.—know their days are numbered is the fact that Feld Entertainment created and heavily promoted a new circus venture, Kaleidoscape, which does not use any exotic animals. Circuses that don't use any animals at all, such as Cirque du Soleil, have seen no end to their skyrocketing popularity. As reported in a 1997 edition of *Circus Report*, another trade publication, "Times are changing, and people are changing, and maybe we need to change also; maybe animals aren't going to be in circuses because people don't want them to be. The majority will rule someday, and maybe that time is here."

# Part 5

# ANIMALS IN AGRICULTURE

# 1: For a Mouthful of Flesh

GENE BAUSTON

SINCE THE GENESIS of agriculture approximately 10,000 years ago, humanity has striven to increase its control over plants and animals to enhance their usefulness as food products. In the United States, this endeavor—fostered by the industrial revolution and induced by agrichemicals—is now exploding into the global marketplace. The number of animals raised and exploited by agribusiness is rising to accommodate expanding populations and higher demand for animal products around the world, exponentially increasing the amount of cruelty involved.

Animals used for food are perceived as commodities on the agribusiness assembly line. Referred to as "units of production," they are treated more like inanimate objects than living, feeling animals. Chickens, pigs, turkeys, cattle, and other animals are subjected to genetic manipulation, severe overcrowding, and intensive confinement in order to produce the most meat, milk, and eggs at the cheapest price. The animals are denied wholesome foods and instead are given rations that can include garbage, manure, industrial byproducts, and even the ground-up remains of other animals, including members of their own species. They suffer routine mutilations, inadequate shelter and veterinary care, and cruelty during handling, transportation, and slaughter.

Before World War II, animals used for food traditionally were raised on small family farms in an indoor/outdoor environment. Farming methods changed after the war because of technological innovations, including the use of drugs and chemicals to enhance growth and deal with disease. Intensive animal agriculture, commonly called "factory farming," has flourished in the United States and is now the primary method for raising animals for food. Despite concerns from a growing number of consumers, environmentalists, animal advocates, and even farmers regarding the widespread environmental destruction, animal cruelty, and human health hazards caused by factory farming, the use of intensive production methods is expected to increase.

Animal scientists, geneticists, pharmacists, and agricultural engineers are at work calibrating the factory-farm machine, subjecting animals to numerous research trials in the quest to maximize production and efficiency. Most agricultural research deals with such rudimentary issues as feed utilization, the effect of growth hormones and drugs on weight gain, reproductive performance, and, increasingly, on preventing dangerous pathogens from entering the human food supply.

**Poultry**
The number of individual animals being subjected to intolerable living conditions and untimely deaths is on the rise, largely because consumers are replacing red meat with poultry, and birds provide less flesh per carcass than mammals. Americans have doubled their consumption of chickens and turkeys over the past two decades, and this pattern is expected to continue. Of the nine billion "farm" animals raised in the United States last year, the vast majority were birds.

In 1999, nearly nine billion meat-type chickens ("broilers") were hatched; about 8.1 billion of these made it to the slaughterhouse, while hundreds of millions died in production. Also in 1999, approximately 273 million turkeys were slaughtered, with tens of millions dying before reaching the slaughterhouse.

The poultry industry has become the model for other segments of animal agriculture. It is vertically integrated, meaning that a large corporate entity maintains control of the production and marketing while exploiting contract "growers" who supply most of the labor and capital. The corporation owns the birds, who are raised by growers in buildings constructed at the growers' expense on their own property. This arrangement has produced enormous profits for Tyson Foods and other poultry industry giants, including Gold Kist, Perdue Farms, and ConAgra Poultry, and is being emulated elsewhere, especially in the pork industry. Most chickens and turkeys are crowded by the thousands in huge sheds called grower houses. Chickens are given about half a square foot of space each, while turkeys are given less than three square feet. Research is under way to study the feasibility of using cages for meat birds so they can be stacked vertically to maximize space, and therefore profits.

Chickens and turkeys bred for meat have been genetically altered to grow twice as fast and twice as large as their ancestors. Chickens are now slaughtered at just six weeks of age, turkeys at 20 weeks. Although this rapid growth rate increases profitability, it also increases health problems. A 1997 *Feedstuffs* article reports that "broilers now grow so rapidly that the heart and lungs are not developed well enough to support the remainder of the body, resulting in congestive heart failure and tremendous death losses."

Putting the growth rate of today's turkeys into perspective, *Lancaster Farming* reports, "If a seven-pound [human] baby grew at the same rate that today's turkey grows, when the baby reaches 18 weeks of age, it would weigh 1,500 pounds." Turkeys have been so altered that they cannot reproduce naturally and must be artificially inseminated.

Such outrageous output has made the United States the world's top poultry exporter. Over the past decade, U.S. chicken exports have increased more than 600 percent to more than four billion pounds per year—one out of every five chickens raised domestically is marketed abroad. Turkey exports have increased more than 1,200 percent to 348 million pounds per year. With the support of the U.S. Department of Agriculture (USDA), agribusiness and fast-food retailers are promoting greater global consumption of animal products. Under the heading, "Producers must get ready to supply chicken for nine billion people," analyst William A. Dudley-Cash predicts a six-fold increase in Asian protein consumption (primarily animal products) within three decades.

**Laying Hens**
More than 300 million laying hens live in the United States. The top three states for production are Ohio, Iowa, and California, which account for 31 million, 28 million, and 24 million birds respectively. The number of layers has remained relatively constant, hovering around 300 million. After dropping slightly from 1960 to 1990, the number of laying hens in the U.S. has increased in the 1990s, reaching nearly 330 million in 2000. The total number of eggs produced increased from about 61.5 million in 1960 to 84.4 million in 2000, the result of genetic alteration and manipulated environments (such as feed and lighting regimens) that cause each hen to lay more eggs. In 1960, the average hen laid 209 eggs; in 2000, she laid 257 eggs.

Before factory farming, laying hens produced 70 eggs per year each. Today the average is more than 250 eggs per year, and animal scientists are trying to boost production further. Cornell University professor Kavous Keshavarz explains that breeders are attempting to add one egg per year to each hen's output, with the ultimate objective being a hen who will produce an egg a day.

In contrast, domestic egg consumption dropped from 321 eggs per person in 1960 to 235 eggs per person in 1995, causing U.S. egg producers to rely more heavily on exports for their profits and compelling the American egg industry to spend millions on public relations campaigns aimed at convincing consumers to eat eggs. Meanwhile, per capita consumption of eggs in the U.S. increased from 236 eggs per person in 1995 to 258 eggs per person in 2000. The egg industry has actively encouraged food processors to add eggs to their products, and this has increased per capita consumption of eggs in the U.S., even among consumers who do not purchase whole eggs. The American egg industry is also spending millions of dollars on public relations campaigns aimed at convincing consumers that eggs are not as unhealthy as was previously thought. Between 1960 and 1995, exports increased from 35 million dozen to more than 200 million dozen.

Nearly all laying hens are confined in small "battery" cages that are lined up in rows and stacked in tiers inside huge warehouses. Typically, five hens are packed into a wire cage measuring 18 by 20 inches. These overcrowded birds experience severe feather loss from constant rubbing against the wire. Every normal chicken behavior—including nest building, dustbathing, even walking and stretching their wings—is thwarted. Because the frustrated hens are driven to excessive pecking, they are painfully debeaked with a hot cauterizing blade. Hens commonly suffer from "cage layer fatigue," caused in part by insufficient calcium in their bodies, and researchers have found that 30 percent experience broken bones.

Animal behaviorists know that crowding hens in battery cages causes suffering, increases deaths, and even lowers egg production. But as Bernard Rollin, professor of physiology and biophysics at Colorado State University, explains, "it is nonetheless more economically efficient to put a greater number of birds into each cage, accepting lower productivity per bird but greater productivity per cage. In other words, though each hen is less productive when crowded, the operation as a whole makes more money with a high stocking density; chickens are cheap, cages are expensive."

After one year, the hens' laying rates drop off and they are considered "spent." Half are slaughtered for human consumption; the others are ground up alive, manually decapitated, crushed, composted, or otherwise discarded because, with an abundant supply of meat birds on the market, slaughterhouses have little use for them. One in five spent hens is force-molted, which involves keeping the birds in darkness and withdrawing food and water to shock their systems into another egg-laying cycle.

At the hatcheries, the male chicks of egg-laying strains are discarded because they can produce neither eggs nor quality meat. The chicks are crushed, ground up alive, suffocated in trashcans, or gassed. Thus, the U.S. egg industry is responsible for killing half of its animals right after birth.

## Dairy Cows and Beef Cattle

Over the past decade, the number of dairy cows in the United States has dropped by nearly one million, and is now about nine million. But more milk is being produced because per-cow production is increasing by about 400 pounds every year. In 1999, the average dairy cow produced nearly 18,000 pounds of milk.

To produce such huge quantities, cows are given highly concentrated feed. This unnatural diet contributes to serious metabolic disorders, including ketosis (which can be fatal) and laminitis, which causes lameness. Other diseases now rampant on America's dairies include mastitis (udder infection), bovine immunodeficiency virus, Johne's disease (whose human counterpart is Crohn's disease), and bovine leukemia virus, which afflicts 89 percent of U.S. dairy herds. In a healthy environment, cows can live for more than 20 years, but on modern dairy farms, most are sent to slaughter after just three or four years in production.

Some farmers who question the merits of intensive production are turning to rotational grazing programs whereby they rotate their cows between different fields and use pasture as a significant part of the cows' diets. This approach may yield less milk per cow but can improve the health and well-being of the animals. Despite this mini-revolution, however, USDA statistics show that every year there are fewer but larger dairies, the vast majority of which do not use grazing.

In recent years there has been a steady shift of dairies from traditional northeastern and Midwestern states to more western regions. With this has come a trend toward "dry-lot" dairies, where the cows are kept in filthy, manure-laden holding pens that look a lot like beef feedlots. In California, where dry-lot dairies dominate, the average production per cow was approximately 20,000 pounds in 1995. With its large dairies and high-production cows, California has replaced Wisconsin as the country's top milk-producing state.

Cornell University Dairy Science professor Dave Galton explains that the dairy industry is driven by supply and demand, and he predicts that the level of milk production per cow will continue to increase, possibly to between 70,000 and 80,000 pounds per year. Galton says that milk production increases will be supported by new technologies, genetic improvements, and a better understanding of the "lactation mechanism." Dairy industry scientists are also looking for new ways to enhance consumers' regard for dairy products. One such proposal is to feed cows a diet spiked with certain plant oils, as this is purported to imbue the cows' mammary secretions with anti-cancer properties.

Dairy cows may be the most likely "farm" animals to be cloned, especially because high-producing cows can be very valuable. In 1997, scientists at ABS Global in Wisconsin unveiled a cloned Holstein calf named Gene, who already has two fellow clones, Gene Two and Gene Three. It took at least 150 attempts and cost about $15 million to "create" Gene.

Like other mammals, cows must have babies in order to produce milk. On modern dairy farms, cows are forced to give birth once a year. The calves are taken from their mothers soon after birth. The females are raised to replace older cows in the milking herd; the males are raised and slaughtered for meat. Most are killed for beef, but about one million per year are killed for veal. The veal industry was created as a direct byproduct of the dairy industry to take advantage of an abundant supply of unwanted male calves.

To produce "milk-fed" or "white" veal, calves are chained by the neck in small wooden crates just two feet wide. The calves are not given their mothers' milk but instead are fed a liquid diet devoid of iron and fiber to keep them borderline anemic, which produces the pale flesh desired in upscale restaurants. Since the 1970s, animal protection groups have worked to educate consumers about veal, causing U.S. per-capita veal consumption to drop 300 percent. The use of veal crates has been banned in much of Europe, and some animal scientists believe the United States will follow.

In addition to being responsible for veal, the dairy industry is closely intertwined with the beef industry, as ultimately all dairy cattle are eventually slaughtered for beef. The dairy industry bears the primary responsibility for downed animals (animals too sick to walk) and for drug residues found in meat—problems that have upset beef industry representatives concerned about the beef industry's deteriorating public image.

Most beef cattle have not been subjected to factory-farm conditions, but still endure painful mutilations like castration and hot-iron branding without anesthesia. Range cattle are not adequately protected against inclement weather or disease; they die of dehydration during droughts and freeze during harsh winters. Animals who are injured, ill, or otherwise ailing do not receive proper veterinary attention, and may suffer for weeks without treatment. One common ailment is called "cancer eye"; left untreated, the cancer eats away at the animal's eye and face, eventually producing a crater in the side of the head.

Most beef cattle spend their last few months at a feedlot, where they are crowded by the thousands into dusty, manure-laden holding pens with inadequate shelter. Most feedlot cattle are given growth hormones, and are fed unnaturally rich diets to fatten them quickly and profitably. Feedlots are the domain of corporate agriculture, which is controlling a growing percentage of U.S. cattle and concentrating it into fewer and fewer hands. Five percent of the feedlots now control approximately 90 percent of U.S. cattle. Meanwhile, four corporations—IBP, ConAgra Red Meat Cos., Excel, and National Beef Packing Co.—slaughter 81 percent of the market, up from 41 percent in 1980.

## Pigs

The number of pigs slaughtered in the United States is approaching 100 million per year, an increase of more than 10 percent over the past decade. Iowa is still the top hog producer, but North Carolina has moved into second place. The so-called "North Carolina Model" of hog production, patterned after the vertically integrated poultry industry, is spreading rapidly. Corporate interests own and control pigs from birth to slaughter, and they exploit contract growers who house and feed the pigs.

Although this type of hog production can generate quick profits, it can also generate lasting problems. North Carolina has suffered extensive water pollution, including a 1995 spill of 25 million gallons of hog manure—more than twice the volume of the Exxon Valdez spill. The state's waterways are also contaminated with pfiesteria, a toxic algae that has killed hundreds of millions of fish. Pfiesteria causes open sores, nausea, memory loss, fatigue, and disorientation in humans and other animals, and is often fatal. In March 1997, the North Carolina legislature was forced to enact a two-year moratorium on the construction of new hog farms, and this moratorium has now been extended until September 2003.

As intensive hog farms create social and environmental havoc, they have been forced to move out of populated areas in search of unregulated, unprotected lands. Many have gone west, and more are sure to follow. But even in less populated states, people are objecting to the pork industry. For example, the governor of Oklahoma instated an emergency order to curb the exploding expansion of hog farms, while Wyoming citizens have banded together to fight corporate hog farms.

Some pig farmers, upset by intensive production methods and threatened by corporate control, are returning to outdoor farming. There have been numerous conferences, meetings, and community organizations formed to oppose corporate hog farms. In 1996, there was a conference in Iowa to discuss such options for small farmers. Unfortunately, despite this, the move toward intensification and vertical integration appears to be the dominant trend. The pork industry is trying to emulate the poultry industry, and is in a position to command strong profits in a global economy.

In addition to destroying local communities and the environment, modern pork production is hell on pigs. Within days of birth, piglets endure painful mutilations: their ears are notched for identification, and their tails are cut off to minimize tail-biting, an aberrant behavior that occurs when these highly intelligent animals are later confined in deprived factory-farm environments. At two to three weeks of age, the piglets are taken from their mothers, by which time approximately 15 percent will have died from starvation, crushing, or disease.

During most of their lives, factory-raised pigs are packed into metal and concrete pens, and crowded by the thousands in huge warehouses. The indoor air is laden with dust, dander, and noxious gases produced by the animals' urine and feces. Slaughterhouse surveys have found that up to 70 percent of pigs have pneumonia, and employee surveys show that 60 percent of farm workers experience breathing problems.

Living in these stressful and unhealthy conditions, the pigs suffer from ulcers, arthritis, and other health problems. They are at constant risk for infectious diseases like salmonellosis, which is increasing in both incidence and virulence. New diseases such as Porcine Stress Syndrome (PSS) are the result of genetic manipulation. As industry expert and Colorado State

University professor Temple Grandin describes them, "These are the animals that start shaking and die of a heart attack."

Most pigs are slaughtered when they reach a weight of 240 pounds at six months old, but breeding sows endure years in intensive confinement. They are artificially inseminated and held in small pens or metal gestation crates only two feet wide for four months. Just before giving birth, they are moved to metal farrowing crates, where they can barely stand up or lie down, and often suffer from lesions caused by rubbing against the bars. Some large hog operations are developing even smaller farrowing crates so they can fit more sows per building.

## The Meat Market

Most people are appalled when they learn of the cruelty endured by animals in agriculture. However, this sentiment has yet to translate into legal protection, because agricultural interests have maintained a stranglehold over legislative committees responsible for addressing farm animal issues. Farmed animals are specifically excluded from the federal Animal Welfare Act, and so their primary legal protection is in state anti-cruelty laws. Unfortunately, most state anti-cruelty laws are similarly inadequate. As attorney David Wolfson explains, "states have enacted laws that create a legal realm whereby certain acts (and in most cases any act), no matter how cruel, are defined as outside the reach of the anti-cruelty statute as long as the acts are deemed 'acceptable,' 'common,' 'customary,' or 'normal' farming practices."

Besides being at odds with a growing number of consumers who are offended by animal abuse, agribusiness faces other profound challenges. In recent years, a myriad of international news reports have linked human illnesses and deaths with animal agriculture, ranging from "mad cow disease" in Britain, E. coli bacteria poisoning in the United States, and avian flu in Hong Kong. Agribusiness cannot ignore the fact that people are dying because of its practices, and it is now in a position similar to that of the tobacco industry 20 years ago. The meat, dairy, and egg industries are selling items that are not essential for human survival, and often prove downright hazardous. Efforts to deal with contaminated animal products range from developing helpful bacteria to using radiation to treat meat before sale. One outrageous proposal reported in *Food Chemical News* suggested "using Superglue to seal the 'vents' on poultry before slaughter to prevent the birds from reflexively excreting fecal material at the time of death." (Thankfully, this procedure has not been approved by the Food and Drug Administration.)

While U.S. agribusiness seeks to enhance its profitability in the global marketplace, it also faces serious obstacles. Along with concerns about the effects of an animal-based diet on human health and the environmental hazards associated with factory farms, animal suffering is a growing issue affecting animal agriculture. Several major universities have now established institutes to study farm animal welfare. And although the vast majority of such animals still endure factory farms, a handful of farmers are attempting to market "humane" meat, milk, and eggs. Such "free-range" farms might not be as bad as factory farms, but both ultimately exploit and slaughter animals for profit, and reduce living animals to salable commodities. The only consumer choice that can truly free cows, pigs, turkeys, chickens, and other animals from unnecessary suffering is a lifestyle free of all animal products: veganism.

# 2: The Plight of Poultry

KAREN DAVIS

CHICKENS WERE THE first agriculturally raised animals to be permanently confined indoors in large numbers in automated systems based on intensive genetic selection, antibiotics, and drugs. Until World War II, chickens were raised in towns and villages and on farms, and many city people kept them in back lots. Following the war, the U.S. chicken industry became the model for poultry production throughout the world.

Working through the Peace Corps and other channels, the U.S. government exports intensive poultry and egg production technology to developing countries, according to *Feedstuffs* magazine. This is carried out under the guise of a demand for "high-protein meat- and poultry-based diets" to feed the world's rapidly expanding population, which is projected to double in the next 40 years, tripling food needs. According to the WATT Publishing Company *2000 Executive Guide to World Poultry Trends*, worldwide chicken production accounts for more than 85 percent of world poultry production, which totaled 65.6 million tons in 2000. The total number of broiler (meat-type) chickens and spent egg-laying hens killed worldwide in 2000 exceeded 40 billion, an increase of about 1.3 billion birds per year through the 1990s. Industry analysis hopefully predicts that worldwide poultry meat production will continue to grow at about four percent per year—and egg production at about three percent per year—through 2006.

Since the 1950s, chickens have been genetically divided into two distinct types: broiler chickens for meat production and laying hens for egg production. Battery cages for laying hens—consisting of identical confinement units arranged in rows and tiers—and confinement sheds for broiler chickens came into standard use during the 1940s and 1950s. World War II, urbanization, and a growing human population produced a demand for cheap, mass-produced poultry and eggs. In 1950, broiler chicken sales surpassed egg sales for the first time. The April 13, 1995, edition of *The Washington Post* reported that the U.S. broiler chicken business had become a $25 billion industry, compared to a $4.2 billion egg industry.

The turkey industry took a similar course. The domestic turkey is derived from imported Bronze and Black turkeys from

Europe that were crossed with wild turkeys at the beginning of the 19th century. During the 1930s and 1940s, demand for a smaller turkey for smaller families and ovens led the U.S. Department of Agriculture (USDA) to develop the Beltsville (Maryland) White with subsequent strains of large, medium, and small birds.

As the poultry industry expanded in the 1950s, birds genetically selected for breast meat and fast growth had mating and fertility problems. This led to the adoption of artificial insemination, which is now the sole method of reproducing turkeys for human consumption. In the 1970s, the turkey stud farm concept was adopted. The toms are isolated from the hens and manipulated for their semen by "milkers," who inseminate the hens with a hypodermic syringe, or the milker's breath pressure blown through a tube. This has led to a pathology in turkeys and chickens subjected to the process known as "deep pectoral myopathy." As described in the book *The Health of Poultry*, the condition results from the bird's chest muscles being exerted beyond the body's ability to supply oxygen due to the bird's "struggling and wing beating associated with catching for artificial insemination."

These birds suffer from birth to death. The April/May 1993 issue of *Turkey World* magazine documents the trauma of a baby turkey: "Very few animals go through the stresses of turkey poults in their first three hours of life. They are squeezed for sexing, their toes are removed, and they are injected, vaccinated, and debeaked."

Modern poultry—chickens, turkeys, ducks, and such domestic "game" fowl as guineas, pheasants, and pigeons—are confined by the thousands in stressful, densely packed houses permeated with accumulated droppings, feed ingredients, and excretory ammonia fumes. Disease is inevitable. In 1991, *The Atlanta Journal-Constitution* noted that every week, "millions of chickens leaking yellow pus, stained by green feces, contaminated by harmful bacteria, or marred by lung and heart infections, cancerous tumors, or skin conditions are shipped for sale to consumers." On October 30, 2001, *The New York Times* noted that food-poisoning "[b]acteria called campylobacter contaminate most chickens that go to market in the United States," and in 1999, the General Accounting Office noted that eggs contaminated by the *Salmonella enteritidis* bacteria have been acknowledged as a public health problem since 1988, with over three-quarters of *Salmonella enteritidis* outbreaks linked to eggs between 1985 and 1998, according to the Centers for Disease Control and Prevention.

Despite this, domestic consumption of poultry and egg products continues, resulting in more and more areas of the country being spoiled by the prevalence of poultry complexes. U.S. consumption is linked to the global expansion of the poultry industry through GATT, NAFTA, the World Trade Organization, and related trade agreements that aggressively export domestically produced poultry products to other countries. In February 1996, *Feedstuff* reported that exports represented 15 percent of the total U.S. chicken production, of which Russia represented a third. Since then, a decline in U.S. poultry meat exports to Russia has been offset by increased shipments to Latvia, Estonia, Ukraine, and Hong Kong. The United States remains the leading exporter, followed by Brazil. Exports to Russia and Asia further enrich the U.S. broiler industry by increasing the demand for dark meat. The sale of chicken legs and feet to Hong Kong and China, as noted in April 1995 by *The Houston Chronicle*, is now a $100 million business.

Between 1990 and 2000, the number of laying hens in the world increased from 3.8 billion to five billion, a number that includes hens used for commercial egg production and those used to produce hatching eggs (seven percent of total egg production) for the broiler chicken and egg industries. The huge increase in the number of laying hens reflects the growth of egg production in developing countries, especially China. Although U.S. egg consumption has dropped 40 percent over the past 35 years, consumption of dried and liquid egg products in such foods as pasta and salad dressings has grown. Of the 300 million laying hens in the United States (up from 2.4 million hens in 1995), 99 percent are confined in cages in which eight or nine hens have a total average space of 48 square inches per hen. It was reported at the International Egg Commission's annual conference in Stockholm, Sweden, in 1995 that 75 percent of the world's laying hens are now kept in cages. Although the number of floor-kept ("free-range") birds is increasing in some European countries, *Egg Industry* magazine reported in October 1995 that "the total proportion of caged birds is likely to increase even further because of installations in the developing countries."

Since then, increased welfare standards for commercial egg-producing hens have been set by the European Union (EU), which in June 1999 announced a Europe-wide ban on battery-hen cages by the year 2012. Currently, 90 percent of the 350 million laying hens in the EU are kept in cages. More far-reachingly, the German Parliament voted on October 19, 2001 in support of the 1999 finding by the German Constitutional Court that battery cages violate German law. The new German law is expected to ban conventional battery cages by the end of 2006. In addition, the McDonald's Corporation announced on August 22, 2000 that the producers that supply the company with 1.5 billion eggs each year will have to provide 50 percent more space for each caged hen, ban the practice of withholding food and water from hens to manipulate egg production (known as forced molting), and gradually phase out debeaking. The McDonald's action is important because it is the first time that a major U.S. food company has admitted that the treatment of farmed animals merits attention in its own right.

As noted, the number of birds being slaughtered worldwide is almost inconceivable. In the United States, of the 10 billion farmed animals slaughtered in USDA-inspected facilities in 2000, more than 8.7 billion were birds, including 8.2 billion broiler chickens, 165 million spent commercial laying hens and breeding chickens, 268 million turkeys, and 25 million ducks. In addition, 14,307,000 pounds of "other poultry" were slaughtered including ostriches, emus, geese, pigeons, rabbits (rabbits are classed as "poultry" by the USDA), and other miscellaneous categories of birds. Still more birds die by the millions each year, including those slaughtered in state-inspected facilities and live poultry markets, and the half billion male chicks and defective females destroyed by the U.S. egg industry each year because they are commercially useless. Millions more birds suffer and die prematurely before going to slaughter.

In the United States, broiler chickens and turkeys are not stunned immediately before slaughter but are immobilized with a very painful electric current. The cruelty of poultry slaughter has increased in recent years because younger and heavier birds with extremely fragile capillaries are now being processed for the fast-food and rotisserie trade, resulting in a greater susceptibility to hemorrhage under an electric current. Consequently, poultry companies have reduced the electrical current used to "stun" the chickens to even lower levels. The controversial technique of gas stunning is not employed in America, although a 2001 amendment to the 1995 Welfare of Animals Regulations in the United Kingdom permits the voluntary use of nitrogen and other inert gases mixed with low concentrations of carbon dioxide to presumably improve welfare, because birds can be gassed to death in the trucks and thus be spared the cruelty of live shackling.

Spent laying hens are so osteoporotic from lack of exercise and from calcium drainage for eggshell formation that the U.S. industry does not "stun" them, and slaughter plants don't want them. Consequently, the egg industry is investigating on-site killing of these hens in portable gas units. Meanwhile, the majority of hens are buried alive in landfills, and about 26 million hens are trucked to Canada each year to be gassed in the trucks on arrival, as reported in the May 2000 issue of *Animal People*.

To date, there are no federal welfare laws governing the raising, transport, or slaughter of poultry in the United States. It is inexcusable that the vast majority of animals raised and killed for food in this country are excluded from legal coverage. To those who say that vegetarianism will not come overnight, it can be said with even greater assurance that humane treatment of poultry will never come at all, because the commodification of a living creature is inherently inhumane, and because the poultry industry (even in countries where welfare laws exist) is, for all practical purposes, ungovernable. At best, "humane" improvements are, as poultry specialist Dr. Lesley Rogers points out, "attempts by an industry designed for profit to make some concession to the welfare of the animals."

Rhetoric about how the public isn't ready for vegetarianism has got to be replaced by active promotion of the peaceful palate and equal justice for all animals. The worst thing, as Canadian animal activist Harriet Schleifer points out in the book *In Defense of Animals*, is to lull the public "to feel that the use of animals for food is in some way acceptable, since even the animal welfare people say so." Rather, the advocate's role is to speed the day when regarding a fellow creature as food is no longer an option.

# 3: The Battery Hen

Karen Davis

THE CAGING OF laying hens was successfully prosecuted in 1993 in a private suit brought by Hobart, Tasmania, Australia.

Activist Pam Clarke and the Australian organization Animal Liberation brought charges against Golden Egg Farm following a covert investigation in 1991. During this investigation several hens were purchased from the farm, and videos and photographs were taken documenting the horrible conditions under which Golden Egg hens were forced to live.

On February 24, 1993, Hobart Magistrate Phillip Wright found Golden Egg Farm guilty on seven counts of cruelty under the Tasmanian Cruelty to Animals Prevention Act of 1925. Wright delivered a historic 18-page judgment against the farm and the battery system. He ruled that the hens were unable to exercise and were in chronic pain because they were forced to rub continuously against the cage wire. He stated that confinement causing the state of the hens submitted in evidence "could not be called other than cruel: if a bird is unable to move without affecting physically others in the cage, nor to lay or rest without affecting itself deleteriously, the cruelty is constant and continual and without relief and, I have no doubt, caused stress in all these birds." Wright later commented in a letter to me, "If I have done a little to hasten the abolition of this vile trade by 'civilized' peoples, I am well satisfied and handsomely rewarded with that knowledge."

Shortly after the Golden Egg ruling, Clarke was charged with trespassing at Hobart Parliament House. She was there protesting government efforts to amend the Tasmanian Prevention of Cruelty Act of 1925 to exempt poultry from protection. This amendment would allow the government to override the court judgment. She was sent to prison for three weeks.

In August 1993, Australian industry ministers agreed to a national review of battery hen farming, with a view to seeking alternatives. Animal Liberation branches were poised throughout Australia to launch similar private prosecutions against battery hen farms. To this day, they continue their undercover investigations and media exposures of battery hen farms in Australia. Although Australian state and territory agriculture ministers rejected a national ban of the battery cage system in 2000, this was, according to Animals Australia, "the closest that Australia has *ever* been to liberating the battery hen."

The modern Leghorn hen laying eggs for human consumption is far removed from both the Burmese jungle fowl from whom she derives and the active farmyard fowl of recent memory. While normal and lively in a sanctuary setting, the modern hen is an anxious, frustrated, fear-ridden bird when forced to spend 10 to 12 months or more squeezed inside a small wire cage with eight or nine other tormented hens. The cages are piled in gloomy tiers in sheds holding 50,000 to 125,000 debeaked, terrified, bewildered birds. By nature an energetic forager, the laying hen should be ranging by day, perching at night, and enjoying dust baths with her flock mates—a need so strong that she pathetically practices "vacuum" dust bathing on the wire floor of her cage.

Confined for life without exercise while constantly drained of calcium to form eggshells, battery hens develop the severe osteoporosis of intensive confinement known as "caged layer fatigue." Calcium-depleted, millions of hens become paralyzed and die of hunger and thirst inches from their food and water.

In the 20th century, the combined genetic, managerial, and chemical manipulations of the small Leghorn produced a bird capable of laying an abnormal number of large eggs—250 per year in contrast to the one or two clutches of 12 eggs per year laid by her wild relatives. The laying of an egg has been degraded by the battery system to a squalid discharge so humiliating that ethologist Konrad Lorenz compared it to humans being forced to defecate in each others' presence. Researchers have described the futile efforts of caged hens to build nests and their frantic efforts to escape the cage by jumping at the bars right up to the laying of the egg.

Disease and suffering are inherent features of the battery system, in which the individual hen is obscured by gloom and by thousands of other hens in an environment deliberately designed to discourage perception, labor, and care. Battery hens suffer from reproductive maladies that afflict female birds deprived of exercise: fragments of eggs clog their oviducts, which become inflamed and paralyzed; eggs are formed that are too big to be laid; uteruses prolapse, pushing through the vagina of small birds forced to strain day after day to expel huge eggs. The battery cage has created an ugly disease in laying hens called "fatty liver hemorrhagic syndrome," characterized by an enlarged, fat, disintegrating liver covered with blood clots, and pale combs and wattles covered with dandruff. In recent decades, hens' oviducts have become infested with *Salmonella* bacteria that enter their eggs and cause food poisoning in consumers.

Battery hens live in a poisoned atmosphere. Toxic ammonia rises from the decomposing uric acid in the manure pits beneath the cages to cause ammonia-burned eyes and chronic respiratory disease in millions of hens. Studies of the effect of ammonia on eggs suggests that even at low concentrations, significant quantities of ammonia can be absorbed into an egg.

Hens to be used for a second or even a third laying period are force-molted to reduce the accumulated fat in their reproductive systems and to regulate prices by forcing the hens to stop laying for a couple of months. In the forced molt, producers starve the hens for 10 to 21 days, causing them to lose 25 to 30 percent of their body weight, along with their feathers. Water deprivation, drugs such as chlormadinone, and harsh light and blackout schedules can be part of this treatment. Forced molting significantly impairs the hen's cellular immune system, which may increase *Salmonella enteritidis*, the bacterial infestation of eggs that makes people and chickens sick. Force-molted hens are driven to pluck and consume each others' feathers in order to obtain nutrients, and many hens choke to death when their food is restored as a result of atrophied muscles and crop impaction.

However, eating is always gruesome for the battery hen, who must stretch her neck across a "feeder fence" to reach the monotonous mash in the trough. Repeating this action over time wears away her neck feathers and causes throat blisters. In addition, the fine mash particles stick to the inside of the hen's mouth, attracting bacteria and causing painful mouth ulcers. A mold toxin, T-2, can taint the mash, creating even more mouth ulcers in the hens, who have no choice but to consume what is in front of them.

Battery hens are debeaked with a hot machine blade once and often twice during their lives, typically at the hatchery and again at seven weeks old, because a young beak will often grow back. Debeaking causes severe, chronic pain and suffering that researchers compare to human phantom-limb and stump pain. Between the horn and bone of the beak is a thin layer of highly sensitive tissue. The hot blade cuts through this sensitive tissue, impairing the hen's ability to eat, drink, wipe her beak, and preen normally.

Debeaking is done to offset the effects of the compulsive pecking that can afflict birds designed by nature to roam, scratch, and peck at the ground all day, not sit in prison. Debeaking prevents birds from grasping their food efficiently, thereby saving feed costs. It also distresses the birds, causing them to lose their appetite; therefore they eat less, fling their food less, and "waste" less energy than do intact birds. *Diseases of Poultry* states that "a different form of cannibalism is now being observed in beak-trimmed birds kept in cages. The area about the eyes is black and blue due to subcutaneous hemorrhage, wattles are dark and swollen with blood, and ear lobes are black and necrotic."

The battery system includes antibiotics, used to control the rampant viral and bacterial diseases of chickens in crowded confinement; many antibiotics also can be used to manipulate egg production. For example, virginiamycin is said to increase feed conversion per egg laid, bacitracin to stimulate egg production, and oxytetracycline to improve eggshell quality, extend the period of high egg production, and improve feed efficiency in the presence of stress and disease. In *Factory Farming*, Andrew Johnson says that virtually all laying hens in the United States are routinely dosed with antibiotics, though the U.S. egg industry denies treating hens subtherapeutically with antibiotics the way broiler (meat-type) chickens and turkeys are dosed to increase growth rates artificially.

At the end of the laying period, hens are flung from the battery to the transport cages by their wings, legs, head, or feet. Many bones are broken. Chicken "stuffers" are paid for speed, not gentleness. Half-naked from feather loss and terrorized by a lifetime of abuse, hens in transit embody a state of fear so severe that many are paralyzed by the time they reach the slaughterhouse. At slaughter the hens are a mass of broken bones, oozing abscesses, bright red bruises, oviduct tumors, and internal hemorrhaging. Their condition makes them fit only for shredding into products that hide the true state of their flesh and their lives: chicken soups and pies, school lunches, and other food programs developed by the egg industry to dump dead laying hens onto consumers in diced-up form.

To date, there are no federal welfare laws in the United States or Canada regulating poultry raising, transport, or slaughter. The U.S. egg industry opposes humane slaughter legislation for poultry, claiming that spent commercial laying hens cannot be rendered insensible to pain economically prior to having their throats cut or being decapitated. The California Humane Poultry Slaughter Act, passed in 1991, excludes laying hens. Because there is little or no "meat" market for spent laying hens, the majority of birds in the United States are buried alive in landfills. Some are processed and fed to captive minks on fur farms. About 26 million spent hens are trucked each year into Canada, where the survivors of the journey, which may be thousands of miles, are gassed in the trucks on arrival.

British law requires that livestock and poultry must be rendered instantaneously insensible to pain until death supervenes. At least one British researcher, Dr. Neville Gregory, thinks the law should delete the reference to pain, because "following electrical stunning one can have analgesia where there is conscious perception of non-painful stimuli." In other words, a bird at slaughter can have dreadful sensations of breathlessness and terror over and above bodily pain.

The battery cage is legal in the United States and Canada, although Canada has had a "Recommended Code of Practices" for confinement systems since 1980. Under intense animal welfare pressure at home and abroad, the United Egg Producers (the U.S. egg industry's trade group) formed a Scientific Advisory Committee in 1999, which resulted in a recommendation that U.S. egg producers should increase cage space per hen from 48 square inches to 67 square inches by 2012. This is five square inches less per hen than McDonald's is now requiring of its egg suppliers. In 2000, McDonald's (followed by Burger King and Wendy's) announced that each hen owned by the company's suppliers would have to have at least 72 square inches of living space, that forced molting by food and water deprivation was prohibited, and that the company would not support the practice of "beak trimming."

Switzerland banned battery cages in 1992. Groups of 40 or more Swiss hens must have access to perches and nest boxes and a minimum of 120 square inches of wire-grid floor space each. Currently, about 65 percent of eggs sold in Switzerland are domestically produced; the rest are imported battery eggs. In June 1999, the European Union announced a ban on battery cages by 2012, and in October 2001, the German Parliament voted in support of the 1999 finding by the German Constitutional Court that battery cages violate German law. The new German law is expected to ban conventional battery cages by the end of 2006. "Enriched" cages furnished with perches, nest boxes, and scratching areas will be banned by 2011.

Regarding the European ban on battery cages by 2012, European activists worry that in 2005 or so, the World Trade Organization (WTO) will decide, after its secret tribunal has met, to fine European nations billions of dollars a day if they do not toe the WTO line. The battle against battery cages includes all of us. Wherever we are, we are morally obligated to end the oppression. While working to improve the conditions under which chickens are raised, transported, and killed in current society, consumers should boycott battery eggs and discover the variety of egg-free alternatives in cooking and eating.

# 4: Abolishing Intensive Livestock Agriculture: A Global Imperative

RICHARD H. SCHWARTZ

MODERN LIVESTOCK AGRICULTURE and animal-centered diets not only contribute to the cruel treatment of billions of animals annually, but they also have devastating consequences for people, for the environment, and for scarce resources. Non-vegetarian diets are a major factor behind the present widespread hunger and malnutrition that result in an estimated 20 million people dying each year. Seventy percent of the grain grown in the United States and almost 40 percent of the grain grown worldwide is consumed by animals destined for slaughter, while hundreds of millions of the world's people are chronically hungry. To make matters worse, the United States is a major importer of meat, much of which comes from countries where there is extensive hunger.

While an average Asian consumes between 300 and 400 pounds of grain a year, the average middle-class American consumes about 2,000 pounds of grain, 80 percent of which comes in the form of meat from grain-fed animals. U.S. livestock consume more than six and a half times as much grain as the U.S. human population does. The grain fed to animals to produce meat, milk, and eggs could feed five times the number of people that it currently does if it were consumed directly by humans. While one hectare (about 2.5 acres) of land growing potatoes can feed 22 people, and one hectare growing rice can feed 19 people, that same area producing beef can feed only one person. Feeding grain to livestock wastes 90 percent of the protein and almost all of the carbohydrates and fiber of the grain. While grains are a rich source of fiber, animal products have no fiber at all.

This evidence indicates that the food being fed to animals in the affluent nations could, if properly distributed, end hunger and malnutrition throughout the world. A switch from animal-centered diets would free up land and other resources, which could then be used to grow nutritious crops for people.

Intensive livestock agriculture is a substantial contributor to many environmental problems. Mountains of manure produced by cattle raised in feedlots wash into and pollute streams, rivers, and underground water sources. U.S. livestock produce an astounding 1.4 billion tons of manure per year (this amount works out to almost 90,000 pounds per second!), or about 130 times the amount excreted by the entire U.S. human population. Food geographer Georg Borgstrom has estimated that American livestock contribute five times more organic waste to the pollution of our water than do people, and twice as much as does industry. In addition, huge amounts of chemical fertilizers and pesticides used in the production of animal feed crops end up in surface and ground waters.

Current intensive livestock agriculture and the consumption of meat contribute greatly to the four major gases associated with the greenhouse effect: carbon dioxide, methane, nitrous oxides, and chlorofluorocarbons. The burning of tropical forests for grazing, among other uses, releases tons of carbon dioxide into the atmosphere and eliminates the ability of these trees to absorb carbon dioxide. Also, the highly mechanized agricultural sector contributes to carbon dioxide emissions by using an enormous amount of fossil fuel to produce pesticides, chemical fertilizer, and other agricultural resources. Cattle emit methane as part of their digestive process, as do the termites who feast on the charred remains of trees that were burned to create grazing land and land to grow feed crops for farmed animals. The large amounts of petrochemical fertilizers used to produce feed crops create significant quantities of nitrous oxides. Likewise, the increased refrigeration necessary to prevent animal products from spoiling adds chlorofluorocarbons to the atmosphere.

Nearly six billion of the seven billion tons of eroded soil in the United States has been lost because of cattle and feedlot production. About 90 percent of U.S. cropland is losing soil at a rate at least 13 times faster than the sustainable rate. Lower yields are occurring in many areas due to erosion and the reduction in fertility that it causes.

Grazing animals have destroyed large areas of land throughout the world, with overgrazing being a prime cause of erosion. More than 60 percent of all U.S. rangelands are overgrazed, with billions of tons of soil lost each year. Cattle production is a prime contributor to every one of the causes of desertification: overgrazing of livestock, over-cultivation of land, improper irrigation techniques, deforestation, and prevention of reforestation. In the United States, more plant species have been eliminated due to overgrazing by livestock than by any other cause.

Demand for meat in wealthy countries leads to environmental damage in poor countries. Largely to turn beef into fast-food hamburgers for export to America, the earth's tropical rain forests are being bulldozed at a rate of a football field per second. Each imported quarter-pound fast-food hamburger patty requires the destruction of 55 square feet of tropical forest. Half of the rainforests are already gone forever, and at current rates of destruction the rest will be nearly gone by the middle of this century. What makes this especially ominous is that half of the world's fast-disappearing species of plants and animals reside in tropical rainforests. We are risking the loss of species that might hold secrets for cures of deadly diseases. Other plant species might turn out to be good sources of nutrition. Also, the destruction of rainforests is altering the climate and reducing rainfall, with potentially devastating effects on the world's agriculture and habitability.

Animal-based agriculture is the major consumer of water; irrigation, primarily to grow crops for animals, uses more than 80 percent of U.S. water. The production of only one pound of edible beef in a semi-arid area such as California requires as much as 5,200 gallons of water, as contrasted with only 25 gallons or less to produce an edible pound of tomatoes, lettuce, potatoes, or wheat. *Newsweek* reported in 1988 that "the water that goes into a 1,000 pound steer would float a destroyer."

An animal-based diet also requires much energy. In the United States, an average of 10 calories of fuel energy is required for every calorie of food energy produced; many other countries obtain 20 or more calories of food energy per calorie of fuel energy. To produce one pound of steak (500 calories of food energy) requires 20,000 calories of fossil fuels, most of which is expended in producing and providing feed crops. It requires 78 calories of fossil fuel to make one calorie of protein from feed-lot-produced beef, but only two calories of fossil fuel to produce a calorie of protein from soybeans. Grains and beans require only two to five percent as much fossil fuel as beef. The energy needed to produce a pound of grain-fed beef is equivalent to one gallon of gasoline.

When one considers the above facts, as well as the soaring health-care costs associated with degenerative diseases conclusively linked to animal-based diets, it becomes increasingly clear that vegetarianism is not only an important individual choice, but also an imperative for national solvency and global sustainability. It is not surprising that the Union of Concerned Scientists (UCS) ranks the consumption of meat and poultry as the second most harmful consumer activity (surpassed only by the use of cars and light trucks). It is critical that people become aware of the far-reaching consequences of animal agriculture and begin to shift away from a diet that is bankrupting the United States and the world, crippling and killing 1.5 million

Americans annually with chronic diseases, threatening the world's ecosystems, wasting scarce resources, contributing to world hunger, and cruelly exploiting animals.

People can contribute to a more humane, peaceful, and healthy planet by further educating themselves on the issues. Such books as *The Food Revolution,* by John Robbins, *Beyond Beef,* by Jeremy Rifkin, and *The Vegetarian Sourcebook,* by Keith Akers, are excellent places to start. We should enlighten others through personal conversations, meetings with opinion leaders in our community, letters and op-ed articles to newspapers and other publications, and calls to radio talk shows. There is a world to be saved, but global sustainability is largely dependent on the demise of intensive animal agriculture. Within an individual's daily choice of diet lies the power to create a better world.

# 5: Making a Killing: The Power and Influence of Animal Agriculture in America

JIM MASON

WHAT IF YOU could make a few phone calls to other animal activists, who would then call a few others, and within a few days your collective efforts could block offensive legislation, put a troublesome entertainer off the air, place one of your own at the head of an important congressional committee, or pass laws making it a crime to say disparaging words about animals and animal advocacy?

Some dream, huh?

Although animal advocates can only dream of such power over law-making and opinion-shaping, animal agribusiness has such powers now. Of course, this comes as no surprise to those who have ever tried to pass a law, get media coverage, persuade a school to use different teaching materials, or otherwise move the powers-that-be to do anything at all friendly to animals—particularly animals used for food.

So how are the meat, dairy, and egg industries able to do so effortlessly what all of our best efforts usually fail to do? What do they have that we don't? The answer is money (hundreds of millions of dollars), tradition (thousands of years worth), and popular demand (the overwhelming majority of it).

Nevertheless, leading farm animal advocates say that cracks are creeping across the castle walls, and new ammunition is empowering the attack on animal agribusiness. Advocates urge activists to refuse to be intimidated by agri-power, and instead to study it more closely for openings. "But never think that the meat industry will fall of its own weight and corruption," cautions Alex Hershaft of Farm Animal Reform Movement (FARM), who urges relentless campaigning against "the despair, disease, death, and destruction [that it is causing] every minute of every hour of every day."

Gene Bauston of Farm Sanctuary also sees weaknesses in animal agribusiness: "It's like concrete—cold, dead, and hard. We're like grass, rising up through the cracks and breaking up its weight." A major source of agri-power, he says, is tradition, in the form of appetites and attitudes. "People eat their products, so they don't want to look too closely at farm animals as worthy of concern." Agribusiness knows this, of course, and takes good advantage of it, playing on meat's special status and the public's reluctance to make changes, Bauston says. "And then there is this sacred image of farmers—never mind that there are very few of them left." It all adds up to entrenched power for the animal industries, Bauston says, and a monumental irony: "When one person abuses an animal, there can be outrage; when millions of people abuse billions of animals in the name of profit, even reasonable people will ignore it."

**The Government Till**

When you combine the great weight of tradition with the huge amounts of money generated by animal agribusiness, it is no wonder that the industries are arrogant. (Remember the Oprah Winfrey/Howard Lyman trial?) To get a handle on the amount of power involved, consider that

- The meat and poultry industries generate revenues of $90 billion a year.
- Meat packers and processors employ more than one million workers—more than fruit and vegetable processors, the pharmaceutical industry, television broadcasting, or news-papers.
- Meat and poultry interests are big contributors to political campaigns to get their loyalists elected. Then they spend still more on lobbying them. In 1996, The American Meat Institute (AMI) spent $244,246 lobbying Congress, and the three largest meatpackers—ConAgra, Cargill, and IBP—spent $286,000, $255,000, and $60,000, respectively.
- The meat and poultry industries are the biggest buyers of grain, chemicals, pharmaceuticals, advertising, machinery, vehicles, energy, and water. This gives animal agribusiness a lot of rich, powerful allies, who work together much like a syndicate to keep it all going. When meat is moving, every-body makes money.

Small wonder, then, that agribusiness interests are able to get Congress, state legislatures, and the media to do just about whatever they want. Sadly, this holds true even when the most compelling public interests are on the opposite side, as when children are dying from eating tainted meat. A 1998 study by the Center for Public Integrity (CPI), titled "Safety Last: The Politics of E. Coli and Other Food-Borne Killers," traced in great detail the food poisoning epidemics of the past decade and

their links to modern factory farming and slaughtering methods. The report also followed the efforts to change the system
and the maneuverings of meat industry lobbyists and politicians
to thwart those efforts. According to the report, "Congress has
consistently ignored the growing threat to public health posed
by the slaughter and meatpacking industry....During the escalating public-health crisis of the past decade, the industry has
managed to kill every bill that has promised meaningful
improvement."

The report noted that the meat industry hung tough
through it all, and Congress stayed at its beck and call. What
few hearings were held were stacked with industry witnesses.
Congress blocked stricter rules against using antibiotics in animal feeds and efforts to make the industries pay part of the bill
for meat and poultry inspection. Instead, Congress is allowing
the processors to inspect themselves. The report concluded that
regarding food safety, "the agenda in Congress today is substantially set by the meat industry....The meat interests have overwhelmed the supposedly objective decision-making process in
Washington."

This immense power over government machinery shows up
again and again as the meat industry fights battles over diet,
nutrition, food safety, land use, and other public concerns. For
Hershaft, one battle in particular stands out: the furor over the
1977 McGovern Report, officially called "Dietary Goals for the
United States." After extensive hearings in 1976, the Senate
Select Committee on Human Needs and Nutrition (chaired by
Sen. George McGovern, D-SD) recommended that Americans
"eat less meat." The meat industry "went ballistic," according to
Hershaft. Industry leaders and lobbyists brought out their
biggest guns to pressure McGovern and other committee members. All the arm-twisting brought on a new round of hearings
at which meat industry hacks padded the record with the red-
meat party line. The revised report recommended, "Eat less sat-

urated fat." Never since has a government publication used the word "meat" in such a dietary report.

Most of the time, agribusiness does not have to use its biggest muscles to get things done its way. The great bulk of pro-industry work is done through cozy relationships among lawmakers, government regulators, and industry leaders. A prime example is Rep. Robert Smith (R-OR), a cattle rancher who chairs the House Agriculture Committee and takes trips paid for by the National Cattlemen's Association, the American Meat Institute, and other industry groups. All bills relating to agriculture have to go through (and most are stopped by) his committee. According to CPI's "Safety Last," of the 336 bills that went to the committee and its Senate counterpart in 1995 and 1996, only 13 were enacted into law. One of the losers was the Family Food Protection Act, which would have modernized meat inspection.

A more visible example was the Espy/Tyson affair, which forced Secretary of Agriculture Mike Espy from office in 1994. It seems that while in office, Espy and his girlfriend traveled to Dallas Cowboys games as guests of Don Tyson, head of the world's largest poultry company, Tyson Foods, Inc. The girlfriend, Patricia Jensen, just happened to be an acting assistant agriculture secretary in charge of federal meat and poultry inspection at the time.

Much of the time, though, agribusiness uses its influence to get lawmakers and regulators to do nothing. When the carcinogenic growth hormone diethylstilbestrol (DES) was formally banned in 1979, cattlemen continued to use it illegally. And although numerous countries ban the use of antibiotics as feed additives, U.S. officials ignore the evidence of the drugs' threats to human health and food safety. Our officials won't stop the welfare-for-the-rich scheme that allows cattle ranching on public lands. They have been unable to stop Tyson's poultry factories from polluting the once-pristine waters of the Ozark region. In California, where huge dairy factories have made the state the nation's leading milk producer, officials have not stopped the widespread pollution of streams and groundwater. In the 1920s, Congress was able to break up the meatpacker monopolies, yet today it takes no action to dilute the ownership of 82 percent of the slaughter market by four giant meatpacking firms.

Merciless agribusiness is not content with power over supposedly neutral law- and policy-makers. It knows that the best of all worlds is to have ranchers, meatpackers, and the like sitting in the seats of power (as with Smith heading the House Agriculture Committee). If you serve its interests, the meat industry can offer you a career that moves you from government agency to industry to elected office and maybe back around again. In Washington they call it the "revolving door," and many a bureaucrat has ridden it for life. One was Lester Crawford, who went from head of the federal meat inspection service to a job as vice president for scientific affairs for the National Food Processors Association. Patrick Boyle went from heading the U.S. Department of Agriculture's (USDA) grading, inspection, and marketing program to the presidency of the American Meat Institute. Another AMI president, Richard Lyng, was Ronald Reagan's secretary of agriculture. According to CPI, "the meat industry has created one of Washington's most effective influence machines, partly by recruiting federal lawmakers and congressional aides for its lobbying juggernaut. Of the 124 lobbyists whom the Center has identified as working for the meat industry in 1997, at least 28 previously worked on Capitol Hill."

**Meat the Press**
One would think that such an arrogant use of power would stir up the wrath of the American media, those ever-vigilant watchdogs over truth, justice, and the disaster of the day. Guess what: they, too, are on the take from the agribusiness gravy train. Most of the gravy is in the form of big-budget advertising campaigns, like the dairy industry's "milk mustache" ads and the beef industry's "Beef: It's what you want" ads. These are paid for

through "check-off" programs supervised at the taxpayers' expense by the USDA. Under these, each time a farmer sells eggs, milk, or livestock, a cut of the check is sent to one of the industries' research and information boards. Most of the millions amassed are spent on slick advertising.

The collective agribusiness ad budgets are so huge that publishers and broadcasters quake at the thought of offending one of the industries. In 1991 the *Des Moines Register* suffered an advertising boycott by meat producers after the paper ran a full-page ad by People for the Ethical Treatment of Animals (PETA) likening meat production to murderer Jeffrey Dahmer's serial killings. The paper's owner, Charles Edwards, Jr., caved in, saying, "The PETA advertisement produced widespread unhappiness in the agriculture community that resulted in dropped subscriptions and a decision by the Iowa Livestock Market Association [ILMA] to pull its advertising." Since ILMA had been spending more than $1 million a year on classified ads in the *Register*, Edwards asked the boycotters to change their minds. In 1990, after singer k.d. lang appeared in a television spot as part of PETA's "Meat Stinks" campaign, chains of country music stations in Nebraska, Kansas, and other cattle-producing states joined in pulling lang's records from their playlists. The case of Jane Akre and Steve Wilson illustrates the power of corporate clout over the media. In 1996, the two journalists for a Fox Television affiliate in Tampa, Florida, began studying rBGH, the genetically modified growth hormone American dairies have been injecting into their cows. Their investigation revealed that the drug had been approved by the U.S. government without adequately testing its effects on children. They found other studies that linked the drug to cancer in humans. Just before their report was to broadcast, Monsanto, the hormone's manufacturer, threatened Fox News with "dire consequences" if the stories were aired. Under pressure from Fox lawyers, Akre and Wilson rewrote the story more than 80 times. After threats of dismissal and offers of six-figure sums to drop their ethical objections and keep quiet, the two were fired in December 1997. Akre has won a judgment against the station for violation of Florida's Whistleblower Law, but it is being appealed by Fox Television.

Perhaps the greatest suppression of information ever orchestrated by the meat industry was the dirty tricks operation against Jeremy Rifkin and his Beyond Beef campaign. His plan was to set up 500 action committees all over the United States and to distribute leaflets at 3,000 McDonald's restaurants in 1993. Rifkin himself won't say much about it, but Ronnie Cummins, who directed the campaign with rancher-turned-activist Howard Lyman, says that Rifkin got death threats. Beef industry operatives managed to get details of Rifkin's lecture and talk show itinerary in advance, and then just before his scheduled appearance, one of them would call the host to say that Rifkin had to cancel. When Rifkin showed up for the appearance, the hosts had already booked a replacement.

Industry operatives also hired "Bud," a former intelligence agent and the man who reportedly induced Fran Trutt to plant a bomb at U.S. Surgical Corporation headquarters in Connecticut in the 1980s. Bud spied on Rifkin and the Beyond Beef campaign office and activists, and stole lists and information. In the end, the meat industry was well prepared, says Cummins. "On the eve of the McDonald's action, they were able to get the local media to run stories the day before. This co-opted coverage, because editors felt that they had already 'done' the meat controversy when the April 17 action started. So the action was no surprise, was not considered news, and got little coverage."

Cummins points also to the now-famous food libel laws as another example of how agri-power over the media suppresses information. First enacted in Colorado in 1991 and now law in some 13 states, these laws make it a crime to disparage agricultural products. Cummins says that "the food industry cynically knows that these are unconstitutional, but they forge ahead anyway because they know that they work. Truth is no longer the driving editorial consideration; it is the cost of legal fees and lawsuits." As a result, publishers and broadcasters are re-writing stories, killing stories, or avoiding issues altogether for fear of being sued.

Fortunately, Rifkin's efforts continue. He believes that the agribusiness and pharmaceutical industries are exploding into a giant new superindustrial complex, which he calls the "life sciences industry" (see his 1998 book, *The Biotech Century*). "We are on the eve of a new order of exploitation, a new order of power over nature," Rifkin says. Our use of fossil fuels began changing the world a century ago, but the new life sciences industry's control over the gene threatens even greater changes: It will take control of evolution and shape it and sell it for profit. It will have the ultimate power, Rifkin warns—power over the processes and direction of life on earth.

If that notion seems hazy, it can be explained in dollars and cents. Says Rifkin, "The concentration of power is impressive. The top ten agrochemical companies control 81 percent of the $29 billion global agrochemical market. Ten life sciences companies control 37 percent of the $15 billion per year global seed market. The world's ten major pharmaceutical companies control 47 percent of the $197 billion pharmaceutical market. Ten global firms now control 43 percent of the $15 billion veterinary pharmaceutical trade. Topping the life science list are ten transnational food and beverage companies whose combined sales exceeded $211 billion in 1995."

## Early Brainwashing
So that these moneyed meat magnates may enjoy even greater profits in the generations to come, they make it a point to "reach the children of the land at an early age," as the National Livestock and Meat Board put it in one of their annual reports, and to "prepare them for a lifetime of meat-eating."

For generations, the American Meat Institute, the National Livestock and Meat Board, the American Dairy Association, the National Dairy Council, the American Egg Board (AEB), and other such industry groups and their state counterparts have purveyed their "educational materials" to the nation's classrooms. Many people may remember the materials from their own school years: The "Four Food Groups" (of which two were animal products), sponsored by the USDA under who knows how much lobbying and inside maneuvering by meat industry operatives; the pie charts and other visual aids that exaggerated the value of meat, milk, and eggs in our diet; the coloring books, games, videos, and films that supposedly taught all about the origins of meat, milk, and eggs. By any objective criteria, these materials would be judged as pure propaganda—the purpose of which is to deceive young children about the facts of life on animal farms. In general, they avoid any mention of killing, and the animals are depicted as smiling creatures having fun in barns, fields, and trucks. A coloring book about eggs, for example, shows pictures of smiling hens tending to their broods of baby chicks on cozy straw nests, and its text was approved by the AEB. Surely the AEB officials know that the nation's eggs come from caged hens who never see straw, let alone hatch chicks.

Why, then, one might ask, would animal activists be barred from bringing honest and accurate materials into the schools? The answer is obvious: children would be upset by the violence, suffering, and killing involved in the making of their school lunchmeat and they would stop eating it. By the next day, parents would be upset, and soon some school officials' heads would be rolling.

Although the industries have taken some flack for such blatant salesmanship, and because propaganda loses its effect when the victims learn its source, animal agribusiness has learned to ride on the enduring iconic appeal of the American family farmer (whom, in one of the great ironies of our time, agribusiness has virtually wiped out). One of the slickest new programs is carried out by high school-age Future Farmers of America (FFA) members. These older students take lambs, piglets, chicks, and the like into the elementary classrooms, where of course they make a big hit with younger children. In such a state, the younger kids are wide open to the message: These animals grow up and become food, which farmers sell in order to make a living.

This, of course, is the basic premise that animal advocates challenge and oppose. Some oppose it at the personal level by going vegan. Some become activists, engaging in protests, lobbying, working the media, and doing all kinds of things to puncture the myths peddled by animal agribusiness. In choosing a level of personal commitment and involvement, one should keep in mind that animal agriculture is the cornerstone of all animal exploitation. When domestication and husbandry began nearly 10,000 years ago, they spawned the idea that animals were put here as slaves to serve human purposes. Ever since, our way of relating to animals has been to exploit the useful ones and control or eliminate the rest. Also, the new life sciences industries will, if they succeed, push animal slavery to even greater intensity and massive scale via the use of genetic engineering, cloning, etc.

Knowing how influential and powerful agribusiness interests are may make some people angry and fearful for the future of life on earth—animal, human, and otherwise. For those who want to do something, it will help to get beyond being overwhelmed and intimidated by the enormity and mercilessness of agri-power. Knowledge is power: start learning.

*Special thanks to Mary Finelli, Tracie Reiman of People for the Ethical Treatment of Animals, and Karen Davis of United Poultry Concerns.*

# 6: Victims of Apathy

DAVID J. CANTOR

A STEEL HOOK through the mouth, the wound ripped in the struggle to survive, slow death by suffocation or repeated blows to the head, nets hauling thousands to suffocate in heaps: These are the well-known assaults against billions of fish sold for food each year.

Industry, government, and other literature typically consider these complex animals a "harvest," quantifying the dead by weight, not by number of individuals: a record 9.5 billion pounds "landed" by the U.S. industry alone in 1991, 253 billion pounds by the world industry in 1990. The United Nations Food and Agriculture Organization (FAO) reports that world production of fish, crustaceans, and mollusks reached 117.1 million tons in 1998, a decrease of 4.3 percent from 1997. It projects production of 107 to 144 million tons for 2010.

Commercial fishing has devastated populations of cod, flounder, and haddock—popular species for eating—and has caused extensive environmental damage. The destructive impact of the fishing industry prompted a study by the National Research Council, published in 1999 under the title "Sustaining Marine Fisheries." Meanwhile, humans have begun to eat more fish, mistakenly believing that they need to ingest some form of animal protein and that fish flesh is better for them than chicken or cow flesh.

Less widely known, and now bringing to the marketplace more fish than lost through recent overfishing, is the modern fish aquaculture facility where most trout, catfish, and many others eaten in the United States originate. To meet increased demand—which the industry helps to create through propaganda like that which has kept other animal food products popular, despite the ever-increasing cruelty of production—millions of fish are subject to the same intensive production as chickens, turkeys, calves, and other land animals. Aquaculture is estimated to account for upwards of 20 percent of the human-operated fish industry. Of the fish production anticipated for 2010, the FAO says, "Most of the increase in fish production is expected to come from aquaculture, which is growing rapidly."

"The trend in modern aquaculture," writes Peter Limburg in his prescient "how-to," *Farming the Waters*, "is toward large-scale, highly mechanized, specialized production, much like the chicken industry. In fact, the chicken industry is one that aquaculturists hold up as a model to work toward." He explains, "Fish are a crop just as much as hogs, chickens, or corn, and the greater poundage the fish farmer can produce in the shortest period of time, the more profit he will clear."

One man who learned mass production of animals in the poultry industry later started a $5 million fish farm in Mississippi, naming it SeaChick. SeaChick advertises live tilapia sold to supermarkets from a fish farm using above-ground, circular concrete tanks, geothermal water, liquid oxygen, and computer feeding. It claims to use no fish meal and no antibiotics—supposed advantages, since the use of fish meal diminishes the extent to which aquaculture can replace free-swimming fish, and the use of antibiotics brings problems similar to those of mixing the drugs into chickens', hogs', and other land animals' feed.

Fish factory farms keep five or more 12-ounce (a popular eating size) trout per cubic foot of water in enormous concrete pools called "raceways." About 95 percent of the trout eaten in America are intensively raised in raceways. There are attempts to increase the number of fish per cubic foot as much as possible due to the high cost of land and the enormous amounts of water required to operate a fish farm—some companies need millions of gallons of new water each day.

Diseases spread rapidly in water. In the same way that increased use of antibiotics in land animals threatens human populations, so antibiotics in the water can cause bacteria to become resistant to drugs, producing even more disease. Yet the amount of antibiotics used in aquaculture is not regulated. Densely crowded and unable to seek shade or cooler water, many factory-farmed fish suffer from oxygen depletion due to heat. Workers may not know that oxygen is low until they observe fish gulping for air at the surface. By then it is too late: the fish are so severely stressed that they soon die. Those who survive are more vulnerable to disease.

Fish in raceways are subject to gas-bubble disease, akin to "the bends" in human beings. In human divers, higher-than-normal atmospheric pressure causes nitrogen to dissolve in the bloodstream. Returning to normal pressure upon regaining the surface, a diver experiences excruciating pain when bubbles lodge in the joints. Some raceway conditions lead to supersaturation with nitrogen and other gases. Fish take in these gases but do not expel them. Bubbles form behind their eyes, under their skin, and in their fins. Gas-bubble disease is often fatal.

Fish factory farming causes other animals to suffer, too. Organic waste from raceways and tanks can carry diseases and parasites to fish in the wild. In addition, large open pools of live fish attract egrets, hawks, and other birds who naturally eat fish. Fish companies hire people to kill the birds. In one documented case, a California company with a U.S. Fish and Wildlife Service permit to shoot 50 birds annually throughout the late 1980s was estimated to have unlawfully killed 10,000 to 15,000 birds, including many species not listed on the permit. Poison is also sometimes used to kill fish-eating birds.

Many fish raised for food are killed and quickly refrigerated or frozen before shipping, but many are transported live to processing plants. Live transport of fish requires extremely expensive equipment. Live fish used for food are regularly trucked and transported by jet for breeding purposes. Trucks used to transport live fish are equipped with mechanically aerated, temperature-controlled tanks with monitors for oxygen and ammonia levels. Smaller shipments of fish go in plastic bags.

Like humans, fish suffer from motion sickness. Before travel, they are deprived of food for 24 hours. This is to prevent vomiting, which would foul the water and, on a long trip, kill the fish. The new and frightening environment of the transport tank produces stress, so tranquilizers are added to the water to calm the fish and to keep them from injuring themselves against the sides of the tank in their natural effort to escape. If temperature-control equipment fails, hundreds or thousands of fish can die before the vehicle reaches its destination. And, as with other animals kept captive and exploited, vehicular crashes and other disasters subject fish to suffering and death on a much larger scale than would be the case if these nondomestic animals were not needlessly removed from their natural habitats for human purposes.

Treating fish as if they do not suffer—or as if their suffering is not worth considering—manifests blatant speciesism. Because humans' affinity for fish is less developed than for dogs, cats, sheep, monkeys, apes, and some other land animals, we have all the more reason to assume that fish were made to suffer when we see them beside a lemon wedge on a restaurant plate or on a heap of shaved ice in the supermarket. And all the more reason not to eat them.

# 7: A Holiday Fish Story

BETH GEISLER

IN THE MOVIE *You've Got Mail*, the character played by Meg Ryan rallies to protect her small, endangered family bookshop from the character played by Tom Hanks and his menacing chain of discount bookstores. At an upscale holiday party, the popular protagonists shoot barbs at one another over the buffet—all the while competing for a mere spoonful or two of caviar that garnishes a side dish. In this scene, far more than the bookshop is endangered. The garnish, it turns out, requires protection as well.

In September 2000, the World Conservation Union included several species of caviar-producing sturgeon—including the European (beluga), Russian, and stellate sturgeons—on the Red List of Threatened Species, the most comprehensive analysis of global conservation to date. This is grim foreshadowing for the amazing fish, who can grow to weigh more than 1,000 pounds and live well over 100 years. Hundreds of millions of years old, the species predated and has outlived the dinosaurs. With enthusiasm for caviar—the sturgeon's unfertilized roe, or eggs—at an all-time high, the fish today could be decimated by the demands of the fashionable human taste bud.

Demand for caviar peaks during the holidays. Like the Russian variety, highly prized Iranian caviar comes from the Caspian Sea, a region that produces more than 90 percent of the world's caviar. The decline in the sturgeon population in the Caspian Sea has been notable since the 1970s, and the number of adult sturgeons is estimated to have declined more than 70 percent between 1978 and 1995. Between 1995 and 1997, catch figures dropped an additional 36 percent. The latest numbers confirm this alarming trend: Russia's State Fishing Committee reported in 2000 that their spring sturgeon catch represented a 60 percent drop from 1999, and scientists estimated that the adult sturgeon population, which numbered 1.5 million in 1986, had fallen below 300,000. The population is being harvested at rate that can be sustained for only a few more years.

Today, many varieties of Russian or Iranian caviar can cost more than $100 per ounce, a rate connoisseurs seem ready and willing to pay. And with their dollars they will support fishing and poaching practices that earn an "R" rating for violence. To obtain the roe, fishermen beat the sturgeon on the back of the head, tear open her belly, and remove the sack of eggs. There is no efficient, inexpensive way to remove the eggs without killing the fish. Traditional fishing operations sell the sturgeon meat for human consumption, mostly in Europe; poachers simply discard the fish's body after taking the roe.

One female can produce hundreds of pounds of roe. One record-size beluga sturgeon who weighed 2,200 pounds produced nearly 400 pounds of caviar. Sturgeons who produce the most commercially desirable caviars—beluga, osetra, and sevruga—have become threatened with extinction primarily because of the growing illegal trade. In the decade since the breakup of the Soviet Union, poaching for these varieties in the Caspian Sea has become commonplace. In the frenzy to cash in on the caviar craze, poachers have hooked, netted, and killed many male sturgeons as well as females not yet of reproductive age, leaving the carcasses to rot. Because of their late sexual maturation, which can occur as late as 25 years for beluga females, indiscriminate killing is a serious threat to the species.

According to the U.S. Fish and Wildlife Service (USFWS), international law enforcement agencies report that the illegal wildlife trade is second only to the illegal drug trade in volume and profit. The agency estimates that the total trade in caviar is around $125 million, more than half of which is illegal. According to *The New York Times*, caviar experts estimated that by the close of 2000, the legal yield would be around 160 tons from all producing countries.

Following an investigation initiated by the USFWS, a Maryland caviar importer agreed in 2000 to pay a $10.4 million fine for smuggling illegal caviar into the country and passing off domestic roe as Russian caviar. The fine is the biggest ever in a federal wildlife case. But even with efforts by the U.S. government and the Convention on International Trade in Endangered Species (CITES) to protect the sturgeon, including checks by wildlife inspectors for valid CITES permits and even DNA analysis to confirm the species of origin of a given shipment, buyers still stand to be bamboozled by bogus beluga. And, more importantly, whether or not their contents are poached or smuggled, caviar tins will never qualify for the cruelty-free label.

Overfishing and poaching of sturgeon will stop only when consumer demand for caviar stops. During the holidays, when selecting a delectable treat or a gift for someone who has everything, pass up the caviar. In this fish story, the only happy ending for the sturgeon is, well, no ending.

# Part 6

# ANIMALS IN SCIENCE
# AND EDUCATION

# 1: Vivisection: A Window to the Dark Ages of Sciences

DON BARNES

MANY PEOPLE, FROM college professors to talk-show hosts, continue to scratch their heads and misuse the word "vivisection." *The American Heritage Dictionary* defines vivisection as "the act of cutting into or dissecting the body of a living animal, especially for the purpose of scientific research." However, this narrow definition does not reflect the scope of vivisection practices. When a psychologist puts a chicken on a hot plate and compares the number of seconds the bird remains there before and after being given a drug, he or she is obviously engaging in vivisection. Therefore the definition should be expanded to include any invasive use of nonhuman animals for research, testing, or education.

The definition should also encompass nonhuman animals placed in cages in anticipation of their use as test subjects. After all, the very freedom of these animals is being severely curtailed. Vivisection also refers to the violation (for alleged scientific study) of any basic right accorded to a nonhuman animal to live unfettered, without being used as a tool and without being subjected to stress, pain, suffering, or death for the hypothetical sake of another species or another individual.

Animal exploiters are fond of pointing to a phenomenon that they perceive to be an inconsistency within the animal advocacy movement: While there is constant and impassioned objection to vivisection, and laboratory atrocities are luridly described in fundraising literature, there has been only a relatively small murmur in defense of animals raised for food, who constitute the huge majority of exploited creatures. This observation is not without merit, although more and more voices are now being heard on behalf of the veal calf, the layer or broiler chicken, etc. Historically, however, vivisection has been the practice most publicly decried, as witnessed by the formation of anti-vivisection societies nearly 200 years ago.

Although the reasons for this imbalance of outrage are not entirely clear, one reason may be that vivisection is so deliberate. A nonhuman animal is imprisoned with a clear intent on behalf of the vivisector to inflict stress, pain, suffering, and/or death. Because domestication of animals for food and clothing has been traditional throughout human history, people have become inured to it, and (at least subconsciously) have accepted it because of the belief that "we've always done it and we always will." Vivisection, by contrast, is a relatively new industry, coming into vogue after World War II and escalating rapidly for the next 40 years, showing signs of tapering off and maintaining some degree of stability throughout the 1990s, and then rocketing upward with the advent of genetic engineering.

**Numbers**

The exact number of nonhuman animals used in vivisection each year is not known. The Office of Technology Assessment estimated in 1986 that 17 to 22 million animals are used in U.S. laboratories annually, but private companies and universities that do not receive federal funding may not report all animal use. Ninety-five percent of the nonhuman animals used in laboratory research are mice and rats, and these species (as well as birds and "farm" animals) are not covered under the Animal Welfare Act. It is not unrealistic to assume that at least 40 million sentient creatures are sacrificed in the "temples of science" each year in the United States.

The underlying concept of vivisection is simple: A rat is a pig is a dog is a boy. The entire industry relies on the assumption that biological, physiological, and behavioral phenomena are common across family, genus, species, and even gender lines. For example, researchers assume that by studying a rat they can learn about humans. The term "extrapolation" is used to denote the scientific concept of predictability across these barriers. It is simply assumed that mammalian similarities are sufficient to counteract species differences, even in the face of significant evidence to the contrary.

Nonhuman animals are used to study human responses because the biomedical research community holds a narrow ethic that only includes humans. All through the dark ages of science, other humans (the retarded, the imprisoned, the orphaned, the dispossessed, and members of minority groups) have been used as human guinea pigs. Following the Nuremberg Trials, new ethical guidelines were established to include all humans but to specifically exclude all nonhumans. The rationale was basic: scientists' curiosity about the effects of radiation, poisons, heat or cold sources, brain damage, ocular irritants, etc. (the list is endless) cannot be satisfied with human subjects; consequently the focus shifts to nonhumans who currently have no inviolate legal rights.

Has vivisection led to cures for cardiovascular disease, cancer, stroke, diabetes, or AIDS? The answer is obvious: it has not. Millions of animals have suffered and died in our "War on Cancer," but a human being is more likely to contract cancer today than at any time in history. In the May 8, 1986, edition of *The New England Journal of Medicine*, epidemiologists John C. Bailer III and Elaine M. Smith reported that the mortality rates for more than 98 percent of all human cancers were the same as or worse than they were 40 years before, a finding that remains valid today. For the remaining less than two percent, treatment expectations are higher, but if one examines this finding carefully, successful treatment can be traced to the study of drug and radiation therapies in human patients, not other animals.

As another example, there is no nonhuman animal model for AIDS. After infecting more than 100 chimpanzees with HIV-1, only a single animal progressed to an actual AIDS condition. Although a chimpanzee shares almost 99 percent of human DNA, the differences between this endangered species and *homo sapiens* are obviously more significant than the similarities when it comes to specific disease mechanisms.

The biomedical research community makes dozens of unsupported claims regarding the efficacy of animal research. The truth is that vivisection is based on a faulty premise; despite some similarities between mammals, the vast differences negate the hoped-for extrapolative properties. This results in the vivisectors' failure to understand human disease processes, and causes a significant number of humans to suffer through treatments found "safe" with nonhuman animals, while a potentially greater number may be denied effective treatments because they did not pass animal-based tests.

If the goal of a health-care system is to ensure the best health for the greatest number of people, prevention of disease should be a primary focus; unfortunately it is not. Bailar, Smith, Drs. Neal Barnard and Michael Klaper, medical writer Steven Tiger, and scores of other medical professionals have urged the biomedical research community to concentrate efforts on preventive measures. Little more than lip service is paid to this pressing need, and scientists continue to search through the haystacks of conflicting data from nonhuman animals in the vain hope of finding "magic bullet" cures. In that futile search, they spend billions of dollars that could well be used to help people live healthier and more productive lives.

If one can extend his or her ethical considerations beyond anthropocentricity to include other forms of life, the question of the efficacy of vivisection becomes moot. As one of my fellow animal rights activist friends never tires of telling me, "Don, I realize you can competently refute the claims of the vivisector that the use of nonhuman animals is critical to the health of our population, and you can do so with facts and logic. But you miss the point entirely: the fact is that the practice of vivisection is morally wrong."

# 2: A Current View of Vivisection: Animal Research in America

Martin L. Stephens

F EW ISSUES AROUSE more passion among animal rights activists than vivisection, the practice of using live animals for invasive and/or manipulative research, testing, and educational exercises. Activists have vigorously challenged animal-based experiments carried out by universities, primate centers, the military, and cosmetics companies, as well as the use of live and dead animals in the classroom. In the United States, this opposition began more than 100 years ago, and was reinvigorated during the late 1970s and early 1980s when vivisection emerged as a key issue in the modern animal rights movement.

Despite the contentiousness of animal experimentation and all that has been written about it, there is no thorough profile of this practice within the United States. Knowing the who, what, when, where, how, and why of vivisection would not only address public concern about the practice, but would also help in identifying the best priorities for future reform and evaluating the long-term impact of past campaigns.

Vivisection takes place in both publicly and privately funded facilities, ranging from taxpayer-financed government agencies to pharmaceutical companies. Laboratories that use animals covered by the Animal Welfare Act (AWA) fall under the jurisdiction of the U.S. Department of Agriculture (USDA), which is responsible for enforcing the AWA. In addition, the National Institutes of Health (NIH) oversees labs that receive NIH/Public Health Service funding according to its policy and guidebook concerning the care and use of animals in labs. Facilities that are not monitored by the government include those that do not receive NIH funding and do not use USDA-regulated animals (e.g., a biotech company that uses mice only). The principal mechanism for protecting animals in labs is the USDA/AWA. The AWA regulates some aspects of animal experimentation; however, it has little impact on actual experimental procedures.

Information about laboratories and the animals they use is published each year in the USDA's "Animal Welfare Report." Unfortunately, the reports are grossly incomplete and sometimes misleading. They contain no information about the use of reptiles, amphibians, fish, or invertebrate animals, none of whom are covered by the AWA. The reports also lack information about birds and laboratory-bred mice and rats, which the USDA excludes from AWA coverage. The only animals who are currently covered by AWA regulations are dogs, cats, rabbits, guinea pigs, hamsters, nonhuman primates, mammalian "farm" animals, and miscellaneous mammals such as ferrets.

Apart from the USDA reports, most other sources of information about animal experimentation are usually too fragmentary to be of much use in compiling a nationwide profile (e.g., annual reports that research facilities file with the USDA, which are available through the FOIA). These facility reports can be useful to local activists who may be monitoring a specific facility. The following information is compiled mostly from the USDA's composite annual report from 2000, the most recent year for which specific information is available.

## Species and Numbers of Animals
Given the limited number of species tracked by the USDA, the total number of animals used annually in U.S. laboratories can

only be estimated. Since 1986 the figure cited most often by the Congressional Office of Technology Assessment is 17 to 22 million vertebrate animals. This excludes the estimated several million animals (primarily frogs) used in pre-college dissection and vivisection and not covered by the AWA. The overall figure may have risen since 1986 because of the increasing use of genetically engineered mice.

Reliable figures on the different types of animals used in laboratories are limited to the USDA-regulated species. For 2000, these figures are as follows (rounded to the nearest thousand):

| | |
|---|---|
| Guinea pigs: | 505,000 |
| Rabbits: | 259,000 |
| Hamsters: | 174,000 |
| Farm animals: | 160,000 |
| Dogs: | 70,000 |
| Nonhuman primates: | 58,000 |
| Cats: | 26,000 |
| Other: | 166,000 |

Mice and rats account for approximately 85 percent of the vertebrate animals used (based on data from overseas and from early U.S. surveys), but are not included in USDA statistics. However, if we use 17 to 22 million as the total number of animals, then simple math shows that 85 percent of 17 to 22 million total animals works out to 14.5 to 18.7 million mice and rats.

Experimenters themselves usually decide which species of animals they will use. In theory, their choice is based on perceived scientific suitability (e.g., similarity to human physiology). In practice, it is also influenced by other factors, such as the cost of purchase and housing (random-source vs. purpose-bred animals), the history of the field in question (experimenters often stick with the most commonly used species), the researcher's training (again, using familiar species), and animal availability (species to which experimenters have access).

## Trends in Species and Usage

In the mid-1990s, a Tufts University report estimated that animal use in U.S. laboratories had decreased between 23 and 40 percent in the last 20 years. This estimate was somewhat speculative given the lack of reliable data on non-USDA-regulated animals (mice, rats, birds, reptiles, amphibians, and fish). However, the data on USDA-regulated species largely support the Tufts conclusion. For most of these animals, usage peaked in the mid-1980s. Since then, the numbers for rabbits, hamsters, dogs, and cats have declined between 52 and 64 percent. Only primate use has remained more or less the same. Interestingly, the use of guinea pigs declined by 56 percent from the mid-80s until 1999; however, guinea pig use increased 40 percent between 1999 and 2000. For all of these species taken together, use has declined 42 percent since the mid-1980s. The reason for this decline is not evident; it may be attributable to technological advances, economics, an increased acceptance of animals' rights, or other factors.

The USDA also keeps statistics on wild animals, "farm" animals, and others, but these are difficult to interpret. Wild animals (most of whom are wild-caught) such as armadillos were counted as such through 1989, after which they were lumped in a new category ("other") along with miscellaneous species and voluntarily reported data on mice and rats. "Farm" animals (mostly pigs, sheep, and goats) started to be counted only in 1990.

## Number and Types of Research Facilities

According to the USDA, there were 1,231 active research facilities in 2000 that conducted experiments on regulated animals. Prior to 1997, the USDA broke down the total number of facilities into two groups: federal and nonfederal. (Federal facilities include those run by the Department of Defense, the National Institutes of Health, the Food and Drug Administration, and other federal agencies.) In 1996, federal facilities accounted for

12 percent (171) of all facilities. Though the USDA no longer provides a breakdown of federal versus nonfederal facilities, they do distinguish between numbers of animals at federal versus nonfederal facilities. For 2000, these numbers were 117,019 (8.3 percent) and 1,299,624 (91.7 percent), respectively. Interestingly, federal facilities accounted for a whopping 25 percent of all "farm" animals used in 2000.

To gain a better idea of the types of facilities that experiment on animals, The Humane Society of the United States (HSUS) classified the labs listed in the USDA's 1995 compendium of registered research facilities into three categories: nonprofit facilities (universities, colleges, hospitals, medical centers, research institutes, and others); commercial facilities (manufacturing companies, contract testing laboratories, veterinary clinics, and others); and government facilities (state health departments and others). The aim of such categorization was to identify gross trends.

Nonprofits accounted for approximately 50 percent of the total number of facilities, commercial facilities for 35 percent, and government facilities for 15 percent. It is not known if these figures reflect the relative amounts of animal research conducted at each type of facility, but it was estimated that nonprofits account for 45 percent of animal use, commercial facilities for 40 percent, and government facilities for 15 percent—a close fit to what would be expected from looking at the relative abundance of the various facility types.

**Experimental Purposes**
Animal use in biomedical laboratories can be classified in three broad categories: research, product development and safety testing, and education and training. Each of these areas can take many forms. Research can be "applied"—aimed (ostensibly) at advancing the diagnosis, understanding, treatment, or prevention of an existing medical problem—or it can be "basic" or "fundamental"—aimed (for example) at learning more about

how the body works, without necessarily addressing a specific medical problem. Product development and safety testing (hereafter "testing") includes assessing the safety and effectiveness of drugs, consumer products, and other substances. (Some observers would include only safety assessment under testing, and consider effectiveness assessment under research.) Education and training (hereafter "education") include classroom dissection (dead animals) and vivisection (live animals), as well as animal use in teaching or learning such biomedical techniques as surgery. In reality, the three categories of research, testing, and education can overlap, and there are many gray areas.

**Types of Protocols**

Some of the more infamous vivisection projects from recent decades include Harry Harlow's maternal deprivation experiments on monkeys, Edward Taub's nerve-damage experiments on monkeys, and Thomas Gennarelli's head-injury experiments on baboons. Other well-known targets of past animal rights protests include military research (such as Michael Carey's head-shooting experiments on cats) and space research (including the National Aeronautics and Space Administration's BION project, which involves sending monkeys into space).

Based on available data, most animal research takes place at universities, medical centers, and other nonprofit organizations. It is funded by the federal government, primarily the National Institutes of Health, whose research budget in 2001 was $20.3 billion, derived wholly from taxpayer funds. Approximately one-half of the NIH budget funds research in some way involving animals. Private foundations, such as the Howard Hughes Medical Institute, also finance animal experiments. Numerous charities, including the American Heart Association, the American Cancer Society, the March of Dimes, and the Muscular Dystrophy Association, all fund vivisection as well.

## Testing

Animal-based product testing methods have been widely publicized in recent years.

The LD50 test ("LD" stands for "lethal dose") entails poisoning mice and other animals with substances and estimating the amount that kills 50 percent of the animals. The Organization for Economic Cooperation and Development (OECD), an international trade group that consists of representatives from 30 industrialized countries, is on the verge of deleting the LD50 test from its official manual of test guidelines. In the short run, the LD50 test is being replaced by other animal tests that use fewer animals and cause less suffering. In the long run, cell-based procedures are likely to replace all animal use in this field of "acute toxicity" testing.

The Draize eye irritancy test involves putting substances into rabbits' eyes and then evaluating (but not treating) any resulting eye irritation. The Draize skin irritancy test is the counterpart of the Draize eye irritancy test and also involves rabbits. The standard cancer bioassay involves feeding mice and other animals large quantities of substances (e.g., saccharin) and trying to assess cancer-causing potential. The use of live animals to test personal care and cosmetics products is not required by law, a fact that has bolstered animal rights groups' successful efforts to pressure many companies into switching to non-animal methods.

Animals are also used to screen large numbers of potential drugs for their effectiveness in treating medical conditions. Much of this type of testing is conducted by pharmaceutical companies and other commercial facilities, and is funded by the companies themselves. The Food and Drug Administration claims that animal experiments are required for approvals of new drugs, but rules and policies about specific protocols can vary. Drug approvals are also based on clinical trials involving human subjects.

## Education

The only time most people come face to face with animal experimentation is in the classroom. Millions of dead animals (frogs,
sharks, fetal pigs, cats, pigeons, snakes, etc.) are routinely dis-
sected in high schools, colleges, and universities. Live animals
are also vivisected in the name of education, typically in col-
leges/universities, medical schools, and veterinary schools. In
medical school "dog labs," students inject drugs into live dogs
to observe already well-known effects on the heart and other
organs. The Physicians Committee for Responsible Medicine
estimates that two-thirds of all U.S. medical schools, including
Harvard, Stanford, Tufts, and Yale, have eliminated terminal
surgeries on live animals.

Animals are widely used in training exercises. In veterinary
schools, it is traditional and still common for students to practice surgery on live, healthy animals. However, since 1998, six
veterinary schools—Tufts University, Cornell University, the
University of California at Davis, the University of
Pennsylvania, the University of Florida, and the University of
Wisconsin—have decided to end terminal surgical exercises in
their core curriculum. In training courses on Advanced
Pediatric Life Support (APLS) for paramedics and other medical
personnel, trainees often practice intubation (inserting a
breathing tube into the windpipe) using anesthetized cats. In
military wound labs, anesthetized goats are shot and subjected
to other simulated battle wounds, and then treated by medical
trainees.

## Pain and Distress

The USDA's annual reports divide animal use into three categories based ostensibly on how much pain and distress are
caused by experimental procedures. The categories are: (1) no
pain or distress inflicted; (2) pain or distress relieved by drugs,
and (3) pain or distress not relieved by drugs. Unfortunately, it
is not clear which category applies to animals who experience

pain or distress despite the use of anesthetics or analgesics. Nor is it clear how much pain or distress the animals in the second or third categories actually experience. Research institutions sometimes hesitate to list procedures in the politically sensitive third category. Moreover, the categories do not account for any suffering that stems from barren and cramped housing conditions, rough handling, outright abuse, and other non-experimental causes. Notwithstanding these limitations, the 2000 USDA data indicate that 63 percent of regulated animals experienced no pain or distress, 29 percent had their pain or distress prevented or relieved by drugs, and eight percent experienced unrelieved pain and distress. These figures have varied little over the past several years.

## Life in the Laboratory

For the most part, animals' lives in laboratories are characterized by small and austere cages, limited contact with other members of their own species, and impersonal contact with humans. The result is often monotony, boredom, frustration, and anxiety, in addition to any pain or distress associated with the experimental procedures themselves.

Animals are typically housed indoors in rooms with no windows to the outside; there is little if any natural sunlight or fresh air. Most animals are kept in cages, not pens, runs, or other large enclosures. Cage sizes tend to be at or close to the legal minimums, which are indeed minimal. Food is usually in the form of chow pellets.

The animals are fed, watered, and given veterinary care, but little effort is made to enrich their lives. Their impersonal treatment ignores the fact that these animals are individuals with personalities and emotions, and that laboratory conditions can affect the outcome of experimental procedures.

Dogs and nonhuman primates are exceptions, at least according to the 1985 amendments to the Animal Welfare Act. Dogs are required to be given regular "opportunity to exercise," but unfortunately, the USDA left the specifics of this mandate up to the facilities themselves. Consequently, it is not known how often, for how long, and under what conditions dogs are given the opportunity to exercise, and whether the conditions are such that the dogs actually avail themselves of that opportunity. Any dogs housed in pairs or groups in regulation-sized enclosures do not have to be given opportunities to exercise.

The situation for primates is similar. The AWA calls for housing these animals in environments that promote their "psychological well-being" (PWB). Here again the USDA abdicated its responsibility: it merely identified some key aspects of PWB (e.g., contact with other members of the species), but left all of the details to the facilities themselves. Again, the extent to which primates are being housed in groups, infants are left with their mothers, cages/enclosures are enriched with devices that decrease boredom, etc is unknown. In 1999, the USDA did publish a draft policy on environmental enhancement for primates. It attempted to clarify what is expected of institutions in terms of environmental enhancement to promote psychological well-being of nonhuman primates. This policy was expected to be implemented by the end of 2001. However, on January 30, 2002, the Office of Management and Budget returned the policy to the USDA for reconsideration, thereby thwarting implementation. The USDA is expected to confer with the National Institutes of Health on the policy to iron out areas of disagreement and create an alternate policy for reconsideration. This process will likely weaken the policy considerably.

Fortunately, some progressive facilities are taking these mandates to heart and adopting a "best practices" approach to housing dogs and primates. Rather than simply opening a dog's cage and giving him/her the opportunity to explore a room, these facilities have their personnel interact with the dogs at exercise time. Similarly, rather than simply tossing a hard plastic ball into a monkey's cage as a diversion, some facilities are replacing individual housing with group housing and improving the animals' lives in a variety of ways. The added attention to dogs and primates is also having a positive spillover effect on the treatment of other species.

## Public Criticism and Concern

Many observers of the vivisection scene have a vague sense that the situation is changing for the better: that animal use (with the exception of mice) is generally dropping, that alternative approaches are gaining in popularity, that housing conditions are improving, etc. Defenders of animal experimentation are quick to point to indications of such positive changes. Ironically, the existing reporting system in the United States does a poor job of tracking this critical information. Observers can only sketch the barest outline of the status quo. This situation is completely unacceptable given the level of public concern about, and funding of, animal experiments.

The HSUS tried to remedy this situation in 1992 by submitting an administrative petition to the USDA, recommending a thorough overhaul of the current reporting system. The USDA took no action. In 1999, The HSUS renewed its call for changes in the reporting system, this time focusing on the widely criticized pain and distress classification system. The USDA seemed receptive and, in July 2000, solicited public input on making such changes. As of May, 2002 the USDA had not issued a formal proposal.

Concerned U.S. citizens can obtain information about vivisection by using the federal Freedom of Information Act to obtain documents about grants and laboratory inspection reports. The CRISP (Computer Retrieval of Information on Scientific Projects) and MEDLINE systems, accessible by computer, contain information about a facility's ongoing research and/or its government funding. Medical journals and similar periodicals also describe vivisection procedures and offer insight into who is doing what, and where, and why.

As long as vivisectors rely to a large extent on public support and funding, the issues of public accountability, disclosure, and concern for animal welfare and rights must be addressed.

# 3: The Business of Animal Research

JILL HOWARD CHURCH

IT IS NO wonder that many animals used in biomedical experiments are kept in cold, hard cages made of steel. That environment fits well with the cold, hard cash that buoys the animal research industry by creating a network of businesses that thrive on vivisection.

Unfortunately, any attempt to quantify exactly how many businesses profit from breeding and transporting animals, supplying food and cages, equipping the laboratories, and paying the salaries of researchers and caretakers is like counting bats in a dark cave: you know they exist by the hundreds, but they stay in the shadows and find safety in the lack of scrutiny.

By national standards, the vivisection industry is not overly large, but it is diverse and rather insular. Some businesses—breeders, dealers, and certain manufacturers—focus exclusively on supplying research and testing labs, while others—such as those selling equipment, food, and various supplies—devote only part of their overall market to animal experimentation.

"It's an industry that there's not much information about," admits John McArdle, Ph.D., director of the Alternatives Research & Development Foundation. "Industry [leaders] learned real early to keep their mouths shut."

Some of the secrecy is due to professional competition, so that businesses don't learn too much about each other. But Susan Gaines, a former educator with People for the Ethical Treatment of Animals (PETA), says another reason for the reticence, especially by breeders, stems from companies' desire to keep themselves as far from public view as possible. "It wouldn't be in their best interest for these numbers to be known," Gaines explains. "It makes people uncomfortable." Although polls show that most people still support many forms of vivisection, publicizing the numbers and types of animals harmed and killed in laboratories makes them think twice, which is something experimenters and their supporters don't encourage. Even when details do leak through to the public, Gaines says, "it's impossible for people to understand the sheer magnitude of the deaths involved."

A primary resource for those interested in seeing the big picture is *Lab Animal* magazine, published 11 times a year by Nature Publishing Company of New York. Perusing its pages or web site (www.labanimal.com) offers a glimpse into a world where dogs, rabbits, rats, mice, and the proverbial guinea pigs are advertised simply as products, described like machines with customized features. One such ad for Marshall Farms, which breeds beagles in the United States and Europe, touts the dogs' "predictable performance" and declares them "your best investment."

*Lab Animal's* 2001 online Buyer's Guide contains more than 800 products and services offered by more than 500 companies that sell animals, housing, cage accessories, food and supplements, diagnostic materials, equipment, surgical supplies, building furnishings, veterinary services, and more. The vast majority are private companies that are not required to disclose information about profits or production, so what follows are examples that offer at least partial insight:

**Breeders and Dealers**

According to the U.S. Department of Agriculture (USDA), the number of animals used in U.S. experiments during fiscal year 2000 was just over 1.4 million dogs, cats, rabbits, guinea pigs, hamsters, sheep, pigs, nonhuman primates, and "other" species.

However, this figure does not include the approximately 20 million rats, mice, and birds who are not currently covered under the federal Animal Welfare Act (and thus not reported), yet account for 95 percent of all animals used. All of these animals are classified as either purpose-bred, random-source (obtained from pounds or through other means), or wild-caught. In any case, breeders and suppliers rarely disclose exactly how many animals they turn out each year.

"There's no hard and fast studies on any of that," says Richard L. Crawford, D.V.M., former staff director and assistant deputy administrator for the U.S. Department of Agriculture's (USDA) Animal and Plant Health Inspection Service (APHIS). APHIS publishes an Animal Welfare Enforcement report every year that details the number and species of animals (excluding rats, mice, and some "farm" animals) used in U.S. labs.

In 2000, there were 4,612 USDA-licensed dealers selling animals to laboratories and the "pet" trade, up slightly from 4,325 such dealers in 1995. They are divided into two categories: Class A dealers, who sell only animals they breed themselves, and Class B dealers, who are not breeders but instead sell animals obtained from brokers, auctions, or other sources. There are currently 3,433 Class A dealers and 1,179 Class B dealers operating in the United States. APHIS reports that of these, 23 Class B dealers are involved in supplying cats and dogs for research, down from about twice that number in 1995.

Crawford says the number of Class B dealers has fallen, due in part to increased scrutiny of the animals' origins, including a "traceback" program conducted by APHIS. Numerous animal rights and welfare groups—including PETA, Last Chance for Animals, In Defense of Animals, and others—have documented cases in which Class B dealers obtained companion animals from people called "bunchers," who stole animals or obtained them fraudulently from "free to good home" ads or by other shady means. Crawford says some of the Class B dealers "have not been too truthful and honest in the past," and have kept poor records to conceal unscrupulous practices. Author Judith Reitman documented such abuses in her 1992 book, *Stolen for Profit*. The book also details the enormous profits reaped by Class B dealers, who buy animals for as little as $10 and then resell them to government agencies, universities, and hospitals for up to $500 apiece.

Because of the issue of pet theft, in 2001 Sen. Daniel Akaka (D-HI) introduced the Pet Safety and Protection Act (S. 668) into Congress, a measure that would ban Class B dealers from selling cats and dogs for research. As of Spring 2002, the bill is still pending.

Class A dealers, however, continue unaffected. According to Crawford, their numbers have remained fairly constant. The largest worldwide animal breeder is Charles River Laboratories, a former subsidiary of Bausch & Lomb that became an independent, publicly traded company in 1999. It specializes in breeding and selling more than 130 varieties of mice, rats, hamsters, gerbils, guinea pigs, rabbits, and miniature swine, and also sells veterinary and testing services. Founded in 1947, Charles River has 70 facilities in 15 countries and reported an income of $306.6 million for fiscal year 2000, up 33 percent over 1999. The company claims to be "number one in total market share in many of the niche markets that make up the approximately $1.7 billion biomedical products and services industry." Despite its position atop the purpose-bred pyramid, Charles River does not disclose exactly how many individual animals it "produces" each year.

Information about lab animal breeders "is a black hole, frankly," says Andrew Rowan, the former director of the Tufts University Center for Animals & Public Policy who now serves as senior vice president for Research, Education, and International Issues for The Humane Society of the United States. He says that extrapolation from what few statistics exist is about the only way to even guess at actual numbers.

"Anything that anybody has ever done [to estimate production or profits] is not based on primary information," Rowan says.

He cites studies indicating that the overall laboratory use of some animals is declining, but says companies like Charles

## Animal Prices

Charles River Laboratories is the world's largest breeder and supplier of animals used in biomedical experiments. Its annual report shows that 61.2 percent of its 2000 income came from "research models" (animals), sales of whom totaled $187.7 million. Biomedical products and services brought the company another $118.9 million for the same year. Some sample prices (per animal, depending on size, age, sex, and variety):

Inbred mice: $10 to $41.95; lactating mouse with litter: up to
    $120.60
Transgenic mice: $75 to 220
Inbred rats: $14 to $72.05
Hamsters: $8.65 to $20.85
Gerbils: $10.15 to $13.25
Guinea pigs: $33.25 to $148.20
New Zealand white rabbits: $60.85 to $132.35
Miniature swine: $345 to $795

For an additional charge, Charles River will surgically alter animals before they arrive at the laboratory door. Forty-two different options are offered. For $10.05, technicians will give a rat a vasectomy; to give the same animal a bilateral brain cannulation costs $96.45. To inject a single rat with a drug to induce an Alzheimer's-like illness costs $160. Putting a carotid artery catheter in a mouse costs $64.80 per animal; for a guinea pig, $57.85.

River still profit well because they sell highly specialized animals with altered genes and other physical attributes. "Fewer units [animals] are being sold," he explains, "but they're more expensive. In the old days, you could buy a mouse for $1—now it's $15 a mouse." (See "Animal Prices.")

In 1989, the Connecticut-based Theta Corporation prepared an independent marketing report on the sale of animals to laboratories. The report included detailed profiles of the market shares and sales estimates of the nation's largest animal breeders, including Charles River, the Buckshire Corporation, Harlan Sprague Dawley, Hazelton Research Products, and Taconic. It reported that in 1988, 27.5 million animals were "produced" and sold for an industry-wide total of $209 million. The company projected an annual market growth rate of between eight and nine percent a year, estimating that by 1995, 48.1 million animals would be sold for $338 million. Because the company never did a follow-up study, it is not known whether any of its projections are accurate. The advent of cloning, genetic engineering, and xenotransplantation has created sizeable new markets for purpose-bred animals.

**Staff and Stuff**
The business of animal research follows the same supply-and-demand principles of other industries. Breeders and other suppliers simply respond to the markets available to them. The USDA licenses all non-governmental research facilities, including hospitals, colleges and universities, diagnostic and contract testing labs, and private corporations such as those who make pharmaceuticals and medical/household products. According to APHIS, there were 1,231 such facilities as of 2000, with many facilities operating at multiple sites.

Corporations and other private laboratories do not publicly itemize the cost of running their laboratories. As for colleges and universities, Ray Greek, M.D.—a former researcher who came to oppose vivisection—claims they profit well from housing animal laboratories. Now president of Americans for Medical Advancement, Greek once worked as a technician in a University of Alabama psychology lab, and says that lucrative research grants are used to pay for more than just gloves and guinea pigs. "When a Ph.D. gets a $100,000 grant to look at obese mice," he explains, "the university's going to take 25 percent of that off the top" to pay for salaries, work space, and even programs in other departments that have nothing to do with animal research. "The university really profits from having a successful researcher on board."

The National Institutes of Health (NIH) is the nation's largest funder of medical research, distributing enormous sums of money through grants and federal programs. Its research

## Monkey Markets

In 2000, U.S. laboratories used 57,518 nonhuman primates for research, testing, and teaching at registered and federal sites. These monkeys and apes are bred at domestic and foreign facilities, and are also taken from the wild. The USDA reports that 25,029 of these primates were used in experiments "with pain or distress" and received drugs for relief, but another 915 primates used in similar experiments were given no drugs for pain or distress.

Among the companies dealing in such animals is Primate Products, Inc. (PPI), which sells baboons, capuchins, and macaques. PPI has a 3,000-acre breeding facility on uninhabited Deli Island off the coast of Java, where approximately 15,000 macaques are raised and sold for more than $850 each. The company also raises rhesus monkeys in China; those animals sell for approximately $1,200 each. In late 2001 the company announced plans to establish a 660-acre macaque-breeding colony in Hendry County, Florida. Numerous groups are opposing the plan, both for humane reasons and grant funding grew rather slowly from 1950 to 1975, but has skyrocketed since then. Greek estimates that 40 to 50 percent of NIH funding goes to animal research in one form or another. For fiscal year 2000, the top five NIH grant recipients—Johns Hopkins University, the University of Pennsylvania, the University of Washington, the University of California at San Francisco, and Washington University—were awarded more than $258 million each, with all of the top ten recipients getting at least $209 million apiece. In early 2002, President George W. Bush announced plans to increase NIH's fiscal year 2003 budget to $27.3 billion, including a fivefold increase in anti-bioterrorism research.

because they fear the monkeys—imported from Indonesia and Africa—could escape into nearby Big Cypress National Preserve and cause environmental havoc.

PPI's catalog includes most of the accoutrements needed for primate research. A stainless steel cage measuring 36 inches wide, 79 inches high, and 46 inches deep (divided into two housing areas only 32.5 inches high each) costs about $5,300. Up to ten monkeys can be kept in a 45-square-foot caging module that costs more than $17,000. Restraining chairs used to immobilize macaques and baboons cost between $2,700 and $3,500. Laws requiring psychological enrichment for captive primates created new markets for related products, ranging from $3 toys to $1,500 activity monitors.

According to the U.S. Fish and Wildlife Service, more than 41,400 monkeys and apes were imported into the United States from 1995 to 1999. Charles River Laboratories remains the largest importer, followed by Covance Research Products, Inc., Hazelton Research Products, Inc., Primate Products, Osage Research Primates, LABS of Virginia, New Iberia Research Center, and the Buckshire Corporation.

NIH's pro-animal research bent is readily apparent in a series of 24 classroom-ready posters put out by its Animal Research Advisory Committee. Cartoonish images accompany such slogans as "NIH Research Animals Get TLC" and "Without Animal Research, We Would All Be Guinea Pigs."

In their book *Sacred Cows and Golden Geese,* Greek and his co-author and wife, Jean, a veterinarian, state, "As the medical experimentation status quo is, everyone profits. Money drives education. Money drives research. Money drives industry. Money drives the media. Hence, money is the reason that animal experimentation exists." The cycle is one Greek decries as a self-perpetuating system that consumes vast resources and animal lives while producing few tangible results applicable to advancing human health. "Once the American people understand that a large percentage of their tax dollars—meant to find cures and treatments for disease—are being spent on a form of white-coat welfare, then Congress will come under enormous pressure to redirect those funds into viable research projects," he says.

Greek notes that animal laboratories spend much of their available money on equipment, chemicals, and other operating expenses. "In my lab probably half the budget went to non-animal supplies," he explains. "There's a certain amount of 'stuff' that's in every lab." Big-ticket items like electron microscopes and other complex equipment are expensive, as is the laboratory building space itself.

Laboratory personnel include the researchers—M.D.s, Ph.D.s, and V.M.D.s—as well as technicians who handle the animals and perform non-experimental procedures. According to the American Veterinary Medical Association, approximately 600 of its 60,500 member veterinarians practicing in the United States are employed in the field of laboratory animal medicine. Thousands more people, ranging from graduate students to accredited technicians, also are employed by research facilities.

Other individuals and companies earn their living by transporting or otherwise handling animals going from breeders and suppliers to laboratories. In 2000, the USDA registered 86 carriers (including airlines, motor freight lines, railroads, and shipping lines) at 800 sites, as well as 302 intermediate handlers (including kennels and ground freight companies).

Specialized food for a variety of species is available from about a dozen companies, including Harlan Teklad (affiliated with Harlan Sprague Dawley, a major rodent breeder) and Purina Mills, Inc. A sales brochure for Purina's Baby Pig Milk Replacer quoted a Kansas hog farmer as saying, "I took four 'throwaway' pigs, [and] instead of knocking them in the head, put them on Purina Baby Pig Milk Replacer, and they kept right up with the pigs the same age [nursing] on the sow." Purina produces an entire LabDiet line for all types of animals used in experiments.

## The Future

Animal researchers routinely defend their trade by claiming to have only the benefit of humanity at heart. But there are purse strings attached to those heartstrings. Regardless of whether vivisection is deemed nasty or necessary, it is indisputably a major business interest. Multiply just the purchase prices times the millions of animals used each year and the financial lure of vivisection becomes clearer. Add the cost of feeding, housing, medicating, operating on, and disposing of each laboratory "subject" and the cost in dollars becomes almost as egregious as the cost in lives.

The number of animals being used for research may or may not be going down, but institutions like Emory University and the University of California are still building expensive animal labs, and the use of transgenic and pathogen-free animals is keeping the specialty market thriving. However, says Rowan, "I don't think anyone sees the lab animal market as a growing market." Even Charles River markets non-animal testing methods and products. "The biggest indicator to me about where the [vivisection] business is going is when the biggest lab animal breeder invests in *in vitro* technology."

But as long as animal use is still measured in the millions, the profits will be, too.

# 4: The Politics of Animal Research

JILL HOWARD CHURCH

A N ADVERTISEMENT SHOWS a young boy lying limply on a hospital table, eyes closed, chin cradled in the hand of a gowned doctor. Below, the caption asks, "Will the Animal Rights Activists Fight for His Life?" The ad states that "virtually every major advancement in medicine and surgery has depended upon animal research," and that "if animal rights activists have their way, we will never find cures for AIDS, Alzheimer's, cancer, heart disease, and birth defects."

This and other advocacy materials—full of images of children and families but conspicuously devoid of maimed animals—are packed with rhetoric that praises animal researchers as saviors of humankind while labeling animal rights groups and their leaders as devils without disguise.

The increase in such aggressive campaigns that appeared in the 1990s was a counterattack against the anti-vivisection exposés of the 1980s, when graphic images from medical and product testing laboratories gave the public a glimpse of the animal experiments that stained the image of vivisectors like blood on a white lab coat. Now, coalitions of researchers, medical associations, pharmaceutical and biotechnology companies, government agencies, and others with vested interests have learned from their adversaries and are using high-profile means to assert themselves.

Organized vivisection advocacy groups have existed in the United States since the end of World War II, when the National Society for Medical Research (NSMR) was formed in Chicago to combat the programs of the National Anti-Vivisection Society (NAVS), which was founded in Chicago in 1929.

## National Association for Biomedical Research

The trenches of vivisection advocacy were dug by the National Association for Biomedical Research (NABR), which began in 1979 as the Research Animal Alliance and was renamed the Association for Biomedical Research (ABR) two years later. The organization was founded by Francine "Frankie" Trull along with her employer, Henry Foster, founder of Charles River Laboratories, the world's largest supplier of animals used in experiments. In 1985, ABR and NSMR merged to form NABR, which focuses on lobbying and political campaigns while its branch organization, the Foundation for Biomedical Research (FBR), works as a nonprofit "educational" mouthpiece to promote and defend animal research.

Based in Washington, D.C., only two blocks from the White House, NABR limits its membership to institutions, organizations, and companies directly involved in using animals in research; the group claims more than 350 members whose dues range from $500 to $12,000. Past and present members of the FBR board of directors include representatives from pharmaceutical companies, university research centers, and medical schools, as well as actor Tony Randall, former Surgeon General C. Everett Koop, and Marilyn Quayle. In 1999 FBR reported an income of $1.6 million, with assets totaling more than $9 million.

NABR publishes a "crisis management manual" that "provides the blueprint for implementing effective strategies to counter the animal rights movement." FBR compiled a 290-page *Educational Resource Directory* that lists hundreds of publications, videotapes, and other materials provided by NABR and dozens of state and professional biomedical groups/companies to promote vivisection and denounce animal rights concerns. NABR opposed implementation of the 1985 amendments to the Animal Welfare Act, among other reforms, claiming that increased regulation of animal laboratories is too restrictive and costly.

Trull's vigorous efforts on behalf of vivisectors may not be as altruistic as her impassioned pleas for humankind imply. In addition to her paid duties at NABR/FBR, Trull runs her own lobbying organization called Policy Directions, Inc. (conveniently located in the same building as NABR/FBR). In 1999, FBR paid Policy Directions $72,751 for "management services."

According to documents filed with the U.S. Senate in 2001, Trull is a registered lobbyist for 31 organizations, mostly pharmaceutical and biomedical companies but also including the American Feed Industry Association, the National Renderers Association, Burger King, and Kraft Foods. In the first half of 2001 alone, Merck & Co. paid Trull $60,000; Eli Lilly & Co. paid her $40,000; and the Cosmetic, Toiletry & Fragrance Association (which supports the use of animals to test personal care products) paid her $20,000—to name just a few.

Christine Stevens, president of the Animal Welfare Institute and secretary of the Society for Animal Protective Legislation, has butted heads with Trull over legislation for years. Stevens and Trull are both veterans of the Washington political circuit, and during the 1980s, Stevens says, "Frankie got around a lot," using her friendship with former National Institutes of Health chief James Wyngaarden (who remains on the FBR board) to shore up federal support for animal researchers.

Stevens says NABR's arguments about the high cost of laboratory compliance with animal welfare law are merely a political tactic: "They have to use an illegitimate argument [to thwart federal reforms] or they'd lose."

NABR and FBR see the animal rights movement's progress as a direct threat to vivisection. In its information packet, "NABR in the Nineties," David W. Martin, Jr., 1995-96 chairman of the NABR board and president of Lynx Therapeutics, states that "the animal rights movement has matured into a highly sophisticated, all-too-big business even more insidious than it was on the fringe....If this broader approach wins more supporters, especially among the young, animal rights' influence on science will only grow dangerously stronger."

To combat such influence, NABR is using the Internet as a surveillance tool against activists. The January 2002 issue of the *Laboratory Primate Newsletter* reports that "[t]he National Association for Biomedical Research is offering an e-mail news and information service containing a summary of each day's top stories as reported by the *New York Times*, *Wall Street Journal*, and other newspapers, as well as information gathered from Websites and chat rooms maintained by animal activists."

**Americans for Medical Progress**
One of the more contentious vivisection advocacy groups is Americans for Medical Progress (AMP), based in Alexandria, Virginia, and formed in 1992 as a not-for-profit trade association. Its stated mission is "Helping the Public Understand Animal Research in Medicine." Much of its work is carried out by its tax-exempt public outreach arm, known as the Americans for Medical Progress Educational Foundation (AMPEF).

Originally led by Susan Paris until 1998 and now run by Jacquie Calnan, AMP owes its inception and much of its funding to the United States Surgical Corporation (USSC), whose president, Leon Hirsch, serves on AMP's national advisory council. Animal rights groups (particularly Friends of Animals) have for years protested USSC's use of live dogs to demonstrate surgical staples. The AMP/AMPEF board of directors and national advisory council include executives from pharmaceutical giants Pfizer, Merck, Wyeth-Ayerst, and GlaxoSmithKline, plus representatives of several university research and medical centers. Among the politicians on AMP's advisory council are

Sen. Orrin Hatch, former President Gerald Ford, and former U.S. Senators George McGovern and Lowell Weicker, Jr. Notable on the AMP board is Adrian Morrison, a University of Pennsylvania veterinarian whose cat experiments have been the focus of heated protests and prompted an Animal Liberation Front raid in 1990.

Calnan acts as president, secretary, and spokesperson for the group; her 1999 salary was listed as $73,718. AMP publishes a newsletter about current animal research- and animal rights-related events. The group's primary target is People for the Ethical Treatment of Animals (PETA), but it has also aimed its arrows at The Humane Society of the United States and the Physicians Committee for Responsible Medicine.

Lawrence Carter-Long, a former United Fund "poster child" who was born with cerebral palsy and now campaigns against vivisection, refers to AMP as "Americans for Medical Profits." In 1996 he was literally thrown out of an AMP news conference after he objected to the group's views in front of reporters. "If they're capable of assaulting a disabled person," he says, "then it's not surprising what they do to animals."

One of AMP's favorite tactics is to promote the notion that human rights and animal rights are mutually exclusive. As part of its "Hollywood Information Project," AMP placed ads in the California press accusing pro-animal celebrities of "aiding PETA's attack on life-saving research." In particular, AMP promotes the idea that celebrities cannot or should not support animal rights groups and simultaneously promote AIDS-related charities. In 1996, AMP recruited AIDS activists to picket the World Congress for Animals and the March for the Animals in Washington, D.C., trying to redirect media attention toward the alleged rift between AIDS activists and animal advocates.

More recently, AMP and the American Association for Laboratory Animal Science Foundation launched the Women's Health Campaign, which focuses on "the attempts by animal rights activists to block vital women's health research" and addresses what it calls a "paradox: women are responsible for the majority of contributions given to animal rights organizations, many of which are opposing research designed to provide treatments and cures for diseases affecting women." Perhaps not coincidentally, one of AMP's directors is Wendy Neininger, senior director of communications for Wyeth-Ayerst, maker of the most widely prescribed women's hormone replacement drug, Premarin. Premarin is derived from the urine of pregnant mares and is the focus of a widespread animal welfare campaign to end the intensive confinement of thousands of horses and the slaughter of thousands of young foals, the unwanted byproducts of the drug's "production."

AMP produces a large amount of literature filled with emotional warnings about the menace to society posed by animal rights activists. Its "Organizational Overview" boasts that its educational outreach program—consisting of fact sheets, newspaper columns, speakers' bureaus, videos, and more—"is without parallel," and that its programs reflect "AMP's key conviction that saving and improving the quality of life is the number-one priority of every sane, sensitive, thinking person." Said former AMP president Susan Paris in a 1996 news release, "[Animal rights] groups have no compassion, no sense of decency...they should be exposed as the dangerous frauds they are."

## Other Groups

Many national medical associations and medical charities have brochures or other publications that promote the use of animals for research and testing. These include the American Medical Association, the National Academy of Sciences, the National Research Council, the American Association for the Advancement of Science, the American Cancer Society, and the American Heart Association. Several lesser-known advocacy groups have programs similar in tone but smaller in scale than NABR, FBR, and AMP. The group Incurably Ill for Animal Research (iiFAR), based in Lansing, Michigan, has chapters throughout the country and a board of directors that includes representatives from several university research centers as well as Harlan Sprague Dawley—which breeds and sells dogs, cats, rats, mice, and other animals internationally—and Lab Products, Inc., which claims to produce "the most extensive line of laboratory animal housing and care equipment in the world." The group's *iiFARsighted Report* notes current events and legislation related to animal experimentation of all kinds. Its annual revenue in 2000 was listed as just over $60,000, down from about $100,000 in 1996.

Join Hands, an organization that promotes animal research for both biomedical and consumer product purposes, is located just a block from NABR and is led by Paul R. Ford. Join Hands has two board members each from both Proctor & Gamble and Bristol-Myers Squibb, as well as another director from Johnson & Johnson.

A group called Research!America—which occupies the same building as AMP—promotes a variety of biomedical issues, including animal research. Its president, Mary Woolley, is a past president of the Association of Independent Research Institutes, and its board chairman, Paul Rogers, is a former U.S. congressman from Florida. Other officers and board members include current or former executives of the American Heart Association, the American Medical Association, and the American Cancer Society, as well as Sam Donaldson of ABC News.

Strange bedfellows abound at the National Animal Interest Alliance, headquartered in Portland, Oregon; its board and members include representatives from a host of organizations and companies that promote the use of animals for meat, fur, entertainment, and the pet trade, in addition to medical research.

The Montana-based group Putting People First, which was moderately active in the early 90s, has shown little or no activity since 1996.

More than a dozen states have their own biomedical research organizations that distribute pro-vivisection materials to schools and to the public. These groups also work with the national advocacy organizations, especially in conjunction with legislation related to animals and laboratories. For example, the group Connecticut United for Research Excellence publishes a newsletter and produces a web site called BioRAP aimed at middle school science teachers and students, touting the alleged benefits of animal research.

## The Federal Government

The federal government, through the National Institutes of Health, remains the nation's largest funder of animal experiments. It gives millions of dollars in grants to many institutions both inside and outside federal agencies. The U.S. Department of Health and Human Services distributes a series of "Animals in Science" leaflets that show photos of animals being cuddled and fed but not injected or infected. Its most inventive piece of propaganda is a set of classroom materials, designed for grades 2 to 5, that are worded so convincingly that they make dissecting "Big Bird" sound like a great idea.

On the legislative front, dozens of political action committees support animal research interests. The American Medical Association's PAC was listed by the Federal Election Commission as the fourth largest in 1997-98, giving more than $2.3 million to congressional candidates. Individual pharmaceutical companies have their own PACs, and 10 of them compose the Pharmaceutical Research and Manufacturers Association Better Government Committee, which, for example, gave Sen. Orrin Hatch (who sits on AMP's advisory council) $6,000 in contributions in 2000. In 1998-99, Hatch received another $15,000 in donations from SmithKline Beecham Corporation's PAC alone.

In Congress, Rep. George Gekas (R-PA) founded and cochairs the Congressional Biomedical Research Caucus in the

House of Representatives; Sen. Bill Frist (R-TN) chairs the Senate's Science and Technology Caucus. In March 2000, Research!America gave its Edwin C. Whitehead Award for Medical Research Advocacy to Sen. Ted Stevens (R-AK) and Rep. Bill Young (R-FL).

**Private Industry**
Pharmaceutical companies are among the most outspoken proponents of vivisection in private industry. One notable effort was a book called *Portraits of a Partnership for Life: The Remarkable Story of Research, Animals & Man*, published in the early 1990s by FBR but funded by Ciba-Geigy. The book features testimonials from people who claim that their lives, or the lives of their children, were saved as a result of animal experimentation. The tone and content of materials from DuPont Merck, Eli Lilly, USSC, and other corporations are much the same.

**The Fight for Influence**
Aside from the American Anti-Vivisection Society, the National Anti-Vivisection Society, and the New England Anti-Vivisection Society, most animal rights organizations can devote only a portion of their resources to animal research issues. They face stiff challenges from groups whose sole purpose is to promote, defend, and even increase the use of animals in research and testing—groups that are funded by huge multinational corporations with many lobbyists on Capitol Hill.

In the 1995 book *The Animal Research Controversy*, authors Andrew Rowan and Franklin M. Loew wrote, "Research advocacy organizations have...portrayed themselves as being up against powerful and much better funded opponents, but...research advocacy groups may have the advantage in both resources and connections to established institutions."

Vivisection advocacy groups want to put animal rights proponents on the defensive, thereby diverting attention from the central issue of whether animal experiments are ethical, humane, cost-effective, or productive. This puts anti-vivisectionists in the position of finding new ways to get their message across. Says Carter-Long, "We've got to work twice as hard...and be doubly prepared." But, he notes, "If they're so afraid of us getting our message out, we must be doing something right."


# 5: Whose Health Is It Anyway?

PEGGY CARLSON

AS AN EMERGENCY room physician I often see the suffering of patients ill and dying from diseases that could have been avoided if more resources were devoted to prevention, if healthier dietary guidelines were advocated, and if more research applicable to humans was conducted. I also know that behind this human suffering is another level of suffering, more hidden from view: the suffering of animals used in costly and needless experiments that benefit no one.

The practice of using nonhuman animals to mimic or study human disease is often unreliable, and occasionally misleads scientific investigation. It also squanders precious financial resources that are urgently needed for crucial clinical and epidemiological studies, preventive medicine, public health programs, and in vitro (test tube and cell culture) studies.

**Real Advances**
Claims that people are living longer today primarily because of animal experimentation have been shown to be false. Researchers at Boston and Harvard Universities found that medical measures (drugs and vaccines) accounted for at most between one and 3.5 percent of the total decline in mortality in the United States since 1900. The researchers noted that the increase in life expectancy is primarily attributable to the

decline in such killer epidemics as tuberculosis, scarlet fever, smallpox, and diphtheria, among others, and that deaths from virtually all of these infectious diseases were declining before (and in most cases long before) specific therapies became available. The decline in mortality from these diseases was most likely due to such factors as improvements in sanitation, hygiene, diet, and standard of living.

Certainly, however, medical research has played an important role in improving people's lives. The list of those advances made without the use of animals is extensive, and includes the isolation of the AIDS virus, the discovery of penicillin and anesthetics, the identification of human blood types, the discovery of the benefits of certain vitamins, and the development of x-rays. The identification of risk factors for heart disease—probably the most important discovery for decreasing deaths from heart attacks—was made through human population studies. John Marley and Anthony Michael wrote in the *Medical Journal of Australia* in 1991, "Our formal knowledge about the factors that 'cause' disease comes primarily from epidemiological research, in which systematic comparisons are made between selected groups of representative individuals."

### Reliable or Risky?

A major problem with animal experiments is that the results frequently do not apply to humans. For example, Irwin Bross, Ph.D., former director of biostatistics at the Roswell Institute for Cancer Research, testified before Congress in 1981 that "[w]hile conflicting animal results have often delayed and hampered advances in the war on cancer, they have never produced a single substantial advance either in the prevention or treatment of human cancer."

A 1980 editorial in *Clinical Oncology* asks why so much attention is devoted to the study of animal tumors when "it is...so hard to find a single common solid human neoplasm [cancer] where management and expectation of cure have been markedly influenced by the results of laboratory research." The writer, D. F. N. Harrison, explains that "most cancers behave differently from the artificially produced animal models," and concluded that "it is in the study of human patients where the relevant answers will be found."

Animal tests that attempt to predict which substances cause human cancers have also been shown to be unreliable. A 1981 U.S. Congress Office of Technology Assessment Report on the causes of cancer placed more weight on epidemiological data than on animal experiments because its authors argued that animal tests "cannot provide reliable risk assessments." According to a 1977 *Nature* article, of all the agents known to cause cancer in humans, the vast majority were first identified by observation of human populations.

Neurological diseases are another major cause of death and disability in the United States. Again, animal experiments in this area have not correlated well with human disease. A 1990 editorial in the journal *Stroke* noted that of 25 compounds "proven" effective for treating strokes in animal models over the previous 10 years, none have proven effective for use in humans.

Stephen Kaufman, M.D., reviewed animal models of such degenerative neurological diseases as Alzheimer's and Parkinson's and concluded that "animal models designed to improve our understanding and treatment of these conditions have had little impact, and their future value is highly dubious." Dennis Maiman, M.D., Ph.D., of the Department of Neurosurgery at the Medical College of Wisconsin noted in the *Journal of the American Paraplegia Society* in 1988, "In the last two decades at least 22 agents have been found to be therapeutic in experimental [laboratory] spinal cord injury. Unfortunately, to date none of these has been proven effective in clinical [human] spinal cord injury."

Two other areas where animal experimentation has been both consumptive of health care dollars and unproductive are psychology and addiction. A review of two clinical psychology journals, *Behavior Therapy* and the *Journal of Consulting and Clinical Psychology*, showed that only 0.75 percent of the references were to animal research studies. Yet in 1986 alone the National Institute of Mental Health funded 350 animal experiments in psychology at a cost of more than $30 million. The Alcohol Studies Center in Scotland stated in 1985 that "[n]othing of clinical relevance has been achieved to date for the vast range of experiments in alcoholism" and that "animal models of addiction are not relevant to human addiction."

However, in 1995 the National Institute on Alcohol Abuse and Alcoholism spent $50 million on nearly 300 animal experiments dealing with alcohol abuse. In 1995 the National Institute on Drug Abuse spent $90 million dollars on animal experiments involving drug abuse. Yet alcohol- and drug-abuse treatment centers for human sufferers remain underfunded.

Using animals to test therapeutic drugs has also proven unreliable. There are scores of examples of differing reactions of drugs between animals and humans. Penicillin kills guinea pigs and hamsters, but is very beneficial for humans. Thalidomide, a tranquilizer formerly prescribed for pregnant women with morning sickness, caused serious birth defects in more than 10,000 children but does not cause birth defects in numerous species of nonhuman animals. Acetaminophen (Tylenol), a common human pain reliever, is deadly to cats. The antibiotic chloramphenicol was thoroughly tested on animals before being released for clinical use, but was found to cause an often-fatal blood disease in humans.

Of the 198 drugs that were tested on animals in accordance with Food and Drug Administration guidelines between 1976 and 1985, 51.5 percent caused reactions serious enough to result in withdrawal from the market or, more commonly, substantial labeling changes. These reactions included heart failure, respiratory problems, convulsions, kidney and liver failure, and death. A consequence of using inaccurate animal tests is that drugs that pass animal trials can be approved for human use and later prove harmful to people; conversely, drugs that fail animal tests but might actually be beneficial to humans can be wrongly discarded.

Unreliable animal experiments have led science astray in other ways as well. For example, unsuccessful attempts to induce lung cancer in lab animals by forcing them to inhale tobacco smoke cast doubt on human clinical findings, delaying health warnings and possibly costing thousands of lives. Although not opposed to vivisection, Albert Sabin, M.D., who discovered one of the major polio vaccines, testified before Congress that "the work on the prevention [of polio] was long delayed because of an erroneous conception of the nature of the human disease based on misleading experimental models of the disease in monkeys."

Using animals in health care research also presents another problem of unknown magnitude: the risk of animal viruses infecting the human population. Some primate viruses, when transmitted to humans, can cause disease and even death. Most scientists now believe that the virus that causes AIDS is a variation of a virus found in nonhuman primates. In the case of xenotransplantation (transplants of animal organs or tissues into humans), the risk of animal viruses entering the human population could have devastating consequences.

**Research Budgets**
Despite the problems inherent in using animals in research, billions of U.S. health care dollars are spent on animal experimentation each year. U.S. health care expenditures totaled slightly more than $1.2 trillion in 1999. Included are medical costs for hospitalizations, medicines, physicians, and public health and preventive medicine programs. Also included are expenditures for health (biomedical) research, which in 1999 totaled $22.2 billion. This excludes industry (i.e., drug companies) spending for research and development, which totaled about $16 billion in 1993. Health care research money is divided among such

diverse areas as animal experimentation, human studies, computer studies, and *in vitro* studies.

The vast majority of federal health care research funds are channeled through the National Institutes of Health (NIH), whose 2001 budget was $20.3 billion. At least 80 percent of the NIH budget goes to actual research projects. According to NIH, 40 to 60 percent of its grants currently have an animal component.

While enormous sums of money are being consumed by animal experimentation, greater emphasis on other areas could lead to huge improvements in the health of this nation. These include human clinical and epidemiological studies, prevention initiatives, public health programs, and *in vitro* tests.

## Emphasize Prevention

We can learn how to improve public health by looking first at what threatens it. The three leading causes of death in this country today are heart disease, cancer, and stroke—diseases that can very often be prevented. Heart disease and stroke have similar risk factors, including: high-fat, meat-based diets; cigarette smoking; high blood pressure; obesity; and sedentary lifestyles. In virtually all studies that have looked at the incidence of heart disease among vegetarians and nonvegetarians, vegetarians have been found to have significantly lower rates of the disease.

Cancer also has a highly preventable component. In 1985 the International Agency for Research on Cancer estimated that as much as 80 to 90 percent of human cancer is determined by such factors as diet, lifestyle (including smoking), and environmental carcinogens. John Bailer and Elaine Smith from the Harvard School of Public Health and the University of Iowa Medical Center wrote in the *New England Journal of Medicine* that "thirty-five years of intense effort focused largely on improving treatment [of cancer] must be judged a qualified failure." They further stated that despite progress against some rare forms of cancer (particularly among patients under 30, accounting for one to two percent of total cancer deaths), the overall cancer-related death rate has increased since 1950. They recommended a shift in emphasis from treatment research to prevention research if substantial progress against cancer is to be forthcoming.

The fourth leading cause of death (bronchitis, emphysema, and asthma) also has a very large component that is caused by a preventable factor: cigarette smoking. In addition, other of the 10 leading causes of death—injuries, suicide, AIDS, and homicide—could be reduced through prevention. Clearly, prevention should be a priority for health care funding.

## Problems with Distribution

A look at where our health care dollars are going shows many significant problems. Human clinical and epidemiological studies, prevention initiatives, and public health programs are severely underfunded. Edward Ahrens, in his book *The Crisis in Clinical Research*, reports that in 1987 only 7.4 percent of NIH's RO1 (traditional research) grants dealing with human clinical problems were given to patient-oriented studies of human disease, and only 2.5 percent of the grants were given to human studies of disease management. (For both of these categories the trend had been on the decrease since 1982.) Experiments involving animal models of human health or disease were awarded 27.2 percent of the grants. Ahrens states, "By far the largest percentage of NIH support for new RO1s in clinical research is awarded to applicants for studies of animal (or microbial) models of human disease. Yet, most experienced investigators realize that animal models of arteriosclerosis, diabetes, hypertension, and cancer are different in important ways from the human conditions they are intended to simulate."

Public education initiatives are crucial for eliminating many of the preventable causes of death and disease but are often poorly planned and underfunded. Tobacco use is responsible for one out of every five deaths in the nation, and programs geared toward ending cigarette smoking have been shown to be highly cost-effective, but they need to be increased. Improving public education about dietary causes of disease is another necessity. A 1995 study by Neal Barnard, M.D., estimated the 1992 U.S. medical costs attributable to meat consumption to be $28.6 to $62.4 billion.

It has been estimated that up to 25 percent of all infant deaths and many of the illnesses that afflict newborns could be prevented if all women received adequate prenatal care. However, currently about 1.3 million women receive insufficient prenatal care each year. Some cancer screening programs have also proven to be cost-effective, and their use should be promoted. Despite the importance of prevention, only three percent of U.S. health care dollars are dedicated to it.

Another underutilized tool for improving American health is the public health system. The primary emphases of the public health programs are disease prevention and providing health care to the poor and near-poor. Despite research showing a strong positive correlation between life expectancy and public health expenditures, many public health programs are severely underfunded. In 1993 only 2.7 percent of all health care funding was spent on government public health activities, most of which went to state and local health departments.

In a 1990 article published in the *Journal of the American Medical Association*, the Centers for Disease Control reported on nine chronic diseases responsible for 52 percent of deaths nationwide: stroke, heart disease, diabetes, chronic obstructive lung disease, lung cancer, breast cancer, cervical cancer, intestinal cancer, and liver cirrhosis. These diseases, the authors state, are all partially or largely preventable by eliminating such risk factors as cigarette smoking, hypertension, obesity, high cholesterol levels, lack of exercise, heavy alcohol consumption, and failure to use available cancer screening techniques. The study reported that by eliminating just one risk factor—the one felt to be most important—for each of the nine diseases, U.S.

life expectancy would increase by about four years and more than 500,000 lives would be saved per year. Yet only about 2.6 percent of state public health expenditures are allocated to prevent and control chronic disease.

Research and testing methods that do not use animals have advanced considerably in recent years, replacing and improving upon areas where animals had previously been used. However, there needs to be greater acceptance and implementation of these techniques. In addition, increased funding needs to be directed toward the development of additional non-animal techniques that can replace current, often highly inaccurate animal tests.

Public health is put in danger when inaccurate animal tests are used to determine efficacy of the drugs and to which the public is exposed.

**Conclusion**
The health of this country could be substantially improved if health care dollars were more appropriately distributed. Animal experimentation is currently being inappropriately overfunded at the expense of crucial clinical and epidemiological studies, preventive medicine, public health programs, and *in vitro* studies.

# 6: **Dissection and Dissent**

JONATHAN BALCOMBE

FROG DISSECTION IS a rite of passage in three out of four junior high and secondary schools in the United States. This hands-on learning experience puts young, impressionable hands on more than three million frogs each year and on tens of thousands of cats, dogs, mice, rabbits, pigs, and other creatures.

Unfortunately, inhumane animal treatment is widespread in the dissection procurement industry. People for the Ethical Treatment of Animals' 1990 investigation of Carolina Biological Supply Company, America's largest supplier of dissection materials, yielded undercover video footage of cats being prodded roughly into crowded gas chambers, and cats and rats still moving while strapped to embalming racks. In 1994 and 1995 investigators with the World Society for the Protection of Animals discovered that Mexican cats bound for dissection in the United States were being killed by drowning or by having their throats cut.

At slaughterhouses, fetal pigs used for dissections are plucked from the bellies of sows reared in intensive confinement. Wild turtles are taken from their wetland habitats in the southern United States and kept in crowded holding tanks for several weeks or months, where many succumb to bacterial infections. Survivors may be injected with colored latex while still alive, to distinguish veins from arteries during dissections. Spiny dogfish sharks (*Squalus acanthias*), a popular dissection animal, are hauled from the oceans by the millions, where they die of suffocation in fishing nets or on boat decks. Mink and foxes, whose skinned carcasses some biological supply companies sell for dissection, were raised on fur farms, where tiny cages exposed to the elements and crude killing methods cause severe animal suffering. Investigations by The Humane Society of the United States revealed that during their processing into dissection specimens, frogs are immersed in alcohol solutions, where it takes them about 15 minutes to die. Few students or teachers are aware of these objectionable realities of the dissection supply trade.

In the United States, efforts to combat dissection have focused primarily on providing students the option to use humane alternatives. California high school student Jenifer Graham gained celebrity when she took her school to court in 1987 for not allowing her to learn frog anatomy without dissecting a killed frog. That case spawned the 1988 passage of California's student choice-in-dissection law. Similar laws also exist in Florida, Pennsylvania, New York, Rhode Island, and Illinois, and a number of school boards in other regions have adopted similar policies. In 1995, the courts awarded Safia Rubaii, a former University of Colorado medical student, $95,000 after the university refused to exempt her from a lethal dog lab. Internationally, dissection has faced harsher criticism: Argentina (1987), the Slovak Republic (1994), and Israel (1999) have banned the practice. Italy enacted a law in 1993 recognizing the right of conscientious objectors to refuse to participate in animal experimentation and dissection, and India has recently enacted legislation to eliminate animal dissections.

The assumption that non-animal alternatives are educationally inferior is being scientifically refuted. In the past decade, 30 or more published studies in educational and biological journals have demonstrated that humane alternatives equal or surpass dissection in knowledge gain and speed of learning. Assertions that dissection is the best way to learn biology are unfounded. Nevertheless, in its statement titled "The Use of Animals in Biology Education," the National Association of Biology Teachers (NABT) "urges teachers to be aware of the limitations of alternatives." NABT's statement is poorly aligned with scientific evidence, leaving one with the feeling that the organization's motives are currently more political than rational.

The mounting evidence against dissection's presumed superiority is helping to fuel a burgeoning alternatives market. CD-ROMs are especially prominent, with such titles as "The Digital Frog 2," "Vertebrate Dissection Guides," and "Anatomy Revealed" offering detailed information in an interactive format, and at a reasonable price. Even in the advanced fields of medicine and veterinary medicine, new methods of learning are being adopted that respect rather than reject concern for animals. Virtual reality simulators made by Immersion Medical allow doctors and nurses to acquire and maintain skills in procedures ranging from drawing blood to performing complex endoscopic surgeries. Empirical studies show that these devices can improve learning curves while enhancing patient safety and reducing animal use. Most veterinary schools now offer "alternative track" curricula for students who have no more desire to harm healthy animals in their training than they will as professionals. The new veterinary school scheduled to open at the Western University of the Health Sciences in 2003 aims to have a completely non-animal-consumptive curriculum.

Good dissection alternatives need not be high-tech. Building an organism from clay or coloring detailed anatomical drawings are among many "unplugged" options. Inquiry-based observational and behavioral studies of organisms in their wild habitats will do more to instill an appreciation for the complexity and diversity of life than will most dissections of a formaldehyde-infused animal carcass. Alternatives can now be borrowed from The Humane Society of the United States, the National Anti-Vivisection Society (NAVS), the New England Anti-Vivisection Society, the American Anti-Vivisection Society, and the International Network for Humane Education (InterNICHE). These lending programs provide a service to students and teachers, and hasten the adoption of alternatives. The Dissection Hotline, a toll-free service operated by NAVS that offers information and advice to students seeking humane alternatives to dissection, has logged more than 100,000 calls since it was founded in 1989.

As long as animals continue to be torn from their native habitats, raised in unacceptable conditions, killed by inhumane methods, and cut open for impressionable young minds to see, the debate over dissection must be engaged. Lessons founded on suffering and death are of dubious value to the student, and they are clearly devastating to animals. According to published surveys, most students have reservations about dissection, but only a fraction raise their concerns publicly. One of the goals of the animal rights movement must be to awaken this silent majority. At least as important is to make teachers and curriculum developers aware of the animal suffering caused by dissection, the high quality of alternatives now available, and the published research showing that these alternatives equal or surpass the dissections they were designed to replace.

Like frogs destined for dissection, traditions die hard. Despite progress toward more humane practices, much of life science education today remains mired in the morbid study of dead or dying organisms. The time has come to unite learning with respect for the integrity of life and the planet on which it has evolved. This is the future of life science education.

# 7: Teaching Life without the Knife

MELINDA B. EVERETT

"Habit, often the determinant of teachers' approaches to their classes, is always an enemy of progressive education."—**Theodora Capaldo, Ed.D.**, NEAVS/ESEC President

KERMIT THE FROG, the marvelous Muppet, often laments, "It's Not Easy Being Green." He could also add, "It's not easy being a frog," since only six states have passed laws ensuring U.S. students the right to refuse to dissect an estimated six million frogs and other animals each year. However, there are steady signs of progress as more and more educators, legislators, administrators, students, and parents are supportive of students' rights to choose alternatives to once living "specimens."

As of 2002, California, Illinois, New York, Rhode Island, Florida, and Pennsylvania have dissection choice laws. Illinois' law, the most recently passed, received a unanimous vote of support from the state's Education Committee. Several other states, including Maine, Maryland, Louisiana, Texas, Ohio and Virginia, have state or district policies to similar effect. However, policies set by state departments of education often present only guidelines, not enforceable requirements.

In Massachusetts, the Ethical Science and Education Coalition (ESEC), the educational affiliate of the New England Anti-Vivisection Society (NEAVS), based in Boston, continues to vigorously push for passage of dissection choice. Home to the first vivisection laboratory in the country—and to more biotech companies than 48 other states and all of Western Europe—Massachusetts has some of the country's strongest pro-animal experimentation promoters.

Theodora Capaldo, Ed.D., President of NEAVS and ESEC, says, "A dissection choice bill is long overdue for passage in Massachusetts—and in every state in the nation. Students in an educationally progressive state such as ours need to be ensured an ethically, scientifically, and educationally superior alternative to specimen dissection if they so choose. Protecting students' rights to conscientious objection is a critical first step in developing a humane ethic in science and in one's relationship with animals. Students who want to 'do science' must be allowed, encouraged, and supported to stay in science—this will help guarantee that vivisection will end."

NEAVS/ESEC's efforts to guarantee dissection choice for students of conscience go back to the 1980s, says Capaldo. However, even in an otherwise "animal-friendly" state such as Massachusetts, various biotech lobbying groups hold powerful sway, according to Capaldo. Lobbying is clearly a top priority on biotech agendas, she says, citing a report in the Boston Globe (6/15/01), headlined, "The new lobby: biotechnology sector is spending more money in political circles." In 1997, the Biotechnology Industry Organization (BIO) spent $1.3 million on lobbying, according to the Center for Responsive Politics. In 1999, that figure rose to $2.56 million, she adds. The Massachusetts Society for Medical Research, a pro-animal research organization, has steadily lobbied to defeat dissection choice in Massachusetts.

The consequences of forced dissection can be severe, according to Capaldo, a psychologist. Students' experiences run the gamut from nightmares, avoidance of further science classes, and feelings of helplessness, to distancing of compassion for animals. She notes that it's not only the conscientious objectors who suffer, "Every student who is 'turned off' from science by being forced to dissect is a loss for the field itself." And, sadly, many students who oppose dissection often end up performing the exercise anyway. "Many students are uncomfortable bringing their concerns to the teachers since they are perceived as authority figures and can be intimidating, even if unintentionally," Capaldo says. Students also find themselves having to dissect under penalty of failure. Recalls one Massachusetts twelfth-grader, "This experience was against my beliefs. I feel that I failed myself and I felt like I had no choice."

Notes Capaldo, "Conscientious objection must not just be a theoretical or a legal right but a day-to-day right. Moral development is fostered by being allowed to make decisions based on one's growing values. From high school dissections to the often cruel and harmful use of animals in medical, psychological, and veterinary training, the psyches of our students are harmed when they are asked to do things that they find emotionally and ethically repugnant.

"Since it is an educational truism that 'teachers teach the way they were taught,' for dissection choice to become a reality, teachers themselves will need to be taught the latest 'alternatives.' Every opportunity to teach teachers about the latest CD-ROM computer technology must be realized," Capaldo adds. Workshops on "alternatives" to dissection have been offered by NEAVS/ESEC at science teachers' conferences, professional associations' meetings, and the State House. Further, NEAVS/ESEC will be providing professional training to teachers to help them move beyond traditional dissection.

Habit, often the determinant of teachers' approaches to their classes, is always an enemy of progressive education, Capaldo says. "Helping teachers become aware of, and comfortable with, alternatives to their long history of reliance on once living specimens is a necessary step in getting them to move toward ways of teaching basic principles of anatomy and physiology that are, in fact, better."

Even skeptics are often won over once they see virtual reality dissections such as those offered by Neotek's three-dimensional CatLab and by Digital Frog2. Users respond enthusiastically to the dazzling and detailed graphics and the wealth of anatomical, environmental, and ecological information. As one Massachusetts superintendent for curriculum reports, "I am very impressed with how realistic these new CD-ROM programs are. They are incredibly accurate and authentic."

At the same time, students need to be informed of the right to select alternatives, and of the existence of organizations such as NEAVS/ESEC who will stand behind them in schools where compassion and progressive education are less valued and respected than is the status quo, Capaldo says. "Dissection choice ensures that animal experimenters no longer are able to rely on the simple decree, 'we must do it this way'—the next generation of bright, inquiring, and compassionate scientists will refuse to give blanket approval to killing and cruelty in the name of science and education. And from this generation of students who learned that you can do science and do no harm to other species will come a generation of anti-vivisection scientists committed to scientifically better and ethically more humane science."

*For free copies of dissection choice bills in various states, a free list of companies that provide "alternatives" and do not sell animal specimens, or for general information on dissection, visit our Web site at www.neavs.org/esec.html.*

# 8: The Paradigm of Progress

SARA AMUNDSON

ACTIVISTS FIGHTING THE use of animals in safety and efficacy testing have been wrongly accused. We have been accused of caring more about rats used in laboratories than wildlife hurt by chemicals in their natural environment. We have been accused of caring about rabbits more than mice, because cosmetics-related campaigns focus on the use of rabbits in Draize eye-irritancy tests. We have been accused of not wanting to protect children from harm. Yet, we have never been accused of advocating good science. But on that charge, we have been guilty.

**Moving Mountains**

Chipping away at the many uses of animals in toxicological testing is daunting. For more than 50 years, nonhuman primates, dogs, rabbits, rats, mice, and other species have been used to assess the safety and efficacy of certain chemicals and products used in our homes and environment. It will take nothing less than revolutionary changes in the test methods used to assess skin corrosivity, skin irritation, ocular irritation, and a host of other endpoints to end the use of animals in toxicity testing.

We know that the predictivity of animal methods, such as the LD-50—in which substances are force-fed to groups of animals and the results are based on the point at which 50 percent of them die—is about as reliable as flipping a coin. We also know that existing animal-based test methods have not been scientifically validated. Validation is the relevance, reliability, and reproducibility of a test method used to predict a certain biological outcome. Now, however, the field of toxicology is faced with a new paradigm—one that is predicated on good science, challenging the wholesale use of animals and the inertia allowing the status quo.

Part of that paradigm is the reluctance of federal regulators to embrace non-animal alternative tests as good science. As long as regulators do not approve the non-animal methods, the industries will not use them. Although such tests are often faster to run, cheaper to administer in the long run, and at least as predictive as their animal-based counterparts, these arguments will not sway an industry that is in bed both with federal regulators and with its lawyers.

**Using Industry Arguments to Win**
Between the late 1980s and '90s, California State Senator Jack O'Connell bravely took on the cosmetics and household products industries. He introduced a bill that would have banned the use of rabbits' skin and eyes in irritation tests on cosmetics and household products. The bill overwhelmingly passed three times, only to be vetoed twice. The opposition from the regulated industries and federal regulators was that "there are no validated alternatives to replace the Draize."

Yet the regulated industries have insisted that where there are validated alternatives, they will use them. This is not the case; the institutionalized culture around animal testing has prevailed. Rich Ulmer, president of In Vitro International, which manufactures a non-animal test for skin corrosivity called Corrositex, states, "It is our collective observation, based on nearly 15 years of offering non-animal testing methods to industry, that even after validation has been removed as a barrier to using such methods, there is still quite a bit of reluctance within industry to using a 'new' method."

In 2000, Senator O'Connell's new bill (S.B. 2082) stated that where there are validated alternatives approved by federal regulators, industry must use them. The bill covers a variety of substances, including industrial chemicals, cosmetics, household products, and pesticides. Despite massive opposition, the bill passed, and Gov. Gray Davis signed it into law. Although the new statute is a minuscule step in ending the use of animals in safety and efficacy testing, it sets a precedent for industry.

## Destroying the Double Standard

Perhaps the most significant stride made to change the existing paradigm was the passage of the ICCVAM (Interagency Coordinating Committee for the Validation of Alternative Methods) Authorization Act, which was signed into law by President Clinton in December 2000. The measure is another chip at the bureaucratic and industry inertia associated with animal testing. It codifies ICCVAM and empowers it to require federal agencies to accept validated alternative test methods. The bill also destroys the "validation double standard" that requires non-animal alternatives to meet a high standard of validation, while new and revised animal tests are often simply incorporated into the federal regulatory mandates after a cursory review. The ICCVAM Authorization Act requires for the first time that all new, revised, or alternative methods be validated, a standard that most existing animal-based tests cannot meet.

An industry toxicologist once told me that the only way some companies will embrace non-animal test methods is if they are forced to—and state and federal laws can accomplish this. After efforts in the 1980s to ban the Draize test in several states, fewer cosmetics and household product companies still use this horrific test. The intense focus by animal activists on testing for vanity products prompted an international dialogue between activists, toxicologists, federal regulators, and manufacturers to expand the research funding, validation, and regulatory acceptance of alternative tests. However, some public health advocates, environmentalists, and toxicologists insist that animal tests are simply "the best we have." Sound science demands that, as with every other scientific discipline, significant advances in toxicology must create a new paradigm. And animal activists must insist on good science that involves radical changes in the field of toxicology in order to end the use animals in safety and efficacy testing.

# ❦ Contributors

Sara Amundson is the deputy director and legislative director for the Doris Day Animal League.

Jonathan Balcombe, Ph.D., is research coordinator with Immersion Medical, a Maryland-based company that develops virtual reality simulators for medical education, and author of *The Use of Animals in Higher Education: Problems, Alternatives, and Recommendations*.

Don Barnes is the southern field representative for the Animal Protection Institute and former experimental psychologist who used nonhuman primates.

Kathy Bauch is senior director of project management for The Humane Society of the United States.

Gene Bauston, who has a master's degree in agricultural economics from Cornell University, is co-founder and executive director of Farm Sanctuary.

Marc Bekoff is professor of organismic biology at the University of Colorado, Boulder; editor of *Encyclopedia of Animal Rights and Animal Welfare* and *The Smile of a Dolphin*; and author of *Strolling With Our Kin* and *Respecting Voiceless Animals*.

Peggy Carlson, M.D., practices emergency medicine in the Washington, D.C., area and is a scientific advisor to The Humane Society of the United States.

David J. Cantor is a self-employed consultant working for national animal organizations full time from his home office near Philadelphia.

Jill Howard Church is senior editor of *The Animals' Agenda*.

Karen Davis, Ph.D., is president of United Poultry Concerns and author of *Prisoned Chickens, Poisoned Eggs; Instead of Chicken, Instead of Turkey;* and *More Than a Meal*.

Joan Eidinger is the editor and publisher of *Greyhound Network News*.

Melinda B. Everett is director of media and public relations at the New England Anti-Vivisection Society

Richard Farinato is director of captive wildlife at The Humane Society of the United States.

Camilla H. Fox is national campaign director for the Animal Protection Institute.

Grace Ge Gabriel is China country director of the International Fund for Animal Welfare.

Beth Geisler is a writer and activist in Pittsburgh, Pennsylvania.

Ariana Huemer is a California-based activist and animal cruelty caseworker. She is the caretaker of two pit bulls, Chloe and Tofupup.

Elisabeth Jennings is executive director of Animal Protection of New Mexico.

Michael Markarian is executive vice president of The Fund for Animals.

Jim Mason is co-founder of *The Animals' Agenda*, co-author of *Animal Factories*, and author of *An Unnatural Order*.

Marianne R. Merritt is an attorney specializing in civil litigation, including cases involving animal protection issues, and has taught animal protection law at the George Washington University Law School and the George Mason University Law School.

Melani Nardone is the Connecticut representative of the Greyhound Protection League.

Susan Netboy is director of the Greyhound Protection League.

Wayne Pacelle is senior vice president of communications and government affairs of The Humane Society of the United States.

Norm Phelps is spiritual outreach coordinator of The Fund for Animals.

Adam M. Roberts is senior legislative associate for the Society for Animal Protective Legislation and Animal Welfare Institute in Washington, D.C.

Jeremy Rifkin is president of the Foundation on Economic Trends, president of the Greenhouse Crisis Foundation, and head of the Beyond Beef Coalition.

Jill Robinson is founder of the Animals Asia Foundation.

Naomi A. Rose, Ph.D., is the marine mammal scientist for The Humane Society of the United States.

Nicole Rosmarino is endangered species coordinator for Forest Guardians, wildlife campaigns coordinator for Rocky Mountain Animal Defense, and vice president of the Southern Plains Land Trust.

Richard H. Schwartz, Ph.D., is professor emeritus of mathematics at the College of Staten Island and author of *Judaism and Vegetarianism* and *Judaism and Global Survival*.

Kim W. Stallwood is executive director of the Animal Rights Network Inc. and editor in chief of *The Animals' Agenda*.

Martin L. Stephens, Ph.D., is vice president for animal research issues at The Humane Society of the United States.

Kevin Stewart is an environmental researcher in Edmonton, Alberta, Canada.

Kim Sturla is the education director for The Fund for Animals.

Teresa M. Telecky, Ph.D., is director of the Wildlife Trade Program at The Humane Society of the United States.

Susie Watts is a consultant to WildAid.

Laurel Williams is the Massachusetts representative of the Greyhound Protection League.

# ❦ Organizations

*Please contact the following organizations for more information.*

American Anti-Vivisection Society
801 Old York Road, #204
Jenkintown, PA 19046
Tel: (215) 887-0816
Fax: (215) 887-2088
www.aavs.org

The American Society for the
Prevention of Cruelty to Animals
424 E. 92nd St
New York, NY 10128
Tel: (212) 876-7700
www.aspca.org

Americans For Medical
Advancement
8391 Beverly Boulevard, #153
Los Angeles, CA 90048
Tel: (310) 678-9076
Fax: (310) 362-8678
www.curedisease.com

Animal Protection Institute
P.O. Box 22505
Sacramento, CA 95822
Tel: (916) 447-3085
Fax: (916) 447-3070
www.api4animals.org

Animal Protection of New Mexico
P.O. Box 11395
Albuquerque, NM 87192
Tel: (505) 265-2322
Fax: (505) 265-2488
www.apnm.org

Animal Rescue League of Boston
P.O. Box 265
Boston, MA 02117
Tel: (617) 426-9170
www.arl-boston.org

Animal Welfare Institute
P.O. Box 3650
Washington, D.C. 20007
Tel: (202) 337-2332
Fax: (202) 338-9478
www.awionline.org

Animals Asia Foundation
PMB 506
584 Castro Street
San Francisco, CA 94114-2594
Tel: 1-888-420-BEAR
www.animalsasia.org

Association of Veterinarians for
Animal Rights
P.O. Box 208
Davis, CA 95617
Tel: (530) 759-8106
Fax: (530) 759-8116
www.avar.org

The Center for Public Integrity
910 17th Street, NW, Seventh Floor
Washington, DC 20006
Tel: (202) 466-1300
Fax: (202) 466-1101
www.publicintegrity.org

Compassion Over Killing
P.O. Box 9773
Washington, DC 20016
www.cok-online.org

Defenders of Wildlife
1101 14th Street, NW #1400
Washington, D.C. 20005
Tel: (202) 682-9400
www.defenders.org

Doris Day Animal League
227 Massachusetts Avenue, NE
Suite 100
Washington, DC 20002
Tel: (202) 546-1762
Fax: (202) 546-2193
www.ddal.org

The Elephant Sanctuary
P.O. Box 393
Hohenwald, TN 38462
Tel: (931) 796-6500
Fax: (931) 796-4810
www.elephants.com

FARM
P.O. Box 30654
Bethesda, MD 20824
Tel: 1-888-ASK-FARM
www.farmusa.org

Farm Sanctuary
P.O. Box 150
Watkins Glen, NY 14891
Tel: (607) 583-2225
Fax: (607) 583-2041
www.farmsanctuary.org

Forest Guardians
312 Montezuma, Suite A
Santa Fe, NM 87501
Tel: (505) 988-9126
Fax: (505) 989-8623
www.fguardians.org

The Fund for Animals
200 W. 57th St.
New York, NY 10019
Tel: (212) 246-2096
Fax: (212) 246-2633
www.fund.org

Great Plains Restoration Council
P.O. Box 4846
Forth Worth, TX 76164
Tel: (972) 504-6223
www.gprc.org

*Greyhound Network News*
Greyhound Protection League
P.O. Box 669
Penn Valley, CA 95946
Tel: (800) G-HOUNDS
www.greyhounds.org

The Humane Society of the United
States
2100 L St., N.W.
Washington, D.C. 20037
Tel: (202) 452-1100
www.hsus.org

In Defense of Animals
131 Camino Alto, Suite E
Mill Valley, California 94941
Tel: (415) 388-9641
Fax: (415) 388-0388
www.idausa.org

International Fund for Animal
Welfare
411 Main Street
Yarmouth Port, MA 02675
Tel: (508) 744-2000
Fax: (508) 744 2009
www.ifaw.org

International Network for Humane
Education
6 Cross Road
Leicester LE2 3AA
Leicestershire
U.K.
Tel/fax: (0)116 2109652
www.interniche.internetworking.de

Last Chance for Animals
8033 Sunset Blvd. #835
Los Angeles, CA 90046
Tel: (310) 271-6096
Fax: (310) 271-1890
www.lcanimal.org

National Animal Control
Association
P.O. Box 480851
Kansas City, MO 64148
Tel: (913) 768-1319
Fax: (913) 768-1378
www.nacanet.org

The National Anti-Vivisection
Society
53 West Jackson Blvd.
Suite 1552
Chicago, IL 60604
Tel: (800) 888-NAVS
www.navs.org

New England Anti-Vivisection
Society
333 Washington St., Ste. 850
Boston, MA 02108
Tel: (617) 523-6020
Fax: (617) 523-7925
www.neavs.org

People for the Ethical Treatment of
Animals
501 Front Strett
Norfolk, VA 23510
Tel.: (757) 622-PETA (7382)
Fax: (757) 622-0457
www.peta.org

Physicians Committee for
Responsible Medicine
5100 Wisconsin Ave., Suite 400
Washington, D.C. 20016
Tel: (202) 686-2210
Fax: (202) 686-2216
www.pcrm.org

Performing Animal Welfare Society
P.O. Box 849
Galt, CA 95632
Tel: (209) 745-2606
Fax: (209) 745-1809
www.pawsweb.org

Predator Conservation Alliance
P.O. Box 6733
Bozeman, MT 59771
Tel: (406) 587-3389
Fax: (406) 587-3178
www.predatorconservation.org

Rocky Mountain Animal Defense
2525 Arapahoe, Suite E4-335
Boulder, CO 80302
Tel: (303) 449-4422
Fax: (720) 565-9096
www.rmad.org

Society for Animal Protective
Legislation
P.O. Box 3719
Washington, D.C. 20007
Tel: (202) 337-2334
www.saplonline.org

Southern Plains Land Trust
P.O. Box 66
Pritchett, CO 81064
Tel: (719) 523-6296
www.southernplains.org

Tufts Center for Animals and Public
Policy
200 Westboro Road
North Grafton, MA
Tel: (508) 839-7991
www.tufts.edu/vet/cfa

United Poultry Concerns
P.O. Box 150
Machipongo, VA 23405-0150
Tel: (757) 678-7875
Fax: (757) 678-5070
www.upc-online.org

Washington Humane Society
7319 Georgia Avenue, NW
Washington, D.C. 20012
Tel: (202) 576-6664
www.washhumane.org

WildAid
450 Pacific Avenue, Suite 201
San Francisco, CA 94133
Tel: (415) 834-3174
Fax: (415) 834-1759
www.wildaid.org

World Society for the Protection of
Animals
89 Albert Embankment
London
SE1 7TP
UK
Tel: (0)20 7587-5000
Fax: (0)20 7793-0208
www.wspa-international.org

IUCN - The World Conservation
Union
Rue Mauverney 28
1196 Gland
Switzerland
Tel: 41-22-999-0001
www.iucn.org

# For Further Reading

Adams, Carol. *The Inner Art of Vegetarianism: Spiritual Practices for Body and Soul*. New York: Lantern Books, 2000.
———. *Living Among Meat-Eaters*. New York: Three Rivers Press, 2002.
———. *The Sexual Politics of Meat: A Feminist-Vegetarian Critical Theory*. New York: Continuum, 1991.
Bauston, Gene. *Battered Birds, Crated Herds: How We Treat the Animals We Eat*. Watkins Glen, NY: Farm Sanctuary, 1996.
Bekoff, Marc. *Strolling with Our Kin: Speaking for and Respecting Voiceless Animals*. New York: Lantern Books/AAVS, 2001.
Berry, Rynn. *Famous Vegetarians and Their Favorite Recipes: Lives and Lore from Buddha to Beatles*. New York: Pythagorean Publishers, 1995.
Braunstein, Mark Mathew. *Radical Vegetarianism*. Los Angeles: Panjandrum Books, 1981.
Coe, Sue. *Dead Meat*. New York: Four Walls Eight Windows, 1995.
Chapple, Christopher Key. *Nonviolence to Animals, Earth, and Self in Asian Traditions*. Albany, NY: SUNY Press, 1993.
Coetzee, J. M. *The Lives of Animals*. Princeton, NJ: Princeton University Press, 1999.
Davis, Karen. *Prisoned Chickens, Poisoned Eggs: An Inside Look at the Modern Poultry Industry*. Summertown, TN: Book Publishing Company, 1996.
———. *More than a Meal: The Turkey in History, Myth, Ritual, and Reality*. New York: Lantern Books, 2001.
Donovan, Josephine and Carol Adams, eds. *Animals and Women: Feminist Theoretical Explorations*. Durham, NC: Duke University Press, 1995.
———. eds. *Beyond Animal Rights: A Feminist Caring Ethic for the Treatment of Animals*. New York: Continuum, 1996.
Dunayer, Joan. *Animal Equality: Language and Liberation*. Derwood, MD: Ryce Publishing, 2001.
Eisnitz, Gail. *Slaughterhouse: The Shocking Story of Greed, Neglect, and Inhumane Treatment Inside the U.S. Meat Industry*. Amherst, NY: Prometheus Books, 1997.

Finsen, Lawrence and Susan. *The Animal Rights Movement in America*. New York: Twayne, 1994.

Francione, Gary. *Rain Without Thunder: The Ideology of the Animal Rights Movement*. Philadelphia: Temple University Press, 1996.

Frasch, Pamela D., Sonia S. Waisman, Bruce A. Wagman, Scott Beckstead, eds. *Animal Law*. Durham, NC: Carolina Academic Press, 2000.

Gaard, Greta, ed. *Ecofeminism: Women, Animals, Nature*. Philadelphia: Temple University Press, 1993.

Giehl, Dudley. *Vegetarianism: A Way of Life*. New York: Harper and Row, 1979.

Godlovitch, Stanley and Roslind, and John Harris, eds. *Animals, Men and Morals: An Enquiry into the Maltreatment of Non-humans*. New York: Taplinger, 1972.

Ham, Jennifer and Matthew Senior. *Animal Acts: Configuring the Human in Western History*. New York: Routledge, 1997.

Hyland, J. R. *God's Covenant with Animals: A Biblical Basis for the Humane Treatment of All Animals*. New York: Lantern Books, 2000.

Kalechofsky, Roberta, ed. *Judaism and Animal Rights: Classical and Contemporary Responses*. Marblehead, MA: Micah Publications, 1992.

Kapleau, Philip. *To Cherish All Life: A Buddhist Case for Becoming Vegetarian*, second edition. Rochester, NY: The Zen Center, 1986.

Kowalski, Gary. *The Bible According to Noah: Theology as if Animals Mattered*. New York: Lantern Books, 2000.

Linzey, Andrew and Dan Cohn-Sherbok. *After Noah: Animals and the Liberation of Theology*. New York: Cassell, 1997.

Marcus, Erik. *Vegan: The New Ethics of Eating*, second edition. Ithaca, NY: McBooks Press, 2000.

Mason, Jim. *An Unnatural Order: Why We Are Destroying the Planet and Each Other*. New York: Continuum, 1997.

Mason, Jim and Peter Singer. *Animal Factories: What Agribusiness Is Doing to the Family Farm, the Environment and Your Health*, revised edition. New York: Crown, 1990.

Moretti, Laura A. *All Heaven in a Rage: Essays on the Eating of Animals*. Chico, CA: MBK Publishing, 1999.

Newkirk, Ingrid. *Free the Animals: The Amazing True Story of the Animal Liberation Front*. Lantern Books: New York, 2000.

Noske, Barbara. *Beyond Boundaries: Human and Animals*. Montreal: Black Rose Books, 1997.

Patterson, Charles. *Eternal Treblinka: The Holocaust and Our Treatment of Animals*. New York: Lantern Books, 2002.

Phelps, Norm. *The Dominion of Love: Animal Rights According to the Bible*. New York: Lantern Books, 2002.

Regan, Tom. *The Case for Animal Rights*. Berkeley: University of California Press, 1983.

Rifkin, Jeremy. *Beyond Beef: The Rise and Fall of the Cattle Culture*. New York: Dutton, 1992.

Ritvo, Harriet. *The Animal Estate: The English and Other Creatures in the Victorian Age*. Cambridge, MA: Harvard University Press, 1987.

Rowe, Martin, ed. *The Way of Compassion: Vegetarianism, Environmentalism, Animal Advocacy, and Social Justice*. New York: Stealth Technologies, 1999.

Ryder, Richard. *Animal Revolution: Changing Attitudes Towards Speciesism*. Oxford: Basil Blackwell, 1989.

Sax, Boria. *Animals in the Third Reich: Pets, Scapegoats, and the Holocaust*. New York: Continuum, 2000.

Schwartz, Richard. *Judaism and Vegetarianism*, revised edition. New York: Lantern Books, 2001.

Schweitzer, Albert. *The Animal World of Albert Schweitzer: Jungle Insights into Reverence for Life*, edited by Charles R. Joy. Boston: Beacon Press, 1950.

Serpell, James. *In the Company of Animals: A Study of Human-Animal Relationships*. London: Basil Blackwell, 1986.

Singer, Peter. *Animal Liberation*, second edition. New York: Avon Books, 1990.

Spencer, Colin. *The Heretic's Feast: A History of Vegetarianism*. London: Fourth Estate, 1990.

Spiegel, Marjorie. *The Dreaded Comparison: Human and Animal Slavery*, revised edition. New York: Mirror Books, 1996.

Stallwood, Kim W., ed. *Speaking Out for Animals: True Stories about Real People Who Rescue Animals*. New York: Lantern Books, 2001.

Stepaniak, Joanne. *The Vegan Sourcebook*. Los Angeles: Lowell House, 1998.

Stull, Donald D., Michael J. Broadway, and David Griffith, eds. *Any Way You Cut It: Meat Processing and Small-Town America*. Lawrence: University Press of Kansas, 1995.

Thomas, Keith. *Man and the Natural World: A History of the Modern Sensibility*. New York: Pantheon Books, 1983.

Wise, Steven M. *Rattling the Cage: Toward Legal Rights for Animals*. Cambridge, MA: Perseus Books, 2000.

Wolfson, David J. *Beyond the Law: Agribusiness and the Systemic Abuse of Animals Raised for Food or Food Production*. New York: Archimedian Press, 1996.

Wynne-Tyson, Jon, ed. *The Extended Circle: A Commonplace Book of Animal Rights*. New York: Paragon House, 1989

# ❧ About *The Animals' Agenda*

*The Animals' Agenda* is a bimonthly news magazine dedicated to informing people about animal rights and cruelty-free living for the purpose of inspiring action for animals. *The Animals' Agenda* is committed to serving—and fostering cooperation among—a combined audience of animal advocates, interested individuals, and the entire animal rights movement. *The Animals' Agenda* is published by the Animal Rights Network Inc., an IRS 501(c)(3) federal tax-exempt, not-for-profit organization founded in 1979.

The mission of the Animal Rights Network Inc. (ARN) is to advance the protection of animals and defend their rights by:

- Working as a news organization that gathers, produces, and disseminates accurate information about acts of cruelty and institutionalized exploitation of animals
- Organizing public education programs to empower people to improve the well-being of all animals
- Leading efforts in the animal advocacy community to encourage dialogue, diversity, understanding, nonviolence, cruelty-free lifestyles, and respect for all members of all species

ARN's five primary programs are *The Animals' Agenda*, the companion *Animals' Agenda* web site, the library and archive, the

Summit for the Animals, and international conferences. The long-term goals are to establish an international network of animal advocacy organizations and individuals, and create an international center for vegetarianism and animal rights.

If you would like more information or a copy of *The Animals' Agenda*, please contact us at:

Animal Rights Network Inc. / *The Animals' Agenda*
3500 Boston Street, Suite 325
P.O. Box 25881
Baltimore, MD 21224, USA
Tel: (410) 675-4566
Fax: (410) 675-0066
E-mail: office@animalsagenda.org
World Wide Web: www.animalsagenda.org